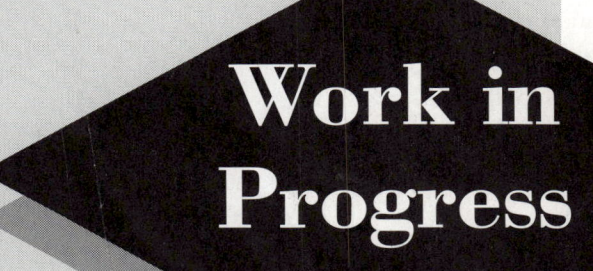

Writing in English as a Second Language

MARTHA J. MCNAMARA

ENGLISH LANGUAGE
INSTITUTE

THE UNIVERSITY
OF AKRON

Heinle & Heinle Publishers
A Division of Wadsworth, Inc.
Boston, Massachusetts 02116
U.S.A.

The publication of *Work in Progress* was directed by the members of the Newbury House Publishing Team at Heinle & Heinle:

Erik Gundersen, **Editorial Director**
Gabrielle B. McDonald, **Production Editor**
John McHugh, **Marketing Development Director**

Also participating in the publication of this program were:

Publisher: Stanley J. Galek
Editorial Production Manager: Elizabeth Holthaus
Project Manager: Rachel Youngman, Hockett Editorial Service
Assistant Editor: Karen P. Hazar
Associate Marketing Manager: Donna Hamilton
Production Assistant: Maryellen Eschmann
Manufacturing Coordinator: Mary Beth Hennebury
Interior Designer: Winston/Ford Visual Communications
Illustrations: Kenneth Urban
Cover Illustrator: Jud Guitteau
Cover Designer: Kimberly Wedlake

Photo Credits
1—Peter Southwick, Stock, Boston; **3**—Michael Lajoie; **10**—Michael Lajoie; **37**—Ulrike Welsch; **54**—Dean Abramson, Stock, Boston; **67**—Bob Daemmrich, Stock, Boston; **73**—Jerry Cooke, Photo Researchers; **93**—Michael Lajoie; **100**—Michael Lajoie; **127**—David R. Frazier, Photolibrary; **129**—Ulrike Welsch; **146**—Alan Carey, The Image Works; **157**—Michael Lajoie; **164**—David R. Frazier, Photolibrary; **169**—Michael Lajoie

Copyright © 1994 by Heinle & Heinle Publishers
All rights reserved. No part of this publication may be reproduced or transmitted in any form or by any means, electronic or mechanical, including photocopy, recording, or any information storage and retrieval system, without permission in writing from the publisher.

Heinle & Heinle Publishers is a division of Wadsworth, Inc.

Manufactured in the United States of America

Library of Congress Cataloging-in-Publication Data

McNamara, Martha J.
    Work in progress : writing in English as a second language / by Martha J. McNamara.
      p. cm.
    ISBN 0-8384-4822-4
    1. English language—Textbooks for foreign speakers. 2. English language—Rhetoric.
  I. Title.
PE1128.M3695 1994
428.2′4—dc20
                                                   93-38195
                                                        CIP

10 9 8 7 6 5 4 3 2 1

Work in Progress
Writing in English as a Second Language

....

Introduction to the Student   vii

To the Teacher   xiii

Part 1: Drafted Works in Progress   1

> **CHAPTER 1**
> Writing an Autobiographical Essay   3
>
> **CHAPTER 2**
> Writing for a Campus Brochure   37
>
> **CHAPTER 3**
> Sharing Your Knowledge or Expertise   67
>
> **CHAPTER 4**
> Taking a Stand   93

Part 2:
Summary Writing and Essay Exams as Works in Progress   127

> **CHAPTER 5**
> Summary/Comment Writing   129
>
> **CHAPTER 6**
> Writing Essay Exams   157

Part 3:
Sentence Structure and Grammar Exercises as Work in Progress **169**

Appendices **241**

Answer Key **A1**

Acknowledgments

When preparing these acknowledgments, I became awed once again by the fact that all writing is collaborative. It really *is* impossible to thank all of the people who contributed to and helped shape this book. These paragraphs acknowledge some of my major collaborators.

Thanks to the people on the publication end of this writing process, who led me through a maze I still do not understand: Erik Gunderson, Editor; Lynne Telson Barsky, Associate Editor; and Karen Hazar, Assistant Editor; Gabrielle B. McDonald, Production Editor; Rachel Youngman of Hockett Editorial Service, Project Manager; and Amy Rose, the Copyeditor. Sincere thanks to the following reviewers for their insightful comments and suggestions for revision: Linda Lonon Blanton, University of New Orleans; Ramón Valenzuela, Boston University; John Kopec, Boston University; Janet Kayfetz, University of California, Santa Barbara; Elizabeth Templin, University of Arizona; and Katherine Schneider, University of Delaware.

I would like to thank all of the ESL writers I have worked with, each of whom has given me insights into L2 writing and invaluable feedback on my own writing. Special thanks go to the following writers, whose work appears in this book: Jasem Ali, Eva Bachor, Kumiko Hasegawa, Yen Lin, Aina Llabres, Noriko Ohara, Shigeki Okuno, Miryung Tai, and Sun Tiensingchai.

I would like to thank all of my colleagues at the English Language Institute at the University of Akron, several of whom used and informally reviewed prepublication versions of this text: David Barkey, Debra Deane, Joanna Grollmus, Melissa Mowder, Terry Pascher, Shirin Sterling, and Monika Tober. Special thanks go to Ken Pakenham and Barbara Robinson Kimyon, for their empathy and words of encouragement. Extra special thanks go to Debra Deane, for always being tuned in and listening; for always hearing and understanding; and for playing such a big role in my professional development.

I would like to thank my friends and family for their never-ending encouragement and support. Special thanks go to Jane Aby and Anne Simoneau, for their cheerleading and confidence in my ability to see this project through to the end. My deepest gratitude goes to Steve Aby, for his loving support, clear-headed perspective, and gentle reminders that, as the title says, this book is a work in progress.

Finally, I would like to dedicate these pages to the memory of my parents, Maurice Michael McNamara and Mary Jane Byrne McNamara, and to their five other works in progress: Mike, Kathy, Tom, Dan, and Mary Ellen.

Introduction to the Student

Learning a second language is like learning to play a new sport or a musical instrument. Sitting at home reading a rule book will NOT make you a better tennis player; reading a book entitled "How to Play the Piano" will not make you a good pianist. Likewise, reading rules about the English language will not make you more proficient in English. The only way to become a better athlete, musician, or user of English is to practice, practice, practice every day. You must practice, make mistakes, learn from those mistakes, practice again, practice again . . . .

Your focus in this course will be on writing. The title of this book, *Work in Progress*, reflects an important, powerful quality of writing: It is a dynamic process, not a static object. A piece of writing can be reworked, changed, added to, subtracted from, and rearranged. A piece of writing expresses your thinking at a point in time; as that thinking changes or develops, your writing can change. In this sense, writing does not have an end point; you can always come back to your written work and revise it. Even published works can be revised and reprinted in subsequent editions.

In addition to being dynamic, writing is a complex activity that requires attention to many different areas: You have to think about your topic, purpose, main idea, and audience (readers).

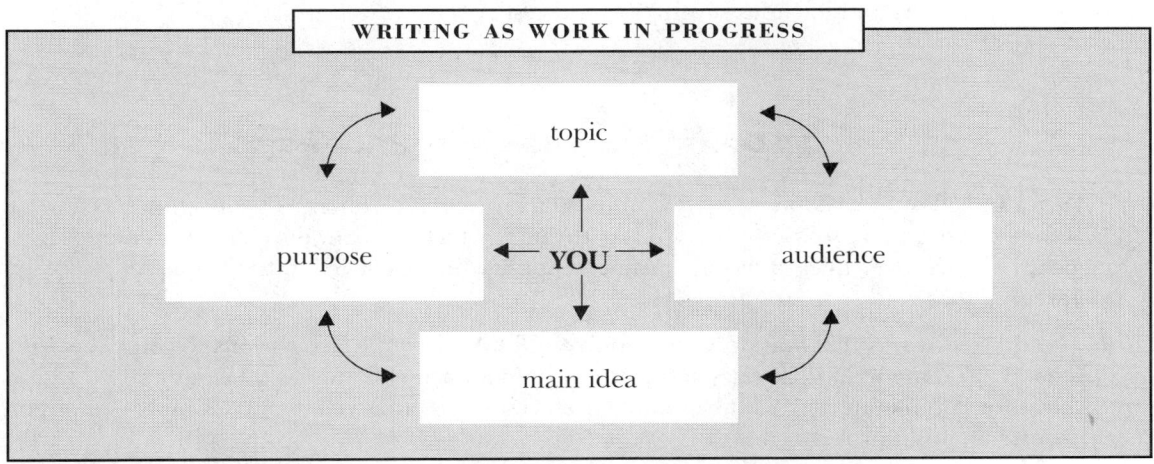

TOPIC:	What are you writing about? This is the subject of your writing.
PURPOSE:	Why are you writing? What do you hope to achieve with your writing?
MAIN IDEA:	What is your most important message? What do you want to say about your topic?
AUDIENCE:	Who are you writing for?

These four elements—your topic, purpose, main idea, and audience—interact with and influence all of the decisions that you make about your writing as a work in progress. They influence your decisions about the development of your ideas, that is, the support and content that you include in your paper. They influence the global structure of your writing, that is, the overall organization of your paper. They also influence your decisions about your paragraphs and their internal organization, your word choice, and your sentence structures. In addition to these decisions, you must also be concerned about grammar, spelling, mechanics, and much more when you write.

Introduction to the Student

Because it is very difficult to pay attention to these concerns and make decisions about all of these aspects of writing at the same time, you should develop strategies to manage your writing process so that you produce effective writing. For any given writing task, the strategies that you use will depend on the situation, or context, in which you are writing.

As a student in the academic context, you will do different types of writing:

1. **Drafted works in progress.** Typically, these assignments are reports, essays, or term papers. Your professor will usually specify a topic, a due date, and some guidelines for completing the assignment. Depending on the due date, you could have, for example, one week, two weeks, or several months to prepare the paper.

2. **Summary writing as work in progress.** With summary writing, you present the main ideas of another writer. Often you are asked to comment on the writer's ideas.

3. **Essay exams as works in progress.** This is writing that you complete in a class period, under a time limit. Typically, you will have to write an answer to a question based on material that you have studied in the class.

To give you the opportunity to develop your strategies for managing these three types of writing assignments and for producing correct English sentence structures, this textbook is divided into three parts and includes several appendices.

Part 1: Drafted Works In Progress

Part 1 includes four chapters, each with its own writing assignment. The assignments and their accompanying exercises provide a context through which you can develop your composing strategies and learn principles of writing. You can apply what you learn in these chapters to other formal writing that you do in English.

The drafted works that you do in this course will take several class sessions to complete. You will probably do some writing in class and some at home. Each assignment specifies a topic and procedures for completing it. Each assignment is structured so that you can work on the different aspects of writing as a process.

INTRODUCTION TO THE STUDENT

STEPS FOR COMPLETING DRAFTED WORKS IN PROGRESS

1. *Prewriting:* When you approach a writing assignment, spend some time establishing your purpose, analyzing your audience, and generating ideas about your topic. This process is called *prewriting* because it is done before you actually begin to write the paper. Prewriting can take many forms, for example, thinking, discussing with others, jotting down notes, freewriting, reading, and interviewing.

2. *Drafting Your Paper: The First Draft:* Once you have a sense of your purpose, audience, and main idea and have gathered some ideas for your writing, write a first draft (or version) of your paper. This first draft is a rough written form of your paper; it is not your final product. In this draft, explore ideas. Focus your attention and energy on clarifying and achieving your purpose and on expressing your main idea. With this draft, do not worry about organization, grammar, or spelling because you can attend to those aspects of writing on later drafts.

3. *Revising Your Writing:* After you have written your first draft, you will study some conventions and patterns of writing in American English. At this point, you will also share your draft with other writers in the class and give each other feedback (suggestions and ideas) about your writing. This collaboration is important: First, your readers can tell you what is especially good or interesting about your first draft. They can also tell you what is unclear or where more information is necessary. They can give you ideas to make your second draft better. Also, by being a reader yourself, you will learn from the other writers in the class.

    After considering the feedback from your readers, revise your first draft and plan to write the second draft. NOTE: Revise does not mean just reread. It means to read the first draft, look at it with fresh eyes, and make changes that will improve your paper. When you plan your revision, you add new ideas, throw out irrelevant ideas, and rearrange or reorganize ideas. In short, you make any changes that you think will improve your work in progress.

4. *Drafting Your Paper: The Second Draft:* After planning your revision, write your second draft. In the second draft, focus on achieving your purpose, clearly communicating your main idea, and organizing your supporting ideas so that they are easy for your readers to follow.

5. *Revising Your Writing:* After you have written the second draft, you will study and practice some sentence structures in English. Then go back to your own writing and revise your sentences as necessary.

6. *Drafting Your Paper: The Third Draft:* When you prepare your third draft, focus on expressing your ideas the way you want to with correct sentence structures and grammar.

7. *Editing Your Writing:* When the third draft is complete, edit it. When you edit, you reread your paper carefully, looking for mistakes and correcting them. Edit for grammar, spelling, and punctuation.

INTRODUCTION TO THE STUDENT

PART 2: SUMMARY WRITING AND ESSAY EXAMS AS WORKS IN PROGRESS

SUMMARY WRITING AS WORK IN PROGRESS Summary writing involves presenting the main ideas of another writer in your own words. In order to be a good summary writer, you must be a good reader. You must understand the global structure (the big picture) of the text you are summarizing, and you must be able to sort out main ideas from supporting details. In the academic context, you will often be asked to comment on what you have summarized. The chapter on summary/comment writing, Chapter 5, illustrates and provides practice with reading and note-taking strategies that will help you write effective summaries and comments.

ESSAY EXAMS AS WORKS IN PROGRESS Essay exams are written under pressure, so you only have time to produce one draft. Some of the steps for the drafted works in progress—prewriting, organizing, writing, reading and editing—will serve you well when writing timed essays. However, you must develop strategies for completing these steps in a very short amount of time. With Chapter 6, you will work on developing and refining those strategies.

PART 3: SENTENCE STRUCTURES AND GRAMMAR PATTERNS AS WORK IN PROGRESS

Part 3 explains select complex sentence structures and grammar patterns and includes exercises for practice. Use this part for review or to learn and practice structures that you may not yet know.

Exercises in Chapters 1 to 6 have been cross-referenced with the explanations and exercises in Part 3 so that you can easily refer to this part when you are revising sentences in your own writing. In addition, a table of contents at the beginning of Part 3 lists all the structures that are covered.

APPENDICES

The appendices include supplemental material that you may find useful when writing.

APPENDIX A Appendix A is an editing checklist. Use it as a reference tool when editing drafted works in progress before you submit them to your readers.

APPENDIX B Appendix B provides a list of editing correction symbols. When editing your own or another writer's work, you can use these symbols to indicate errors. Your instructor or tutor may use these symbols to point out errors in your writing.

APPENDIX C Appendix C offers a few suggestions for writing on a computer.

APPENDIX D Appendix D includes readings for use with the assignments in the book.

INTRODUCTION TO THE STUDENT

FREEWRITING JOURNAL WORKS IN PROGRESS

While you are using this textbook, you will also do an unstructured type of writing called *freewriting*. Freewriting is a technique that many experienced writers use not only to explore ideas for their formal writing (that is, as a prewriting strategy) but also to promote fluency.

Fluency refers to the ability to get ideas out of your head and onto paper, the ability to let ideas flow. The only way for a person to develop fluency in writing is to write often. Freewriting promotes fluency because, as its name implies, it is free, unstructured, uncensored, unedited writing. It is writing to explore.

Throughout this course, you will keep a daily freewriting journal. Your journal will give you a place to develop fluency, explore ideas, and experiment with the language. Some of your freewriting entries will be on whatever topic you want to write about at the time. Sometimes the textbook will specify a topic or pose questions for you to explore in your journal.

SUGGESTIONS FOR KEEPING YOUR FREEWRITING JOURNAL

1. *Write every day for at least ten minutes*. As the course progresses and your fluency develops, try to write for longer periods of time, but always write for at least ten minutes. NOTE: When you are assigned a topic to explore in your journal, you may also be given a time limit.

2. *Write freely*. Because this is a freewriting journal, let your ideas flow. If you write something that you want to change, just cross out what you do not like and keep writing. Do not use an eraser; it will interfere with your fluency. Also, because you will be freewriting, do not be surprised or concerned if you jump from one idea or topic to another. Go where your writing takes you.

3. *Write in English*. You are trying to develop fluency in English, so, of course, you must write in English. Do not use a dictionary or a grammar book while you are freewriting because this will interfere with fluency. If you get stuck for a word or a phrase from time to time, it is o.k. to write that word or phrase in your native language and then shift back to English. If you get stuck for a grammatical structure, write what you think is the correct form, and then continue writing. When you have finished the entry, look up words in your bilingual dictionary and write the English equivalents in your notebook above the words in your native language. Consult a grammar book for correct grammatical structures; write in those correct forms.

4. *Experiment with English*. Use this notebook as a place to try new things in English. Try using new vocabulary and new structures that you are learning. Try writing dialogues, letters, and even poems in English. If you feel that you do a lot of translation from your native language to English, experiment with thinking in English and writing whatever you think.

5. *Skip lines while writing in your notebook*. Write legibly. Date each entry, and write your starting time after the date.

6. *Enjoy!!!!*

To the Teacher

OVERVIEW

Goals

As a process-oriented writing textbook, *Work in Progress* is designed to help its users—developing ESL writers—engage in writing as a dynamic, ongoing process in which the writer interacts with a text and with readers. The main goal of the text is to help students become independent and confident writers in their second language by developing:

- sensitivity to the needs of their readers.
- fluency in writing in English.
- strategies for generating ideas, planning, and putting together a text.
- strategies for organizing ideas, revising content and structure, and editing written work.
- the ability to use the basic rhetorical devices and syntactic patterns of written English.
- the ability to follow the basic writing conventions of the American English academic community.

Audience

Work in Progress is an advanced-level, process-oriented writing textbook for ESL students enrolled in intensive English language and community college programs.

Approach and Rationale

Work in Progress offers an innovative approach to a process-oriented method for writing instruction in that it incorporates elements of form-based and English for academic purposes (EAP) approaches. Because of this synthetic approach, the text is comprehensive: It provides writing assignments and opportunities for developing composing strategies as well as instruction in and practice with select rhetorical devices, sentence structures, grammatical patterns, and editing points.

Work in Progress fosters the idea of writing as a collaborative process by providing many exercises that lend themselves to small-group and pair work. Several of the chapters include peer review worksheets that offer students guidelines for giving feedback to other writers about their work in progress. The text also suggests that students keep a daily freewriting journal as a way to promote fluency. Short freewriting assignments are sprinkled throughout the chapters to encourage this writing for fluency.

To the Teacher

Work in Progress makes use of extensive modeling, not only of final products but also of composing strategies and of work in progress. This modeling offers students a chance to analyze other writers' work and to see possibilities for their own writing—possible drafting and revising techniques, possible organizational structures, and possible rhetorical devices and syntactic patterns. With the insight gained from their analyses, students can be encouraged to experiment with their own writing and discover what strategies and forms work the best for them in any given writing situation.

Work in Progress also utilizes a step-by-step, task-based approach. As students work through a chapter, they are presented with explanations and models, followed by the opportunity to apply what they have just learned to their own writing.

Work in Progress was shaped by the approach described above because of its target audience, ESL students who are preparing to enter universities in the United States. (Prepublication versions of *Work in Progress* were successfully used with groups of prospective undergraduate and graduate students whose placement TOEFL scores ranged from 460 to 550.) These students typically represent a variety of linguistic, cultural, and educational backgrounds. While some of them are experienced writers in their native languages, many characterize themselves as inexperienced L1 writers. Most consider themselves inexperienced writers in English. Although all of the students in a class using *Work in Progress* have studied English in their home countries or in the United States, many are still developing their linguistic competence. Furthermore, any one class may comprise students at different levels of writing and English proficiency. The approach adopted by *Work in Progress* helps inexperienced writers discover and develop their own composing processes in English, and it provides opportunities for experienced writers to practice and expand their strategies. It gives all students material through which to learn about and practice basic rhetorical devices of formal written English and to develop their linguistic competence.

ORGANIZATION AND SUGGESTIONS FOR IMPLEMENTATION

Work in Progress contains more than enough classroom and homework material for a writing course that meets five hours a week for fifteen weeks. The text consists of three parts:

Part 1: Drafted Works in Progress

Part 2: Summary Writing and Essay Exams as Works in Progress

Part 3: Sentence Structure and Grammar Exercises as Work in Progress

This organizational plan reflects the three different writing goals featured in the text: 1) experiencing writing as a process of discovering, shaping, and communicating ideas in order to achieve a purpose; 2) practicing summary writing and essay exam writing as academic study skills; and 3) completing sentence and grammar exercises as a way to develop linguistic competence.

TO THE TEACHER

PART 1

Comprising the core of the text, Part 1 contains four chapters, each with its own focused writing assignment and specific topic:

Chapter 1: *Writing an Autobiographical Essay*

Chapter 2: *Writing for a Campus Brochure*

Chapter 3: *Sharing Your Knowledge or Expertise*

Chapter 4: *Taking a Stand*

Each of the first three chapters can take from 10 to 15 class hours to complete and Chapter 4 can take from 15 to 20 class hours. The amount of time spent on each chapter will vary, depending on how much work you complete in class or assign as homework and on how much depth you go into with the explanations, examples, and exercises.

Chapters 1 to 4 are organized so that students produce a drafted paper over time. While working through the drafting process, students focus on developing their topic, achieving their purpose, and meeting the needs of their audience. For ease of use, each chapter has been sequenced as a lesson plan. While working through the material in the order presented, the students draft, revise, and edit their papers.

A unique feature of Chapters 1 to 4 is that the composing strategies (e.g., generating ideas, revising ideas and structures) and the form-based teaching points (that is, those that present rhetorical devices and syntactic structures) are introduced, illustrated, and practiced during the students' writing process, at a time when the relevance of these topics is readily apparent. Moreover, the four chapters in this part are designed to be covered in order. The assignments in these chapters are sequenced so that students move from working with data of a personal nature (the autobiographical essay) to working with data obtained from external sources (the essay using written sources). Chapters 2, 3, and 4 build on and recycle features of written discourse and composing strategies that were introduced earlier in the text.

Each chapter in Part 1 is organized as follows:

PREWRITING In a section entitled *Setting the Context*, the student writers prepare for the writing assignment with a short freewriting/discussion exercise. In *Understanding the Assignment*, the writing task is described. Students initially consider the needs of their readers in *Analyzing the Audience*, and they begin to generate ideas for their papers in the section entitled *Collecting Data*. Each of Chapters 1 to 4 introduces and illustrates an idea-generation strategy for students to try. As with the treatment of other composing strategies throughout the text, this exposure to a variety of idea-generation techniques is designed to help students expand their strategy options and to find the ones that work the best for them.

DRAFTING YOUR PAPER The First Draft: In Chapter 1, students write their first draft immediately after completing the prewriting steps. In Chapters 2 to 4, a section entitled *Planning Your First Draft* introduces them to several planning strategies to use before they produce a first draft. Students should be encouraged to experiment with these planning strategies to find the ones that suit their approach to writing.

TO THE TEACHER

REVISING YOUR WRITING In each chapter, a section entitled *Developing Your Writing* explains and illustrates one or more ways to develop writing. Models provide the students with the opportunity to analyze these methods of development in other writers' texts. Students then practice these methods in their own writing. *Giving and Getting Feedback* includes a list of peer review questions for students to use when reading and responding to each other's writing.

DRAFTING YOUR PAPER: THE SECOND DRAFT Chapter 1 provides a model of a student's drafting process to show students one way to plan and prepare a second draft. The model and the suggestion box of planning steps represent one of many ways to work from one draft to the next. Students should be encouraged to use the model as a starting point from which to discover their own revising strategies. Chapters 2, 3, and 4 include suggestion boxes with steps for planning and writing a second draft.

REVISING YOUR WRITING In each chapter, this section illustrates and provides practice with sentence revision. Emphasis is given to sentence structures that should prove useful for students given the nature of the writing assignment (e.g., subordination with connecting words of cause/effect, time, and purpose is the focus of Chapter 1, where the students write an autobiographical essay; adjective clauses, reduced adjective clauses, and appositives are the focus of Chapter 2, where the students write a description). Suggestion boxes refer the students to the pages in Part 3 where the emphasized structures, or related ones, are explained and additional practice is provided. The explanations and exercises in Part 3 can be covered by the whole class or assigned to small study groups or individuals depending on the needs of your class.

DRAFTING YOUR PAPER: THE THIRD DRAFT This section of each chapter provides a suggestion box with steps for planning and preparing a third draft. Chapter 1 includes an example of one writer's drafting steps; once again, this example should serve as a starting point for students to find their own best composing strategies.

EDITING YOUR WRITING Chapter 1 introduces editing and suggests ways for students to develop effective editing strategies, including the use of the Editing Checklist found in Appendix A. Chapters 2, 3, and 4 recycle these suggestions.

TO THE TEACHER

PART 2

Part 2 contains two chapters: Chapter 5, *Summary/Comment Writing* and Chapter 6, *Writing Essay Exams*.

While these chapters are self-contained and can be taught any time during the writing course, it is recommended that they be covered after the completion of Chapters 1 and 2 because they incorporate material introduced in those chapters. The following course plan seems to work well:

Chapter 1: *Writing an Autobiographical Essay*

Chapter 2: *Writing for a Campus Brochure*

Chapter 5: *Summary/Comment Writing*

Chapter 6: *Writing Essay Exams*

Chapter 3: *Sharing Your Expertise*

Chapter 4: *Taking a Stand*

Chapter 5 offers suggestions for effective summary writing and an example of one writer's summary writing process. It also provides five high-interest texts for students to summarize. After analyzing the summary-writing strategies and the model, students can practice summary writing with the texts provided. This practice can be done in class or as homework. Students can work in study groups or individually. For additional practice with summary writing, students can summarize the texts in Appendix D, other texts that you provide, or texts that they bring to class.

Chapter 6 presents the students with a process approach to essay exam writing, including strategies for preparing for test day. Recycling many of the writing process steps introduced in Chapter 1, this chapter suggests ways to cope with a stressful and difficult writing task. A short text in Appendix D provides course material for the essay exam practice. Supplementing this chapter with examples of essay exam answers of varying degrees of success will help students develop criteria and standards for effective answers. These examples can come from the students in your class, or you may create a file of representative samples over the course of several semesters or terms.

Because most of the students using *Work in Progress* will not have written essay exams in English, they will benefit from extensive practice with this type of writing. Once Chapter 6 has been covered, other essay exams can be scheduled during the course. Students can prepare for the exams in study groups during class if time permits, or outside of class.

PART 3

Part 3 contains explanations of and exercises for sentence structures and grammar patterns that tend to be challenging for many developing ESL writers. For easy access, the structures and patterns in Part 3 have been arranged in alphabetical order with an index on pages 170 and 171. These structures can be covered during the students' drafting process, when they are focusing on revising their sentences. Chapters 1 to 4 provide cross-references to the structures that may be useful for the students given the nature of the writing assignment.

TO THE TEACHER

SUPPLEMENTAL MATERIAL

Work in Progress includes four appendices and an answer key for the exercises in Part 3.

APPENDIX A: EDITING CHECKLIST provides rules and editing strategies for the following: subject/verb agreement, article usage, mechanics, prepositions, punctuation, and verb tenses and forms. Once students become familiar with the Editing Checklist and learn how to use it, they can refer to it while editing their papers.

APPENDIX B: EDITING CORRECTION SYMBOLS lists correction symbols to use on later drafts of written work. You might find these symbols useful when responding to your students' work. Your students might want to use them when editing their own writing or the work of a peer.

APPENDIX C: WORD PROCESSING offers suggestions for revising work that has been word processed.

APPENDIX D: READINGS AND WORKSHEETS supplies texts for use with Chapters 4 and 6. The first four readings provide background knowledge and some history about the topic in Chapter 4, determining tuition fees for international students. The worksheets that accompany two of these readings guide students through a critical analysis of the ideas presented in the texts, modeling reading skills that will help them evaluate their written sources. The final two readings in *Appendix D* provide course content for the essay exam writing in Chapter 6.

ANSWER KEY Because you may find it desirable to assign work in Part 3 on an individual or small-group basis, an *Answer Key* has been provided for the exercises in this section. Students can use the key to check their own work or to discuss and analyze sentences in pairs or small groups.

TO THE TEACHER

SPECIAL FEATURES OF WORK IN PROGRESS

Work in Progress

- provides a writing course curriculum.

- sequences each chapter to take students through the writing process from idea generation to a final draft.

- provides step-by-step instruction and practice with writing drafted essays, essay exams, summaries, and a documented paper.

- not only explains but also models prewriting, revising, and editing strategies for the students.

- sequences exercises for rhetorical devices and syntactic patterns at relevant points throughout the drafting process.

- fosters collaboration through the use of peer review and exercises that work well for pairs and small groups.

- explains and provides practice with grammatical and syntactic structures that prove challenging to ESL writers.

PART I
Drafted Works in Progress

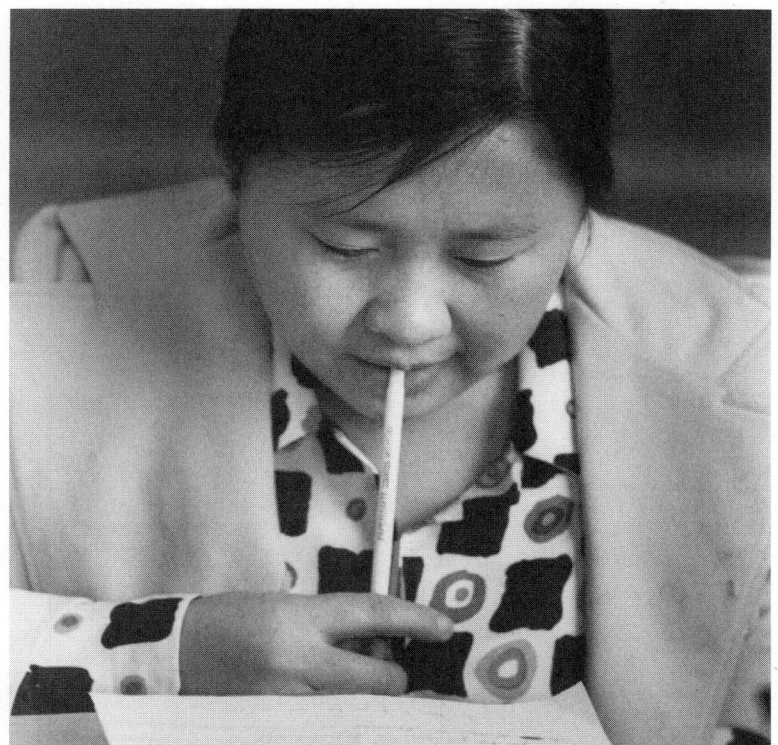

CHAPTER 1   **3**

Writing an Autobiographical Essay

CHAPTER 2   **37**

Writing for a Campus Brochure

CHAPTER 3   **67**

Sharing Your Knowledge or Expertise

CHAPTER 4   **93**

Taking a Stand: Writing from Sources

Chapter 1

Writing an Autobiographical Essay

PREWRITING
- Setting the Context
- Understanding the Assignment
- Analyzing the Audience
- Collecting Data

DRAFTING YOUR PAPER: THE FIRST DRAFT
- Writing Your First Draft

REVISING YOUR WRITING
- Developing Your Ideas
- Giving and Getting Feedback

DRAFTING YOUR PAPER: THE SECOND DRAFT
- Planning Your Second Draft
- Writing Your Second Draft

REVISING YOUR WRITING
- Focusing on Your Sentence Structures

DRAFTING YOUR PAPER: THE THIRD DRAFT
- Planning and Writing Your Third Draft

EDITING YOUR WRITING
- Developing a Strategy for Editing

PART I: DRAFTED WORKS IN PROGRESS

PREWRITING

SETTING THE CONTEXT

Exercise 1.1 Freewrite answers to the following questions. Then discuss your answers with your classmates.

① What is an autobiography?

② Why do people write autobiographies? Think of and write about as many reasons as you can.

③ Have you read any autobiographies? If yes, whose? In what language? What was the purpose of the autobiographies that you have read?

UNDERSTANDING THE ASSIGNMENT

For this assignment, you are going to write a brief autobiographical essay (about 300–500 words) that would be appropriate for one of the situations described below. Read and think about each situation carefully and then choose the *one* that you wish to write for. After you decide, specify the details of the situation by answering the questions with information of *your choice*.

① Applying for admission to undergraduate or graduate school.

You are applying for admission to an undergraduate or graduate program at a university or college in the United States. In addition to filling out an application form and sending your grades and your TOEFL score, you must write an essay about yourself, including information about your past life, education, practical experience, and special interests. The admissions office also wants to know why you chose your major field of study, why you chose their institution, and what your future plans and career goals are.

If you decide to write for this situation, answer the following questions:
  a. What is the name of the university or college?
  b. Are you applying for an undergraduate or graduate program?
  c. What is your major field of study?
  d. What other details would you like to specify?

② Applying for a scholarship.

You are applying for a scholarship sponsored by a major multinational corporation. Every year, this company awards full-tuition scholarships to four students for whom English is a second language. The recipients are selected on the basis of merit; in other words, the scholarships are awarded to highly motivated and successful students with well-defined career goals. The company is looking for people who will do well in their studies and who will be successful when they graduate. To apply for the scholarship, you must send an application form and your grades as well as an autobiographical essay.

If you decide to write for this situation, answer the following questions:
  a. What is the name of the corporation?
  b. What is the name of the university where you will use the scholarship?
  c. What other details would you like to specify?

③ Applying for a job in your field.

You are applying for a job with an American company in your country. In addition to filling out an application form and sending your grades and TOEFL score, you must send an autobiographical essay. This essay should include information about your education, training, work experience, special qualifications for the position, your reasons for wanting the position, and your reasons for wanting to join the company.

If you decide to write for this situation, answer the following questions:
  a. What is the name of the company?
  b. What is the position that you are applying for?
  c. What is the starting date for the position?
  d. What other details would you like to specify?

④ Applying for a student or graduate assistantship.

You are applying for a teaching, research, or student assistantship in a department in a university or college in the United States. In addition to submitting an application form, your high school or undergraduate transcripts, TOEFL score, and three letters of reference, you must send an autobiographical essay. This essay should include information about your education, training, any work experience, and special qualifications for the assistantship. The assistantship selection committee also wants to know what your future plans and career goals are.

If you decide to write for this situation, answer the following questions:
  a. What is the name of the university and the department?
  b. Are you applying for a teaching, research, or student assistantship?
  c. What other details would you like to specify?

⑤ ?????

If none of the situations above is appropriate or relevant for you, craft your own. Think of a situation in which you may have to write an autobiographical essay in English. Specify the details of that situation.

PART I: DRAFTED WORKS IN PROGRESS

ANALYZING THE AUDIENCE

Before you begin to write, think carefully about who is going to read your autobiographical essay. Discuss these questions with your classmates:

1. Who are your readers?
   For Situation 1?
   For Situation 2?
   For Situation 3?
   For Situation 4?
   For Situation 5?
2. You do not know them personally. How will that affect your writing?
3. What do your readers want/need to know about you?
4. Why do the readers need this information?

COLLECTING DATA

Now collect some ideas to use in your essay. Since all of the ideas will come from your head, that is, from your memory, what are some ways for you to tap those ideas and get them on paper?

DRAWING AN IDEA MAP An *idea map* (also called a tree diagram) is a technique that some writers use to collect ideas. It is a way to generate information about your topic before you start writing. Experiment with this technique for this assignment to see if it is a strategy that works for you.

Exercise 1.2 To draw an idea map, take a blank sheet of paper. In the middle, write your topic. For this assignment, the topic is YOU, so write "ME" in the middle of the page. Then put your memory to work and let the ideas flow. From the center circle, write and circle words about you and your life. Join these circles with lines to show the connections. When you get to the end of one "branch," go back to the center circle, to ME, and head off in a different direction. Write as quickly as you can and as much as you can. Do not worry about order. Do not censor ideas—*write whatever comes to mind*. Study the example on page 7 before you begin.

Chapter 1 : Writing an Autobiographical Essay

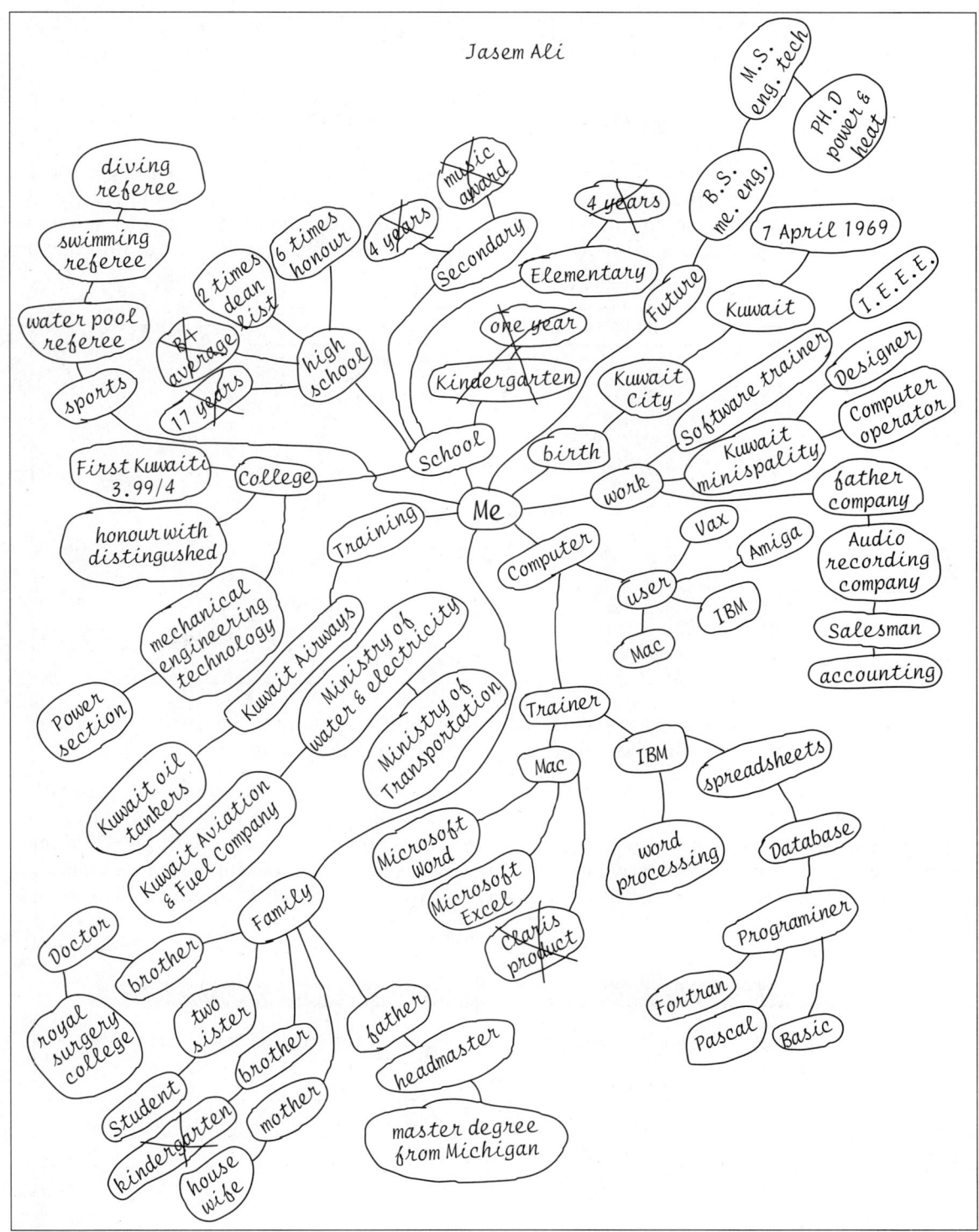

Jasem Ali

PART I: DRAFTED WORKS IN PROGRESS

DRAFTING YOUR PAPER: *The First Draft*

WRITING YOUR FIRST DRAFT

Reread the situation that you have chosen for your autobiography. Think about your topic, audience, purpose, and main idea (to convince your reader that you should be admitted to an undergraduate or graduate program, should win the scholarship, should get the job, or should be awarded a graduate or student assistantship). Complete the chart below to clarify this information for yourself.

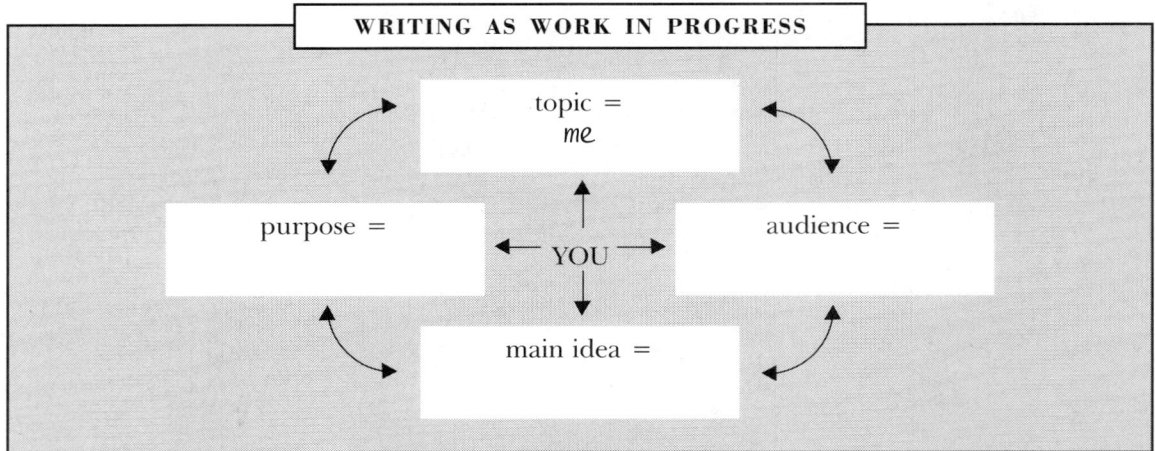

Scan your idea map and select the ideas that you think you should include in your paper. Let your decisions be guided by your topic, purpose, main idea, and audience.

Write your first draft. Concentrate on putting your ideas into sentences. Do not be overly concerned with organization, grammar, word choice, or spelling at this point. For example, do not stop to look up words in the dictionary, because this will break your train of thought. If you do not know a word in English, write it in your native language and then shift back into English. You can consult a dictionary later. Remember, this is *not* your final product; you will have a chance to make changes on later drafts.

SUGGESTIONS • SUGGESTIONS • SUGGESTIONS • SUGGESTIONS

If you are using a computer, see Appendix C, page 263, for suggestions about writing your first draft.

CHAPTER 1 : WRITING AN AUTOBIOGRAPHICAL ESSAY

REVISING YOUR WRITING

DEVELOPING YOUR IDEAS

LEARNING FROM OTHER WRITERS To see some possible ways to develop your own autobiography, consider the work in progress of two other writers. Below you will find the final draft of the essay that one writer wrote as part of his application to a university (Situation #1 above). After you have read the essay carefully, complete *Exercise 1.3*.

I would like to apply as a transfer student to the Department of Mechanical Engineering Technology. I was born in Kuwait City, Kuwait, on the 7th of April 1969. I started my formal education in Kuwait in 1974, and I studied there for the next 12 years. From 1982 to 1986, I was in high school, where I was an honors student and was on the dean's list two times, in 1983 and 1986. During school vacations, I worked at my father's audio and video showroom as a salesman and as an accountant.

In 1987, I entered Kuwait Institute of Technology (K.I.T.), which is a two and a half year college. I took a placement test which indicated that I had a high aptitude for mechanics. Because of that, I chose mechanical engineering technology to be my major at K.I.T., with a minor in the power section. During my studies, I took courses in engines, turbines, design, and thermodynamics. I used to write my reports, solve problems, and write scientific programs using computers, so I became familiar with different computer systems and their capabilities and with different computer languages. I graduated from the Institute in 1989 with a G.P.A. of 3.99 out of 4.00 and received a distinction with honor. Since I was the first Kuwaiti to achieve that G.P.A. in my major, the government of Kuwait awarded me a full scholarship to the U.S.A. to finish a B.S. in mechanical engineering technology.

While I was studying at K.I.T., I had a chance to do a co-op program in which I applied what I had learned during my studies to my work in companies and ministries. I worked as a trainee at Kuwait Airways, Kuwait Aviation and Fuel Company, the Ministry of Water and Electricity, the Kuwait Oil Tanker Company, and the Ministry of Transportation. After graduation, I worked for a short time with the Institute of Electrical and Electronic Engineers (I.E.E.E.) as a software trainer. I also worked for the Kuwait Municipality as a computer operator and a designer. In this job, I developed mechanical projects using computer aided design (C.A.D) workstations.

I chose your university for my undergraduate studies because a lot of my friends recommended it and because it has a good reputation back in Kuwait for its mechanical engineering technology program. Moreover, the chairman of my department at K.I.T. highly recommended it to me. My long term goal is not only to receive a B.S. degree but also to earn an M.S. and eventually a Ph.D. in engineering technology. A higher degree will enable me to become involved in industrial planning and design, which Kuwait is relying on for the future of its industry. I would also like to achieve one of my childhood dreams to be a professor at Kuwait University in mechanical engineering technology.

PART I: DRAFTED WORKS IN PROGRESS

Exercise 1.3 Imagine that you are the admissions officer at the university to which this writer is applying. Freewrite answers to the following questions. Then discuss each one with your classmates.

① What impression do you get of this writer? What kind of person does he seem to be?

② Why do you get that impression? In other words, how does the writer make that impression?

③ How many parts or sections does the writer have in the essay? How do you know?

④ Why does the writer divide this essay into parts?

⑤ What does he discuss in the first part? in the second part? in the third part? in the fourth part?

Now read and analyze another writer's autobiographical essay. This writer applied for a job in an international company, so she was writing for Situation #3 above. After you have read the essay carefully, complete *Exercise 1.4*.

CHAPTER 1 : WRITING AN AUTOBIOGRAPHICAL ESSAY

I would like to apply for the position of international secretary in your company. I know that Proctor and Gamble is a world-famous and growing company and that it already has several offices in Japan. While living in the United States, I have become familiar with your products at supermarkets. I would like to work at your company using my job experience and English language skills.

I became interested in foreign languages when I was in high school, so I decided to major in English in college because it is the common language in the world. In 1984, I received a B.A. in English from Kyoto University of Foreign Studies. While studying in college, I visited the United States and Singapore during vacation.

As soon as I graduated from the university, I began to work for an international trading company, Inoue Shoji Company, because I was interested in foreign countries from my travel experience. For a year, I worked in the export section, where I booked vessels, made shipping documents, and conducted negotiations at the bank. Then I was transferred to the import section, where my duties included opening letters of credit, arranging the delivery of goods, and communicating with the American manufacturers in English using telex and facsimile equipment. In addition to these responsibilities, I worked with the chairman of this section and assisted him as a secretary. From my five years at Inoue Shoji Company, I could learn a great deal about the import/export business.

After getting married in 1990, I registered with Temporary Center and worked for the export company Act, Inc. for 6 months. My job was making shipping documents and negotiations at the bank. This company had the latest office machines, so I worked using a Japanese word-processor, English word-processor, and computers. This training allowed me to get used to the latest machines. My typing speed is 40 w.p.m.

Now I am studying English in an intensive language program in the United States. After I brush up on my English language skills, I am going to take some courses in business communication at a local two-year college. I will be returning to Japan in August 1992, so I would be available for employment beginning in September.

Exercise 1.4 Imagine that you are the personnel manager for the Proctor and Gamble office to which this writer is applying. Freewrite answers to the following questions. Then discuss your answers with your classmates.

(1) What impression do you get of this writer? What kind of person does she seem to be?

(2) Why do you get that impression? In other words, how does the writer make that impression?

(3) How many parts or sections does the writer have in the essay? How do you know?

(4) Why does the writer divide this essay into parts?

(5) What does she discuss in the first part? in the second part? in the third part? in the fourth part? in the last part?

(6) Compare the two essays. Look for differences in the type of information that each writer focused on and in the way each one organized the essay. What are the differences? Why do you think the first writer selected the type of information and the organizational plan that he did? Why do you think the second writer selected the type of information and the organizational plan that she did?

PART I: DRAFTED WORKS IN PROGRESS

USING SPECIFIC DETAILS   In this assignment, you want to prove to the readers that *you* are the best applicant for the university, the scholarship, the job, or the assistantship. You want to convince them that *you* stand out from the other applicants. One way to convince them is to *show* them what your qualities and attributes are. It is true that you could say, "I'm hardworking, serious, intelligent . . ." but will that convince your readers? Probably not. You must show them through details and specific information exactly what your strong points are.

Details are *specific* ideas. When writers develop their writing with details, they make their ideas more precise for the readers; they "show" the readers what they mean rather than just "tell" them. Study the examples below.

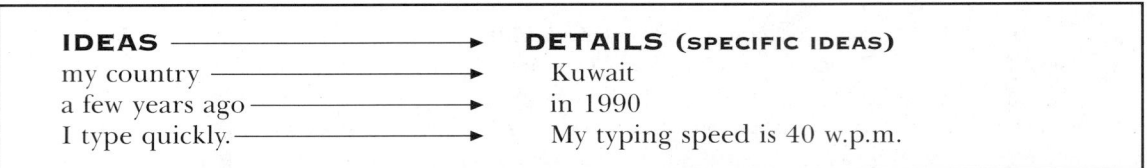

Exercise 1.5   Read through the draft written by the student from Kuwait. Circle the specific details that give you an indication of this writer's qualities. What qualities does he possess?

Now read through the draft written by the student from Japan. Circle the specific details that give you an indication of this writer's qualities. What qualities does she possess?

Exercise 1.6   Below is the first draft of an essay written for Situation #2, the scholarship application. There are several places in this draft where the writer will be more convincing if he adds specific details and information for his second draft. Identify these places in his draft. With your classmates, discuss what additions you think the writer should make.

I was born in 1964. From 1978 to 1982, I attended secondary school. My favorite subjects there were science and math. I was an officer of one of my classes. I also belonged to a school club. One year I participated in our annual science fair and won a prize. I also played sports. We had school vacations every year. At that time, I always worked part time. I graduated from high school. I began to work full-time. I also helped with bookkeeping and accounting.

I have always been interested in science and math, and I enjoyed my jobs. I decided to continue my studies in computer science and to concentrate on computer applications in business. I am in my second year at this university and am a member of two clubs on campus. In addition to my studies and club activities, I work twenty hours a week. Next semester, I will work in the computer center on campus.

I will finish my undergraduate studies, and I will return to my country. My father is planning to computerize his business, so I will work for him for a few years. I will be in charge of the entire computerization process, so this job will provide me with very good experience. I would like to move on to a larger business or corporation. I want to be able to use both my computer skills and my English language skills.

GIVING AND GETTING FEEDBACK

Share your first draft with another writer (or a small group) from your class.

When you are reading another writer's first draft, read through the entire paper carefully. If you have trouble with vocabulary or handwriting, ask the writer for clarification. Once you have read and understood the draft, write answers to the following questions. Write your answers on a separate sheet of paper so that you can give them to the writer.

1. What part of this first draft do you like the best? Why?
2. Do you see any places in this first draft where the writer used strong specific details to develop ideas? If yes, where?
3. Where would you like more explanation or more development? Where would you like more specific details? Why?
4. Are there any sentences or ideas that you feel the writer should omit from a later draft? If yes, which ones? Why?
5. Comment on the organization.
   a. How many paragraphs does this first draft have?
   b. Are the paragraph divisions effective?
      If yes, what is the focus of each one?
      If no, what changes would you recommend for the next draft?
   c. Are the ideas within each paragraph grouped properly?
      If no, what changes would you recommend?

Part I: Drafted Works in Progress

DRAFTING YOUR PAPER: *The Second Draft*

PLANNING YOUR SECOND DRAFT

When writing your first draft, you got some ideas out of your head and down onto paper in sentences. Since you wrote the first draft, you have analyzed the work of other writers and have gotten feedback about your own writing from some readers. Look at your first draft again and plan how to shape it into a second draft.

SUGGESTIONS • SUGGESTIONS • SUGGESTIONS • SUGGESTIONS

Here are some suggestions for one way to plan your second draft:

1. Turn back to pages 4 to 6 and reread the situation for which you are writing your autobiography.

2. Reread your first draft and your readers' comments carefully.

3. Cross out any information that you think should be omitted from the next draft.

4. Number the remaining sentences (or groups of sentences).

5. Identify places where you should add information or specific details. At the end of your first draft, list this additional information in note form, and somehow indicate where you want it to appear in your second draft.

6. Decide how many parts—or paragraphs—you want to have in your second draft and how you would like to group your information.

7. Write a plan for your second draft on a separate sheet of paper. In your plan, group and arrange the sentences from your first draft in the order that you would like them to appear in your second draft. You can do this by referring to the number of each sentence from your first draft.

8. Review your plan carefully.

9. Determine what part(s) of your first draft and/or your plan you would like to receive more advice or suggestions about before you write the second draft. At the bottom of your plan, write specific questions seeking that feedback.

10. If you are using a computer, follow the suggestions above by marking your changes on the computer printout of your first draft.

LEARNING FROM ANOTHER WRITER Below is one writer's first draft and what he did to follow the suggestions above. Study this example before you begin to plan YOUR second draft.

On pages 15 and 16 you will find the writer's first draft exactly as he wrote it in class. (Do not be surprised to see many errors in the first draft. Remember—it is a work in progress.) On pages 17 and 18 you see that same draft with some information crossed out and the remaining sentences numbered (suggestions 3 and 4). On page 19 you see the list of information that the writer wishes to add (suggestion 5), his plan for organizing his second draft (suggestion 7), and questions that he has about his work in progress (suggestion 9).

I was born in Kuwait City, the State of Kuwait, ~~in~~ on the 7th of April 1969, from a Kuwaiti parents. I joined the formal education in Kuwait in 1974 where I studied for the next 12 years. at high school I was listed two times on the Dean list and I was awarded 6 times ~~for my~~ as an honour student. During school vacations, I worked ~~at~~ in my father's audio & vido showroom as a salesman and as an accountant.

Since I was a child I showed big intrest in mechanisims & mechanics, as a result I did an I.Q. test which told me that I got a high ~~grper~~ percentage in mechanics.

I joint then ~~the~~ Kuwait Institue of Technology which is a two & half years college and my major was mechanical engineering technology. ~~at the college~~ in my major I took a lot of courses about heat engines, design and thermodynamic courses. during ~~the~~ my study, I ~~went to~~ joined many training courses (as a bart of my study) ~~such as~~ which were in Kuwait Airways, Kuwait Aviation & Fuel Company, Ministry of Water and Electricity, Kuwait Oil Tanker and Ministry of Transportation.

~~I also~~ as a prize for my distingshin honor graduation G.P.A. (3.99 out of 4) the Government of Kuwait gave me a free scholarship to the U.S.A. to finish a B.S. in Engineering Technology.

During my study at the college I became familiar with computers such as Apple Macintosh, I.B.M., Amiga and Vax with an experience in word processing (MS Word), spreadsheet (MS Excel), programing languages (Fortran, Pascal, Basic).

at my free time I'm a first class referee in water pool, diving and swimming and I have been doing that since 1987. Also at my free time I like to see my family which consest of my father who works as a headmaster in an elementary and hold a master degree in education from Michigan and there is my mother who is a housewife and two sisters who are student and finally two brothers, the older one is studying at the Royal Surgary College in Dublin, Ireland.

after the college, I worked for a short time with (IEEE) as a software trainer and I worked with Kuwait minucipality as a computer operator and a designer.

Part I: Drafted Works in Progress

My goal is not to have a B.S. only be it extend to a M.S. and a PhD. in engineering technology which is my country is relaing on for the future of Kuwait Industry as one reason and as another reason so I can achive one of my childhood dreams to be a proffissional lecturer at Kuwait University in Engineering Technology.

I choosed your university because a lot of my frieds recommended it for me and because your university has a got reputation back in Kuwait in for it engineering technology and as a matter of fact the chairman of my Mechanical Engineering Technology Department at my college recommended it to me.

also by looking to the program contents and by comparing your program to other available programs in other university I have found that is was more suitable and fruitefull for me.

CHAPTER 1 : WRITING AN AUTOBIOGRAPHICAL ESSAY

① I was born in Kuwait City, the State of Kuwait, ~~in~~ on the 7th of April 1969, ~~from a Kuwaiti par-~~ ② ~~ents~~. I joined the formal education in Kuwait in 1974 where I studied for the next 12 years. ③ at high school I was listed two times on the Dean list and I was ~~awarded 6 times for my as~~ an ④ honour student. During school vacations, I worked ~~at~~ in my father's audio & vido showroom as a salesman and as an accountant.

⑤ *placement*
~~Since I was a child I showed big intrest in mechanisims & mechanics~~, as a result I did an ~~I.Q.~~ test
aptitude
which told me that I got a high ~~grper percentage~~ in mechanics.

⑥ I joint then ~~the~~ Kuwait Institue of Technology which is a two & half years college and my major ⑦ was mechanical engineering technology. ~~at the college~~ in my major I took a lot of courses about ⑧ *took*
heat engines, design and thermodynamic courses. during ~~the~~ my study, I ~~went to joined~~ many training courses (as a bart of my study) ~~such as~~ which were in Kuwait Airways, Kuwait Aviation & Fuel Company, Ministry of Water and Electricity, Kuwait Oil Tanker and Ministry of Transportation.

⑨ ~~I also~~ as a prize for my distingshin honor graduation G.P.A. (3.99 out of 4) the Government of Kuwait gave me a free scholarship to the U.S.A. to finish a B.S. in Engineering Technology.

⑩ During my study at the college I became familiar with computers such as Apple Macintosh, I.B.M., Amiga and Vax with an experience in word processing (MS Word), spreadsheet (MS Excel), programing languages (Fortran, Pascal, Basic).

⑪ at my free time I'm a first class referee in water pool, diving and swimming and I have been doing that since 1987. ~~Also at my free time I like to see my family which consest of my father who works as a headmaster in an elementary and hold a master degree in education from Michigan and there is my mother who is a housewife and two sisters who are student and finally two brothers, the older one is studying at the Royal Surgary College in Dublin, Ireland.~~

⑫ after the college, I worked for a short time with (IEEE) as a software trainer and I worked with Kuwait minucipality as a computer operator and a designer.

PART I: DRAFTED WORKS IN PROGRESS

(13) My goal is not to have a B.S. only be it extend to a M.S. and a PhD. in engineering technology (14) which is my country is relaing on for the future of Kuwait Industry as one reason and as another reason so I can achive one of my childhood dreams to be a proffisional lecturer at Kuwait University in Engineering Technology.

(15) I choosed your university because a lot of my frieds recommended it for me and because your university has a ~~got~~ *good* reputation back in Kuwait ~~in~~ for it engineering technology and as a matter of fact (16) the chairman of ~~my Mechanical Engineering Technology~~ *my* Department at ~~my college~~ *K.I.T.* recommended it to me.

~~also by looking to the program contents and by comparing your program to other available programs in other university I have found that is was more suitable and fruitefull for me.~~

Additions

Before sentence 1, add a sentence to state my purpose: I would like to apply as a transfer student to the Department of Mechanical Engineering Technology.

③ Add dates: from 1982 to 1986   ⑥ Add date: In 1987

⑥ Add minor: in power section

⑧ Explain that the training courses were a co-op program in which I applied what I have learn during my studies to my work in companies and ministries.

⑨ Add date of graduation: 1989

⑨ Add that I was the first Kuwaiti to achive a 3.99 out of 4.00 G.P.A. in my major.

⑩ Explain how I became familiar with the computers and programs: I used to write reports, solve problems and write scientific programs using computers.

⑫ Explain I.E.E.E. = Institute of Electrical and Electronic Engineers.

⑫ Add details about my job as an operator and designer: I developed mechanical projects using computer aided design (C.A.D.) workstations.

Plan for 2nd Draft: Paragraph 1: include statement of purpose (see above) and early education and work = 1, 2, 3, 4

Paragraph 2: studies at K.I.T. = 6, 5, 7, 10, 9

Paragraph 3: work at K.I.T. and after = 8, 12

Paragraph 4: reasons for this university & future plans = 15, 16, 13, 14

Questions: 1. Should I include the information about hobbies? See ⑪. I don't think it will fit.

2. Do I need all the details about the different computers and programs? This seems too detailed.

PART I: DRAFTED WORKS IN PROGRESS

WRITING YOUR SECOND DRAFT

At this point in your work in progress, you have written a first draft, received feedback from a reader, and developed a plan for a second draft. Now begin to write your second draft.

SUGGESTIONS • SUGGESTIONS • SUGGESTIONS • SUGGESTIONS

Here are some suggestions for how to proceed when writing your second draft.

1. Begin to write your second draft according to your plan. Use any of the sentences from your first draft that work well. Make changes and rewrite any of the sentences that you feel should be changed. Be sure to skip lines.

2. Reread your second draft when you are finished. If you would like to make any changes, feel free. Just cross out what you would like to change and rewrite.

3. If you are using a computer, see Appendix C, page 263 for suggestions about revising your paper to produce a second draft.

Freewriting Journal Assignment

Where do you spend your free time on campus or in the local community? Why do you go to these places? What attracts you to these places?

For the next few days, make freewriting journal entries about your favorite place or places on campus or in the local community.

For each of the journal entries, go to the place that you will be writing about. Write while you are actually at this place. For each entry, observe and freewrite for at least ten minutes. Write down as much information as you can. Write about what is happening in this place and about your impressions of it. Write about how you feel here. In your freewriting, try to capture what it is that you like about this place.

Your freewriting can take any form; that is, you can write notes, idea maps, sentences, or a combination of all three forms.

SUGGESTIONS • SUGGESTIONS • SUGGESTIONS • SUGGESTIONS

To help focus your freewriting sessions, you might try the following:

1. Freewrite about what the place looks like, that is, about its *physical appearance*. Describe what you see in the place: size, shapes, dimensions, the objects that you see, and their arrangement. You might even draw a rough sketch of the layout of this place in order to keep a visual record of what it looks like.

2. Freewrite about the *activities* that are going on in this place. What is happening right now? What are typical activities for this place?

3. Freewrite about the *kind of people* that you see in this place. Who is there? How many people are there? What ages are the people? How are they dressed?

4. Freewrite about *how you feel* in this place and *why*.

5. ?????????????????

CHAPTER 1 : WRITING AN AUTOBIOGRAPHICAL ESSAY

REVISING YOUR WRITING

FOCUSING ON YOUR SENTENCE STRUCTURES

In your autobiographical essay, you describe different times in your life as well as give reasons for your actions and state your future plans or purpose. In the draft that you submit to your reader, you want to use sentence structures that clearly and correctly communicate this information. You also want your ideas to flow smoothly.

This next section of the chapter focuses on using correct and varied sentence patterns to express ideas effectively.

LEARNING FROM ANOTHER WRITER Below are several excerpts of text from different writers' second drafts of their autobiographical essays. As you can see, at this point in the work in progress, each writer focused on the sentences in the draft and penciled in revisions so that they flow well and express the ideas clearly.

Exercise 1.7 Read through the original and revised versions of each excerpt carefully. With your classmates, describe each change that the writers made. Then discuss how each change affects the writing. Discuss:

- how the changes help the readers.
- how the changes help the clarity of ideas.
- how the changes help the flow of ideas.

To facilitate the discussion, the revisions are printed for you below each excerpt. Refer to each revision by its number.

PART I: DRAFTED WORKS IN PROGRESS

Excerpt A: Original

> prize for my exhibit on the formation of crystals. I also played on our high school soccer team for three years. We had school vacations. At that time, I worked part-time in my father's hardware store as a sales clerk. I graduated from high school. I began to work for my father full-time. I also helped with bookkeeping and accounting.

(had) inserted above "I also played"

Excerpt A: Revision

> prize for my exhibit on the formation of crystals. I also played on our high school soccer team for three years. ① Whenever we ~~We~~ had school vacations, ~~At that time~~ I worked part-time in my father's hardware store as a sales clerk. ② As soon as I graduated from high school, I began to work for my father full-time. ③ In addition to sales, I ~~also~~ helped with bookkeeping and accounting.

1. We had school vacations. At that time, I worked part-time in my father's hardware store as a sales clerk.
   ↓
   Whenever we had school vacations, I worked part-time in my father's hardware store as a sales clerk.

2. I graduated from high school. I began to work for my father full-time.
   ↓
   As soon as I graduated from high school, I began to work for my father full-time.

3. I also helped with bookkeeping and accounting.
   ↓
   In addition to sales, I helped with bookkeeping and accounting.

Chapter 1 : Writing an Autobiographical Essay

Excerpt B: Original

my favorite subjects were science and math. I especially enjoyed conducting experiments in the lab and learning how things work. In my final year of high school, I represented our school in the regional science fair and won a third place prize for my experiment.

I decided to major in chemistry and biology in the university. I was so interested in science in high school. My father completed his undergraduate studies at your university

Excerpt B: Revision

my favorite subjects were science and math. I especially enjoyed conducting experiments in the lab and learning how things work. In my final year of high school, I represented our school in the regional science fair and won a third place prize for my experiment.

④ I decided to major in chemistry and biology in the university. *Because* I was so interested in science in high school, My father completed his undergraduate studies at your university

4. I decided to major in chemistry and biology in the university. I was so interested in science in high school.
   ↓
   Because I was so interested in science in high school, I decided to major in chemistry and biology in the university.

PART I: DRAFTED WORKS IN PROGRESS

Excerpt C: Original

why I have chosen computer science for my major.

    I will finish my studies, and I will return to my country. My father is planning to computerize his business, so I will work for him for a few years, and I will be in charge of the entire computerization process, so this job will provide me with valuable practical experience in a small business. I would like to move on to a larger business or corporation. I want to be able to use both my computer skills and my English language skills.

Excerpt C: Revision

why I have chosen computer science for my major.

⑤ *After finishing*
~~I will finish~~ my studies, ~~and~~ I will return to my country. My father is planning to computerize his business, so I will work for him for a few ⑥ *years. Since* ~~years, and~~ I will be in charge of the entire computerization process, ~~so~~ this job will provide me with valuable practical experience in a small business. ⑦ *Once that work is complete,* I would like to move on to a larger business or corporation~~.~~ *so that can* ~~want to be able to~~ use both my computer skills and my English language skills.

5. I will finish my studies, and I will return to my country.
 ↓
 After finishing my studies, I will return to my country.

6. My father is planning to computerize his business, so I will work for him for a few years, and I will be in charge of the entire computerization process, so this job will provide me with valuable practical experience in a small business.

↓

My father is planning to computerize his business, so I will work for him for a few years. Since I will be in charge of the entire computerization process, this job will provide me with valuable practical experience in a small business.

7. I would like to move on to a larger business or corporation. I want to be able to use both my computer skills and my English language skills.

↓

Once that work is complete, I would like to move on to a larger business or corporation so that I can use both my computer skills and my English language skills.

USING CONNECTING WORDS The chart below lists some of the common connecting words and phrases used in written English.

TIME	before, after, when, while, until, whenever, as soon as, as, since, once, as long as, then, next, first, second, third, last, finally, meanwhile, at the same time, simultaneously, at this point, at this time
CAUSE–EFFECT/REASON–RESULT	because, since, as, now that, therefore, as a result, hence, thus, consequently, accordingly, for this reason, for, so
PURPOSE	so that, in order that, to do this, to this end
CONCESSION AND CONTRAST	although, even though, though, however, nevertheless, nonetheless, but, yet, in spite of the fact that, despite the fact that, whereas, while
ADDITION	moreover, furthermore, in addition, and, nor, also, not only . . . but also
CONDITION	if, otherwise

These and other connecting words help you to:

- make the meaning relationships between clauses and sentences explicit for your readers. (See revisions #2, 4, 5, and 7 in Exercise 1.7.)
- show your readers the relative importance of ideas. (See revisions #1, 2, 4, and 5 in Exercise 1.7.)
- vary your sentence patterns. (See revisions #3, 6, and 7 in Exercise 1.7.)
- organize ideas within your paper so that you maintain their flow. (See revisions #3, 4, and 7 in Exercise 1.7.)

PART I: DRAFTED WORKS IN PROGRESS

Each of the words and phrases listed above is used in a certain sentence pattern or structure; in other words, when you use these connecting words, you follow specific rules of structure and punctuation.

Through experience and observation, you can develop instincts about how to use different sentence patterns and connecting words effectively. When you are reading, pay attention to how other writers vary their sentence patterns and build from one idea to the next. Try to analyze why the writers made the choices that they did.

SUGGESTIONS • SUGGESTIONS • SUGGESTIONS • SUGGESTIONS

If you need information about the rules of structure and punctuation for the connecting words listed above or practice using these words, see Part 3 of this text.

Adverb clauses of concession and contrast	see pages 184 to 187
Adverb clauses of time, cause-effect/ reason-result, and purpose	see pages 187 to 191
Adverb clauses: reduced	see pages 191 to 193
Conditionals	see pages 196 to 211
Coordination	see pages 212 to 217
Sentence connectors	see pages 237 to 240

Exercise 1.8 Turn back to page 9 and reread the autobiographical essay by the student from Kuwait. Find and underline places where the writer used some of the connecting words listed above. With other writers in the class, discuss the use of these connecting words and their sentence patterns. Discuss:

- the meaning relationship that the connecting word expresses.
- possible reasons why the writer used the connecting word. Did he use it to clarify meaning? to show the relative importance of ideas? to ensure sentence variety? to maintain the flow of ideas? Did he use it for a combination of reasons?
- the various sentence patterns used with the connecting words.

For additional practice, do the same analysis with the autobiographical essay on page 11.

Exercise 1.9 This exercise will give you practice with sentence revision. It will also help you become aware of what to consider when you are trying to decide on an effective pattern or connecting word for the sentence that you are working on. Your decisions will depend on the meaning that you are trying to convey, on the context of your sentence, and on the flow of ideas.

On page 27, you will see one writer's autobiographical essay. In the essay, some sentences or pairs of sentences are numbered and written in *italics*.

Read the essay carefully. With other writers in your class, discuss possible ways to revise each numbered sentence or pair of sentences. Discuss as many ways as you can think of. Then choose the way(s) that seem most effective within the context of this essay. When you have finished your discussion, write the revised sentences in the blank spaces on the following page. NOTE: There may be more than one appropriate way to revise each sentence or sentence pair.

Chapter 1 : Writing an Autobiographical Essay

Number 1 has been done for you and is explained below. Study this example after you read the essay.

I was born in Medillin, Colombia, in 1960. In Medillin, I attended six years of elementary school and six years of high school. (1) *I decided to pursue an advanced degree in pharmaceutical chemistry. I liked chemistry and biology in high school.* (2) *I graduated from high school. I entered the University of Antioquia.* (3) *I studied at the university for ten semesters. I was awarded a B.S. degree in 1982.*

(4) *I worked in the pharmacy at St. Vincent de Paul Hospital. (1978–1982) I was taking courses at the university. (1978–1982)* (5) *I filled in for staff members who were on sick or vacation leave. My responsibilities there were varied.* As a result, I observed all aspects of running a large hospital pharmacy. (6) *It was difficult to work and study at the same time. I gained invaluable practical experience. The work complemented my studies.*

(7) *I finished my course work at the university, and then I did a three-month practicum in the quality control division of Bayer of Colombia, and I wrote a thesis about good manufacturing practices after I completed this practicum.* Many of the practices that I described have been adopted by Bayer and by other pharmaceutical companies in Colombia.

(8) *I became interested in food science. I was doing research on manufacturing practices and quality control.* (9) *I heard from some colleagues in Colombia that your university has excellent research facilities in this field. I would like to be considered for admission to your master's program in food science.*

(10) *I will finish my master's degree. I will return to Colombia.* I would like to work for the agriculture department of the national government. As my country grows in population, the demand for agricultural products increases. (11) *My country is working to fill that demand through domestic production. We want to be able to reduce our dependence on imports from other countries.*

NOTE: the dates in parentheses give you information to help you decide how to combine the paired sentences. However, you should not use those dates in your new sentences.

Number One

1. I decided to pursue an advanced degree in pharmaceutical chemistry.
   I liked chemistry and biology in high school.

Some Possible Combinations

   a. I decided to pursue an advanced degree in pharmaceutical chemistry because I liked chemistry and biology in high school.
   b. I decided to pursue an advanced degree in pharmaceutical chemistry, for I liked chemistry and biology in high school.
   c. Because I liked chemistry and biology in high school, I decided to pursue an advanced degree in pharmaceutical chemistry.
   d. I liked chemistry and biology in high school; therefore, I decided to pursue an advanced degree in pharmaceutical chemistry.

Option *c* seems most effective for this context. The dependent clause picks up the reference to "high school" in the preceding sentence and leads into the information about the writer's major in the university. Option *d* seems effective, too, because this pattern also uses the phrase "in high school" as a bridge between the previous idea and the next idea.

Part I: Drafted Works in Progress

I was born in Medillin, Colombia, in 1960. In Medillin, I attended six years of elementary school and six years of high school. (1) _____
_____.

(2) _____.

(3) _____
_____.

(4) _____
_____.

(5) _____
_____.

As a result, I observed all aspects of running a large hospital pharmacy. (6) _____
_____.

(7) _____
_____
_____
_____.

Many of the practices that I described have been adopted by Bayer and by other pharmaceutical companies in Colombia.

(8) _____
_____.

(9) _____
_____
_____.

(10) _____
_____.

I would like to work for the agriculture department of the national government. As my country grows in population, the demand for agricultural products increases. (11) _____
_____
_____.

CHAPTER 1 : WRITING AN AUTOBIOGRAPHICAL ESSAY

DRAFTING YOUR PAPER: *The Third Draft*

PLANNING AND WRITING YOUR THIRD DRAFT

Before you begin to prepare the third draft of your autobiographical essay, plan the revisions that you will make in your paper.

SUGGESTIONS • SUGGESTIONS • SUGGESTIONS • SUGGESTIONS

Here are some suggestions for one way to plan your third draft.

1. Reread your second draft carefully.

2. Mark any changes that you plan to make in your third draft.
   a. If you plan to reorganize any ideas, try using brackets and arrows to show the new order.
   b. If you plan to omit any ideas, cross them out with one line.
   c. If you plan to add any information, write it in the margin or in blank spaces, and somehow indicate to yourself where it will be inserted.
   d. Do you want to make any changes in the sentence structures? If yes, cross out the sentences that you want to change; write in the revised sentences above them.
   e. If you see any corrections that you should make in your grammar, spelling, or punctuation, make them on your second draft.

3. After you mark up your second draft, begin to write your third draft. Write this draft neatly; skip lines.

4. Reread your third draft when you are finished. If you would like to make any additional changes, feel free. Cross out what you would like to change and rewrite.

5. If you are using a computer, see Appendix C, page C-264, for suggestions about writing your third draft.

LEARNING FROM ANOTHER WRITER Below is the second draft of the paper written by the student from Kuwait. Before you begin to mark your second draft, study this example to see how the writer followed the directions above. On his paper you see his notes about the changes that he wanted to make for his third draft. As you can see, he decided to throw some ideas away and to add a few more ideas. He also changed some of the sentence structures and words. After marking up his second draft, he produced a clean third draft.

Part I: Drafted Works in Progress

Second Draft

I would like to apply as a transfer student to the Department of Mechanical Engineering Technology. I was born in Kuwait City, ~~the state of~~ Kuwait, on the 7th of April 1969. I ~~joined the~~ *started my* formal education in Kuwait in 1974, ~~were~~ *and* I studied for the next 12 years. From 1982 to 1986, I was in high school ~~were I was listed two times on the dean list (1983, 1986). I was an honor~~ *where I was an honour student and was listed on the dean's list two times, in 1983 and 1986.* ~~student, I graduated from high school with a G.P.A. 3.19 out of 4.00.~~ During school vacations, I work at my father's audio & video showroom as a salesman and as an accountant.

In 1987 I ~~joined~~ *have entered* Kuwait Institute of Technology (K.I.T.), ~~K.I.T.~~ *which* is a two and half years college, I ~~did~~ *took* a placement test which ~~told me~~ *indicate* that I have a high aptitude for mechanics; *Because of that, I choosed* ~~my major was~~ mechanic engineering technology *to be my major at K.I.T.* with a minor in the power section. During my studies, I took courses in engines, turbines design ~~&~~ *and* thermodynamics. I used to write my reports, solve problems and write scientific programs using computers, *so* I became familiar with different computer system and their capabilities and with different computer language. I graduated from the Institute in 1989 with a G.P.A. of 3.99 out of 4.00 *and received a* (distinction with honor). *Since* I was the first Kuwaiti to achive that in my major, ~~as a prize for my distinction with honor~~ the Government of Kuwait awarded me a *full* ~~free~~ scholarship to the U.S.A. to finish a B.S. in mechanical engineering technology.

While I was studying at K.I.T., I have had a chance to do a co-op program in which I apply what I have learn during my studies in companies and ministries, I worked as a training student in Kuwait Airways ~~(overhaul engine workshop)~~, Kuwait Aviation & Fuel Company ~~(pumps & compressor lab)~~, Ministry of Water and Electricity ~~(power generating plant)~~, Kuwait Oil Tanker Company ~~(pneumatic and hydraulic lab)~~, Ministry of Transportation ~~(engine workshop)~~. After graduation ~~from K.I.T.~~, I worked for a short time with the Institute of Electrical and Electronic Engineers (I.E.E.E.) as a software trainer; ~~and~~ I *also* worked with Kuwait ~~minucipality~~ *Municipality* as a computer operator ~~&~~ *and* a designer. I developed mechanical projects using computer aided design (C.A.D.) workstations.

CHAPTER 1 : WRITING AN AUTOBIOGRAPHICAL ESSAY

I choosed your university because a lot of my friend recommend it and because ~~your university~~ has a good reputation back in Kuwait for its engineering technology program~~, and as a matter of fact~~ *Moreover,* the chairman of my department highly recommend it. My long term goal is not *only* to have a B.S. ~~only,~~ but ~~it extend to~~ *also to earn* a M.S. and a P.hd. in engineering technology. A higher graduate degree will enable me to ~~envolve~~ *become involved* in industrial planning *and* ~~&~~ design which ~~my country relay~~ *Kuwait is relying* on for the future of ~~Kuwait~~ *its* industry. ~~Another thing so~~ I *would also like to* ~~can~~ achive one of my childhood dream to be a ~~profesor~~ *professor* at Kuwait University in *mechanical* engineering technology.

(inserted: for my undergraduate studies; it)

EDITING YOUR WRITING

DEVELOPING A STRATEGY FOR EDITING

Once you are satisfied with the content, organization, and overall expression of ideas, it is time to *edit*. Editing is the process of checking over a later draft of a paper to look for and correct mistakes with grammar, spelling, punctuation, and word choice. A responsible writer always edits the draft that will be submitted to the reader.

It is important to keep in mind that all writers make mistakes, so it is not a bad thing to make mistakes. However, remember, too, that it is your responsibility to find and correct as many mistakes as possible before you give your work to your reader.

Why do you make mistakes when writing in English?

> **SOURCES OF ERRORS FOR ESL WRITERS**
> - Carelessness
> - Gaps in your knowledge of English
> - Interference from your first language

For these and other reasons, it can be difficult for you to identify your mistakes. It is always easier to find other people's mistakes; it is hard to "see" your own.

In order to use your editing time well, it is important to develop a system or a strategy for editing your papers. To get started, try this two-part strategy: 1) discovering your most common mistakes, and 2) using an editing checklist.

PART I: DRAFTED WORKS IN PROGRESS

DISCOVERING YOUR COMMON MISTAKES To focus your editing, it will help you to know what your most common mistakes are; in other words, what are your "favorite" mistakes at this point in your development as a writer in English? Once you know what your common mistakes are, you can focus your attention on those problem areas and be more likely to find and correct your errors.

SUGGESTIONS • SUGGESTIONS • SUGGESTIONS • SUGGESTIONS

With this first assignment, it might be useful to begin to compile a list of your own editing mistakes. To help you identify what they are:

1. Your readers (your instructor, tutor, and/or classmates) will indicate errors on your third draft.

2. You can try to:
   - analyze the source of the errors,
   - correct them,
   - and, if possible, identify a pattern to your errors.

If a pattern emerges, you will know what to focus on when editing your next piece of writing.

USING AN EDITING CHECKLIST An editing checklist provides you with a systematic way to proofread a revised draft that is almost ready for submission to your readers. See Appendix A for an editing checklist that you can use when writing. When using the checklist, pay special attention to steps that address your most common mistakes.

LEARNING FROM ANOTHER WRITER To see one way to develop a strategy for editing, study the following example. Below you will find the third draft of the mechanical engineering technologist from Kuwait. If you compare this draft to his first (pp. 15 and 16) and second (pp. 30 and 31), you will see that he made several revisions in content and organization. He also polished up some of his sentence patterns. Now he wants to edit carefully.

Scan through the third draft below. You will see several marks on his paper—underlinings and circles. These marks were made by one of the readers, in this case, the writer's instructor. Each mark indicates a mistake. The writer must go through his paper carefully, find each mistake, and correct it.

Exercise 1.10 For practice, go through this writer's paper and see how many errors you can identify and correct. Use the Editing Checklist in Appendix A to help you focus your editing. When you find an error, cross out the incorrect form and write in the correct one above it.

When you have finished editing this draft, try to see if there is a pattern to the writer's errors. Which types of errors does he make most often? Try to find his three most frequent errors. These are probably three mistakes that he makes often at this point in his acquisition of English. As this writer progresses in English, learns more about the language, and has more experience with reading and writing, he may stop making these mistakes; he may find that other types of errors replace them.

Chapter 1 : Writing an Autobiographical Essay

I would like to apply as a transfer student to the Department of Mechanical Engineering Technology. I was born in Kuwait City, Kuwait, on the 7th of April 1969. I started my formal education in Kuwait in 1974, and I studied there for the next 12 years. From 1982 to 1986, I was in high school, where I was an honors student and was on the dean's list two times, in 1983 and 1986. During school vacations, I work at my father's audio and video showroom as a salesman and as an accountant.

In 1987, I have entered Kuwait Institute of Technology (K.I.T.), which is a two and a half year college. I took a placement test which indicate that I have a high aptitude for mechanics. Because of that, I choosed mechanical engineering technology to be my major at K.I.T., with a minor in the power section. During my studies, I took courses in engines, turbine design & thermodynamics. I used to write my reports, solve problems and write scientific programs using computers, so I became familiar with different computer system and their capabilities and with different computer language. I graduated from the Institute in 1989 with a G.P.A. of 3.99 out of 4.00 and received a distinction with honor, since I was the first Kuwaiti to achive that G.P.A. in my major, the Government of Kuwait awarded me a full scholarship to the U.S.A. to finish a B.S. in mechanical engineering technology.

While I was studying at K.I.T., I have had a chance to do a co-op program in which I apply what I have learn during my studies to my work in companies and ministries. I worked as a trainee at Kuwait Airways, Kuwait Aviation and Fuel Company, the Ministry of Water and Electricity, the Kuwait Oil Tanker Company, and the Ministry of Transportation. After graduation, I worked for a short time with the Institute of Electrical & Electronic Engineers (I.E.E.E.) as a software trainer. I also worked for the Kuwait Municipality as a computer operator and a designer, in this job, I developed mechanical projects using computer aided design (C.A.D) workstations.

I choosed your university for my undergraduate studies because a lot of my friend recommend it and because it has a good reputation back in Kuwait for its mechanical engineering

PART I: DRAFTED WORKS IN PROGRESS

technology program. Moreover, the chairman of my department at K.I.T. highly <u>recommend</u> it to me. My long term goal is not only to receive a B.S. degree but also to earn an M.S. and eventually a Ph.D. in engineering technology. A higher degree will enable me to become involved in industrial planning <u>&</u> design, which Kuwait is relying on for the future of its industry. I would also like to <u>achive</u> one of my childhood <u>dream</u> to be a professor at Kuwait University in mechanical engineering technology.

This writer's most frequent mistakes at this point seem to be verb forms and tenses, noun plurals, and marking sentence boundaries with periods. Whenever he is editing his writing, he should remember to look carefully for these types of errors.

To help him remember, he created his own *editing acronym*. (An acronym is a word created from the first letters of other words. For example, UNESCO is an acronym that stands for <u>U</u>nited <u>N</u>ations <u>E</u>ducational, <u>S</u>cientific and <u>C</u>ultural <u>O</u>rganization. Acronyms shorten the full phrase and are easier to remember.) This writer created the acronym PLU-PER-VER to remind him to edit his later drafts for errors with <u>PLU</u>rals, <u>PER</u>iods, and <u>VER</u>bs.

SUGGESTIONS • SUGGESTIONS • SUGGESTIONS • SUGGESTIONS

Here are some suggestions for editing your own draft:

1. If you had another reader mark mistakes on your third draft, read through your draft carefully. Use the marks, comments, and the Editing Checklist in Appendix A to guide you.

2. When you find a mistake, correct it. If you have any doubts or questions while you are working, ask another writer in the class for assistance.

3. When you have finished making the corrections on the third draft, reread the whole draft carefully. Be sure all of the ideas and sentences read exactly the way you want them to read.

4. Try creating your own editing acronym. When you have finished editing, look over the errors that you corrected on your *third* draft. See if you can identify a pattern to your errors. Do any errors recur? Which types of errors did you seem to make the most often? Find your most common mistakes and write them in the space below. When you have finished this list, create your own *editing acronym* to use when you are editing your writing. Write that acronym in the space provided.

COMMON MISTAKES ON ASSIGNMENT # 1:

_____
_____
_____
_____

EDITING ACRONYM: _____

CHAPTER 1 : WRITING AN AUTOBIOGRAPHICAL ESSAY

Freewriting Journal Assignment

Now that you have written an autobiographical essay in English, take some time out to consider your writing as work in progress. Spend a few minutes looking back over and reflecting on all of the work that you did while drafting your autobiography. In your freewriting journal, write a paragraph describing what YOU like about your work in progress. In other words, celebrate your successes.

Describe:

- what you feel proud of about your work.
- what you have done with this work that you did not think you were capable of doing before you started.
- what you have learned by doing this work.

Write another paragraph describing one aspect of your writing that you want to work on and improve.

Describe:

- why you think that you should work on this aspect.
- what you can do to work on this aspect over the next few weeks.

CHAPTER 2

Writing for a Campus Brochure

PREWRITING
- Setting the Context
- Understanding the Assignment
- Analyzing the Audience
- Collecting Data

DRAFTING YOUR PAPER: THE FIRST DRAFT
- Planning Your First Draft
- Writing Your First Draft

REVISING YOUR WRITING
- Developing Your Ideas
- Giving and Getting Feedback

DRAFTING YOUR PAPER: THE SECOND DRAFT
- Planning and Writing Your Second Draft

REVISING YOUR WRITING
- Focusing on Your Sentence Structures

DRAFTING YOUR PAPER: THE THIRD DRAFT
- Planning and Writing Your Third Draft

EDITING YOUR WRITING

PART I: DRAFTED WORKS IN PROGRESS

PREWRITING

SETTING THE CONTEXT

In the United States, catalogs and brochures are a common way to inform people about places, services, and products. Tourist attractions, hospitals, car and clothing companies, and colleges and universities publish brochures to tell people about what they have to offer.

Exercise 2.1 Freewrite answers to the following questions. Then discuss your answers with your classmates.

1. What are some brochures or catalogs that you have read recently?
2. What qualities in a brochure attract your attention? In other words, what characteristics make you pick up a brochure and read it?
3. Do you think brochures and catalogs are an effective way to inform people about places, services, and products? Why or why not?

UNDERSTANDING THE ASSIGNMENT

Imagine that the admissions office at your school, college, or university is going to print a new brochure to use for its overseas recruitment. The purpose of the brochure will be to tell prospective students about the school: to describe its academic programs, its extra-curricular activities, and different places on campus. The brochure will also tell the readers about the area in which the school is located: to describe resources, facilities, and places of interest in the local community. The brochure will be designed to give its readers—students from all over the world—an idea of what the school and the area have to offer international students.

The admissions office feels that one of the best ways to recruit new students is by "word of mouth;" that is, they feel that new students will be attracted to the school if they hear about it from current students. Therefore, this office has asked international and bilingual students on campus to submit essays about the school and the surrounding area. These essays will be considered for inclusion in the brochure.

For this assignment, you are going to write a brief essay about one of your favorite places on campus or in the surrounding area. You will be writing the essay for inclusion in the recruitment brochure. It must be brief, between 300 and 500 words. Your purpose in writing the essay is to help attract new students to your school, college, or university.

ANALYZING THE AUDIENCE

Think about the audience that you are writing for. Remember that it is international students who are in the process of selecting an American college or university.

1. What places on your campus or in the surrounding area will they want to read about?
2. Why?

CHAPTER 2: WRITING FOR A CAMPUS BROCHURE

COLLECTING DATA

OBSERVATION AND NOTE-TAKING In your freewriting journal, you have already written several entries about your favorite place or places on campus or in the local community. (See page 20.) Reread those entries now. Do you want to write about one of these places for the campus brochure? Do you want to write about another place? Keep your audience and purpose in mind as you make your decision.

Exercise 2.2 Go to the place that you will describe. Find a comfortable spot to sit; be sure that your seat gives you a clear view of the place.

1. If you have not already done so, draw a rough sketch (or diagram) of the place.

2. If you have already freewritten entries about this place, reread them. Keeping your audience and your purpose in mind, take additional notes about the place. Jot down anything about the place that you think international students will find attractive or interesting. If you prefer, write these notes in words and phrases, not in complete sentences.

3. If you have no notes about this place yet, freewrite some now. Keep your audience and purpose in mind as you work.

Study the following example of one writer's notes before you begin. This writer decided to describe the basketball court inside her university's gymnasium, the JAR Arena.

Place: JAR Arena, Basketball Court

Date: 1/17/93

Time: 8:00-9:00 p.m.

fans, coats, cheerleaders, players, coaches, players running back and forth, coach upset at referees, one player fell into the chairs at the side, electronic display board ⟶ flashes ads, messages to the fans. Some crazy fans ⟶ really "into" it. 2 special half-time contests: 1) dollar bills thrown on the floor ⟶ contest = collect as many bills as you can in a time limit ⟶ a young girl won; 2) basket shooting to win a car ⟶ sponsored by a car dealer. TV crews; good place to meet people — ask about the sport. Student sitting next to me asked why I'm taking notes; she explained the rules of basketball to me: foul shots, 3-point baskets, offense, defense. Lots of noise: clapping, cheers, boos, music, announcements. Student next to me: "Oh no!!" "Oooh!" "Aaah!" "Yeah!" New bleachers. fans in blue and gold tee shirts. Shouts Band — lots of music. Blue and gold everywhere: scarves, jackets. Court = new — very clean. Electronic display screen — announcements, ads, score. Noise <u>all</u> the time — roars, shouts; two groups of fans shouting across the court. One fan ⟶ blue and gold hair!! Another ⟶ painted face = $\frac{1}{2}$ = gold;

½ = blue! players dive for the ball — land hard. Time-outs — listen to coaches; several coaches. Coaches meet; make decisions. Players help each other. Lots of excitement, friendly, happy. Determination: players try 100%. Coaches pacing. Motivation — fans and players. Concentration, spirit, love of the team. Strangers talking to each other — giving high fives. Air = taste of dust, wood, pop. ~~Smell~~ Smells of sweat (yuck!), coffee, pop corn, wood, wool from & coats. People everywhere. Mascot = kangaroo called "Zippy." Cheerleaders = gymnastics! Jumps, runs, men throw women into the air. Zippy teases ⟶ referees and players. Fans play close attention to the game — clap and cheer for every point. Yell at referees. Bleachers = wooden benches — hard — not comfortable. More expensive seats = chairs with backs — nice. Modern score board displays messages. Court = shiny finish; highly polished.

PART I: DRAFTED WORKS IN PROGRESS

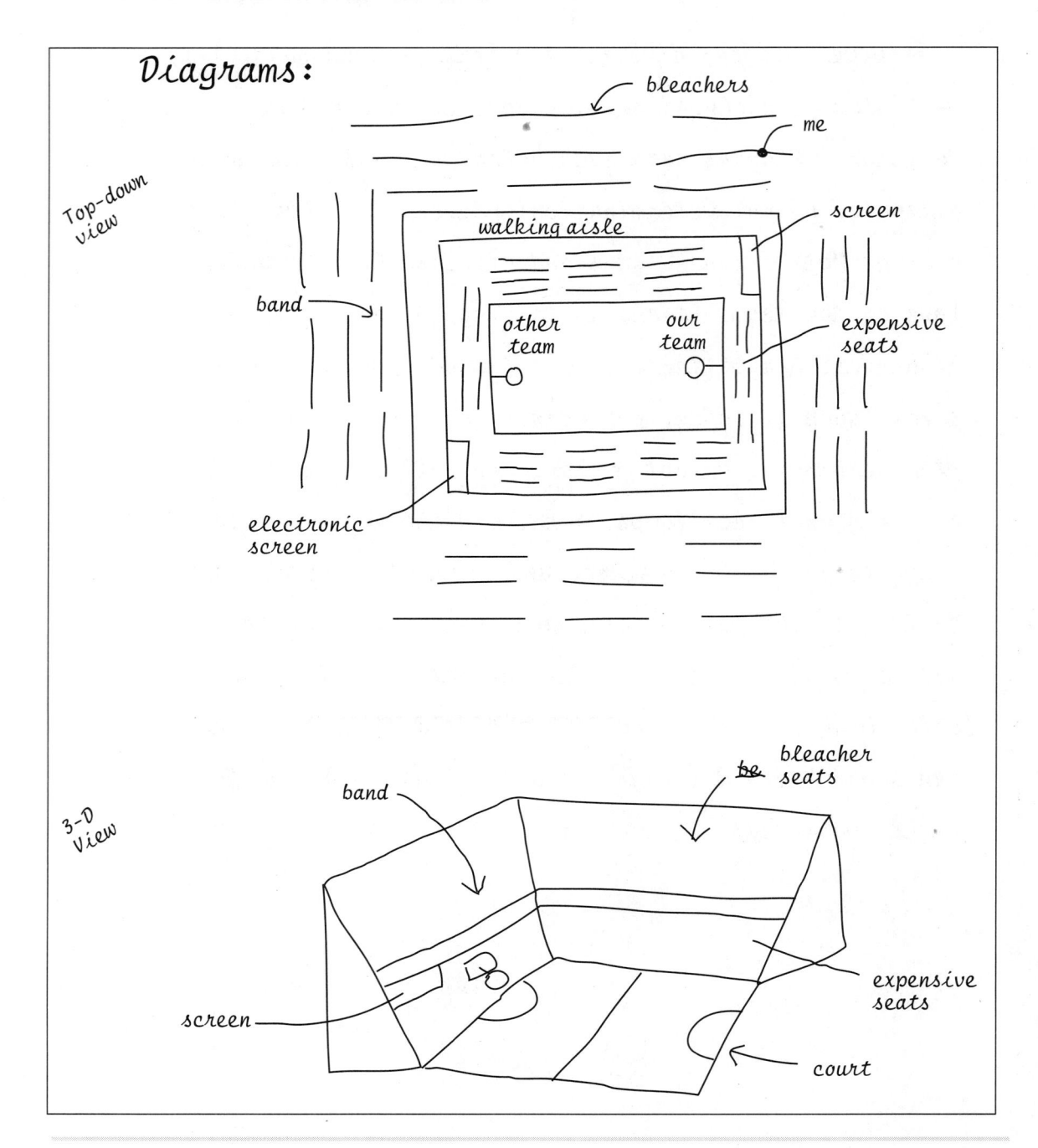

Diagrams:

Top-down view: bleachers, me, walking aisle, screen, band, other team, our team, expensive seats, electronic screen

3-D View: band, bleacher seats, expensive seats, screen, court

CHAPTER 2: WRITING FOR A CAMPUS BROCHURE

DRAFTING YOUR PAPER: *The First Draft*

PLANNING YOUR FIRST DRAFT

For this assignment, you are writing a brief description of one place on your campus or in the local community. The purpose of your description is to help attract international students to your school, college, or university. The text that you submit should be between 300 and 500 words.

In this brief essay, you cannot say everything about the place you have chosen to describe. At the same time, you want your description to be unified, to have some thread or theme holding it all together. Therefore, you should find a *main idea* for your writing—that is, find one characteristic or quality about the place that you can concentrate your writing on. All of the sentences in your description will work to develop or communicate that main idea.

LEARNING FROM OTHER WRITERS To see what we mean by *main idea*, look at some descriptions written by other writers. The first one describes Buchtel Commons, an outdoor area in the center of a university campus.

Buchtel Commons

The campus of the university isn't very big, but it's very clean, convenient and comfortable. The heart of the university is Buchtel Commons, an open mall in the center of campus. During the cold months, Buchtel Commons is deserted except for every hour on the hour, when students and teachers are rushing to their next class. In the summer, the Commons is a pleasant place to relax between classes and feel like you're a part of the university.

Let's take a walking tour of Buchtel Commons, which was named after John Buchtel, the founder of the university. Standing on the east edge of the wide brick street which goes through the Commons, you can see two classroom buildings, Kolbe Hall and Leigh Hall, on your left. Walking west through the Commons, you'll find Bierce Library on your right. This is one of the most important facilities for students on campus. Around the library, there are a fountain and benches where students sit and enjoy the warm weather. Some are reading books; others are listening to the wind chimes that line the Commons and ring out tunes during the day; still others are enjoying their lunch. The Commons has several food and snack stands, where you can buy sandwiches, tacos, gyros and soft drinks if you are hungry.

Opposite the fountain, up a short flight of stairs, there is a large statue of John Buchtel. The area on either side of the statue is covered with green grass and beautiful flowers, and students who have just left the library are relaxing on the grass. Some of them are eating sandwiches, some are chatting with friends, and others are sleeping. After you pass Buchtel's statue, you'll see Zook, Crouse and Ayer Halls, three more classroom buildings. On your right are the three dormitories which provide on-campus accommodations. Straight ahead, you will find a marvelous tall glass building, which is the new Polymer Science Building. The sights of Buchtel Commons are reflected in its shiny glass exterior, which mirrors back to you the relaxation and comfort of the Commons.

This is the end of the tour. The campus spreads out around Buchtel Commons and there are a lot of facilities with which you can enjoy your American student life.

PART I: DRAFTED WORKS IN PROGRESS

Exercise 2.3 Discuss these questions with your classmates.

(1) What seems to be the main idea of this description? In other words, what is the writer's most important message about Buchtel Commons? What one idea do all of the sentences communicate?

(2) What *one* sentence in the description expresses the writer's main idea?

Now read this description of the Chuckery, a student cafeteria at the same university.

The Chuckery

Although the university has many eating and drinking places, the Chuckery is the best place for you to go. Located on the first floor of Gardner Student Center, the Chuckery isn't merely an eating place. It's a good place to "hang out" and enjoy your free time. The Chuckery has two different time zones for you to enjoy: a crowded time and a quiet time.

Whenever you go to the Chuckery before 2:00 p.m. from Monday to Friday, you see many students of diverse ethnic backgrounds crowding there. But you can probably find a vacant seat soon because there are lots of pleasant wooden tables and chairs in the Chuckery. There are McDonald's, the Creamery, Altieri's Zipizza and Del Burrito, where you can find all kinds of food, such as cookies, hamburgers, pizza, egg rolls, tacos, burritos and ice cream. During the crowded time, there are many lines in front of each restaurant counter. The staff is busy serving orders as quickly as possible. They work so fast that the Chuckery provides "fast food" even if it's crowded. The noisiest area is the front of McDonald's, which is located in the center of the Chuckery. The people sitting around there are laughing, smoking, chatting, studying, reading magazines and listening to music. The mere thought of all this noise might make you nervous, but it proves that the Chuckery is the most lively place on campus.

On the other hand, you experience a completely different atmosphere when you go to the Chuckery on weekends or after lunch time has passed on weekdays. It becomes less noisy little by little, and the staff begins to clean the tables. Although you can sit anywhere now, the best place is by the windows, which is the brightest area in the Chuckery. During the quiet time zone, people are talking quietly, reading newspapers over coffee, or taking naps. As this quiet time is completely different from the crowded time, you feel as though you are in another place. Out of the windows, you can see Jackson Field, which has tennis courts, basketball courts and a soccer field, where many people enjoy sports. To watch these people makes you relax when you are tired of studying. Another merit of the quiet time in the Chuckery is the opportunity to get acquainted with American students who have enough time to converse with international students.

If the Chuckery were always noisy, you would probably feel annoyed. If it were always quiet and vacant, you would feel bored. Take advantage of the two time zones offered by the Chuckery.

Exercise 2.4 Discuss these questions with your classmates.

(1) What seems to be the main idea of this description? In other words, what is the writer's most important message about the Chuckery? What one idea do all of the sentences communicate?

(2) What *one* sentence in the description expresses the writer's main idea?

Now read this description of the Eagle Valley Health Club, a fitness center located near the writer's university.

Eagle Valley Health Club

Have you ever counted how many hours you spend sitting at school and studying at home or in the library? Probably a lot. And do you ever feel that you are without energy and freshness? Do you ever feel bored? Does your brain not work fast enough? I have the answer. You need to go somewhere where you can do many different sports activities to keep in shape. You don't know any place like that? I can show you because I do.

That place is a health club called Eagle Valley. It is located in the town of Brecksville, which is around 30 minutes from campus. The club is open seven days a week from 6:00 a.m. to 11:00 p.m. on Mondays through Fridays and from 8:00 a.m to 7:00 p.m. on weekends. The cost and length of a membership can vary, but typical fees are $15.00 to $25.00 per month. It is also possible to negotiate a personal membership. You don't have to be a member to use the facilities, but it costs a lot more to pay for each separate visit.

Do you want to know what you can do there? There are too many choices. At first, I'll show you the second floor. Let's go take a look.

When you feel like jumping, dancing or just somehow shaking your body, you will like the aerobics and step classes. Step classes are a big hit in America right now. They are similar to aerobics, but in step training you use a simple plastic step; you step on and off this platform in rhythm to the music. Is that too slow for you? No problem. In another room you can find a nice running track, where your speed is up to you. When you get tired, you can just walk. There are also stationary treadmills, machines for running or walking at your own pace. If you don't enjoy running but you still wish to have a hard workout, you should choose the stairmaster. It is a hydraulic machine with two steps which move up and down. As you are stepping on each pedal, you hold your body above the ground. In just 15 minutes you will get an exhausting workout. If you like other outdoor activities but the weather is bad, you can use the indoor bikes and rowing machines. Using the rowing machines makes you feel as if you are on a small boat in the middle of a lake. And in the summer, with no snow in sight, ski lovers can practice on the Nordic Track, a machine that lets you feel like you are really skiing. For those of you who wish to build up hard bodies, very modern lifting machines are available. If you prefer only simple lifting, you can find thousands of pounds in free weights. And on the second floor, fans of martial arts can join a judo class.

Does it seem like there is enough to do? Right! But that's not all. Now we will move to the first floor. If you love tennis or racquetball, Eagle Valley has tennis and racquetball courts that will satisfy even very serious players. And after all your jumping, biking, running and sweat producing, you deserve to get some rest. What about sitting down in a hot whirlpool and getting a rich bubbling massage or relaxing in a nice hot sauna or in the steam room? It will become too hot for you after a while, so why don't you go refresh yourself in the pleasant water of the 25 meter swimming pool? And don't forget that Eagle Valley has a beautiful outdoor swimming pool for use in the summer. Are you ashamed to show up in your swimming suit because you look too pale? Don't worry because there's a tanning room in which you can get your skin bronzed.

Finally, your time in the gym is almost over. Take a quick shower and rest for a while by the romantic fireplace while reading some popular magazines. How do you feel now? Do you feel like a new person with lots of fresh energy? Are you ready to get back to your studies? I know you'll be so amazed by the Eagle Valley Health Club that you'll say, "I love this place!"

PART I: DRAFTED WORKS IN PROGRESS

Exercise 2.5 Discuss these questions with your classmates.

① What seems to be the main idea of this description? In other words, what is the writer's most important message about the Eagle Valley Health Club? What one idea do all of the sentences communicate?

② What *one* sentence in the description expresses the writer's main idea?

FINDING THE MAIN IDEA Often the data that a writer collects on a topic could yield many main ideas. Consider, for example, the prewriting notes collected by the student who wrote a description of JAR Arena, the basketball court. (See pages 40 to 42.) When this writer looked through her notes, she saw several different possible main ideas—or most important messages—for her essay.

POSSIBLE MAIN IDEAS

① fans = dedicated
② facilities in the basketball court = modern; show that the university is committed to sports
③ more than just a game = entertainment other than basketball
④ athletes and coaches = dedicated

Exercise 2.6 Of these four possible main ideas, this writer decided on number 3 for her draft because this was the focus she was most interested in writing about. Look back at the notes on pages 40 to 42. Circle all the ideas that she could use in her draft to communicate this main idea.

If she had decided to focus on the dedicated fans in the basketball arena, which ideas would she probably have used for her paper? Which ideas are related to that main idea? Write the number 1 next to each note that relates.

If she had decided to focus on the modern facilities in the basketball arena, which ideas would she probably have used for her paper? Which ideas are related to that main idea? Write the number 2 next to each note that relates.

If she had decided to focus on the dedicated athletes and the coaches in the basketball arena, which ideas would she probably have used for her paper? Which ideas are related to that main idea? Write the number 4 next to each note that relates.

EXPRESSING THE MAIN IDEA: FORMULATING A THESIS STATEMENT A reader has an easier time understanding a text if the writer's main idea is stated directly *in* the text. For a formal essay in American English, it is common to state the main idea at the beginning of the text, somewhere in the introduction. We call this explicit statement of the main idea a *thesis statement*.

CHAPTER 2: WRITING FOR A CAMPUS BROCHURE

CONVENTIONAL STRUCTURE FOR A FORMAL ESSAY IN AMERICAN ENGLISH

| INTRODUCTION / THESIS STATEMENT | → | DEVELOPMENT AND SUPPORT | → | DEVELOPMENT AND SUPPORT |

WHAT IS A THESIS STATEMENT?

It is one sentence within your paper; it tells the reader your TOPIC and YOUR MAIN IDEA.

TOPIC = the subject, or "what" you are writing about.

MAIN IDEA = what you will say about that topic. Your main idea is your most important message.

WHY IS A THESIS STATEMENT IMPORTANT?

- It tells your readers what your paper will be about. It previews or summarizes the contents of your paper and prepares your reader for your ideas.
- It often indicates the organization or arrangement of the ideas in the paper.
- It is common practice to include a thesis statement in a formal paper.

WHAT ARE THE CHARACTERISTICS OF A GOOD THESIS STATEMENT?

- It is a complete sentence.
- It appears somewhere INSIDE your paper, not as a title, but rather, right within the text of the paper. (A thesis statement often appears in the introduction of a formal paper. In a short text, it might appear at the beginning or at the end.)
- It is specific enough to cover the contents of the paper.
- It matches or agrees with all of the information that you include in your paper.

WHERE DOES A THESIS STATEMENT COME FROM?

A THESIS STATEMENT comes from YOU, the writer. One way to determine and formulate a thesis statement is to:

- collect some ideas,
- read through them,
- find a main idea in your data, and
- write a sentence that expresses your main idea.

47

PART I: DRAFTED WORKS IN PROGRESS

Exercise 2.7 The writer of the description of JAR Arena came up with four possible main ideas for her paper. Look at the list of main ideas on page 46. Then, read the following *possible* thesis statements for a brief description of this place. Match each statement with its main idea.

1. A night at JAR Arena is more entertainment than just basketball.
2. JAR Arena is a modern facility that symbolizes the university's commitment to sports.
3. Go to JAR Arena during a basketball game to feel the spirit and friendliness of the fans at the university.
4. An evening in JAR Arena will show you how seriously college athletes take their sports.
5. JAR Arena is a good place to learn about American sports fans.

Exercise 2.8 Now consider your own writing. Read back over your notes and your freewriting journal entries about the place that you are going to describe for the campus brochure. What possible main ideas do you see in those notes? Make a list for yourself. Then reread your list and choose the idea that you think you want to focus on in your description. If several ideas interest you at this point, number them in order of priority; you can make your choice later.

Exercise 2.9 At this point, try to formulate one or more possible thesis statements for your description. To do this,

1. Think about the main idea that you chose in Exercise 2.8.
2. On a piece of paper, compose a sentence that expresses your main idea. Be sure that your statement is a complete sentence, identifies the topic of your paper for your reader, and states your main idea about that topic. NOTE: Remember that you will be able to change your thesis statement later if you want to or need to, so do not feel trapped by the sentence that you write now. Instead, consider this sentence a first attempt at focusing your ideas.
3. You will only have one main idea in your paper, so you will only need one thesis statement. Right now, however, you might want to experiment with a few main ideas and thesis statements so that you can explore more than one possibility.

DECIDING ON AN ORGANIZATIONAL PLAN: THE GLOBAL STRUCTURE OF YOUR PAPER

You have established your topic, purpose, and audience for this paper. You also have some data and a preliminary main idea. Before you begin to write your first draft, give some thought to the organizational plan that you will use to establish the *global structure* of your paper. The *global structure* is the overall arrangement of ideas in your paper. It represents the "big picture" structure of your paper and the way that the ideas build on and relate to one another. A paper with a good, clear global structure is easier to read.

The plan or combination of plans that you use in any essay depends on your topic, purpose, main idea, and audience. You choose the plan that successfully achieves your purpose and that makes your readers' job easy.

There are several standard organizational plans in American English writing. Among the more common plans are the following:

CHAPTER 2: WRITING FOR A CAMPUS BROCHURE

CHRONOLOGICAL ORDER	arranging the ideas by time sequence
SPATIAL ORDER	arranging the ideas according to their relations in space; by location
ORDER OF IMPORTANCE	building the paper from the most important idea to the least important
REVERSE ORDER OF IMPORTANCE	building from the least important idea to the most important
CAUSE/EFFECT OR PROBLEM/SOLUTION ORDER	grouping the ideas by cause and effect or problem and solution
LOGICAL DIVISION	presenting the topic in parts
COMPARISON/CONTRAST	arranging the ideas according to similarities and/or differences

COMMON GLOBAL STRUCTURES

STRUCTURE	SAMPLE DATA	OUTLINE OF PAPER

CHRONOLOGICAL ORDER (time)
 	
Often used:
• to describe historical events
• to explain a sequence, cycle, or process
	Autobiography:
	1969 — born
	1974 — started school
	1986 — graduated high school
	1987 — entered technical school
	1989 — graduated technical school
	1990 — came to U.S.
		I. Through H.S.
		  A. 1969
		  B. 1974
		  C. 1986
		II. During Technical School
		  A. 1987
		  B. 1989
		III. In the U.S.
		IV. In the Future

SPATIAL ORDER (location)
 	
Often used:
• to describe a place
	Description of Buchtel Commons (for a brochure):
	[map showing Polymer science, Dorms, fountain, Library, Ayer, Crouse, Zook, statue, food stand, Leigh, Kolbe with N/S/E/W compass]
		I. On the East Edge
		II. Around the Library
		  A. fountain
		  B. benches
		  C. students
		III. At the Statue
		  A. grass and flowers
		  B. students
		IV. On the West Edge
		  A. classrooms
		  B. dorms
		  C. Polymer Bld.

PART I: DRAFTED WORKS IN PROGRESS

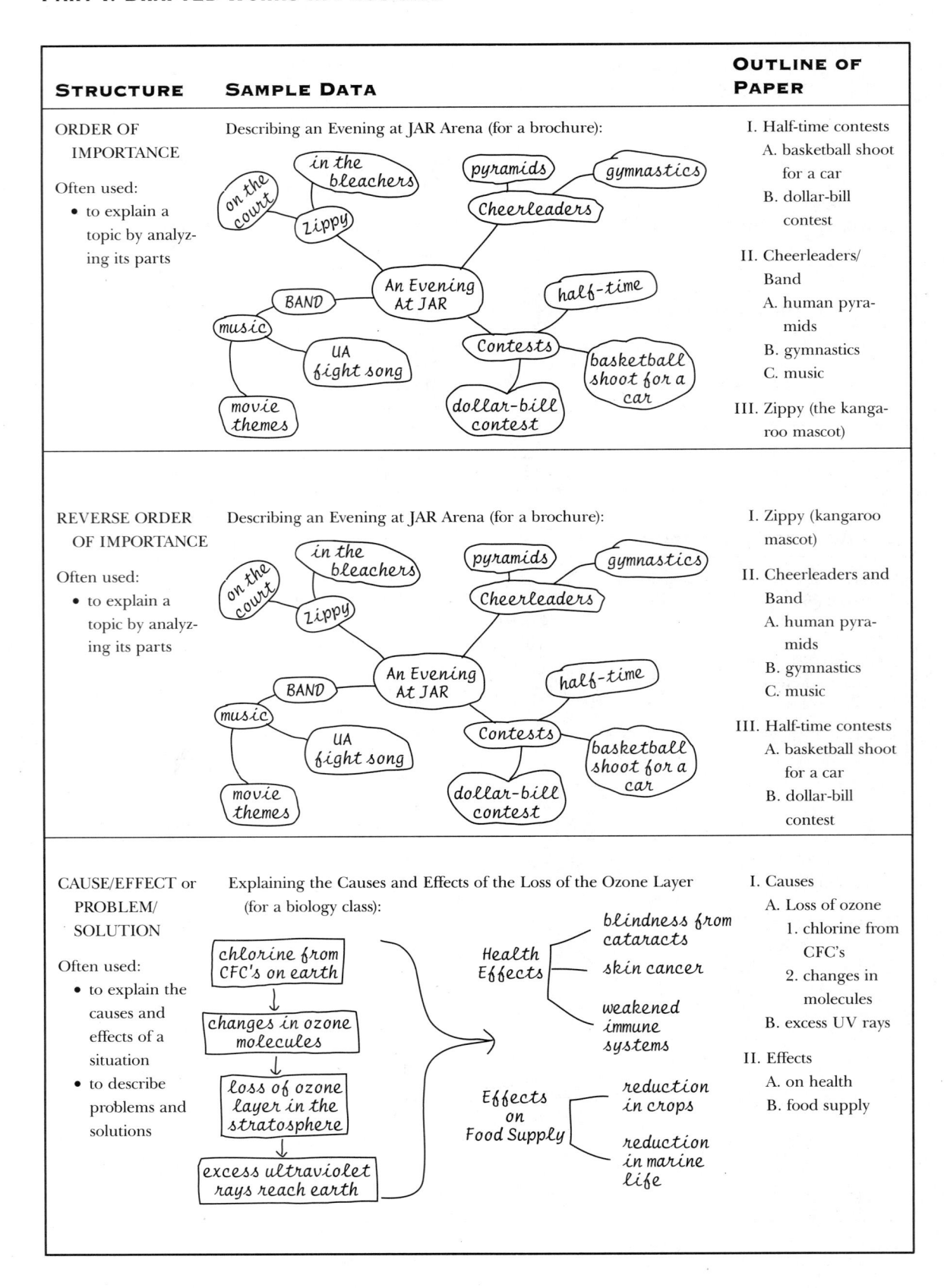

STRUCTURE	SAMPLE DATA	OUTLINE OF PAPER
ORDER OF IMPORTANCE Often used: • to explain a topic by analyzing its parts	Describing an Evening at JAR Arena (for a brochure): *[cluster diagram centered on "An Evening At JAR" with branches to: Zippy (on the court, in the bleachers); Cheerleaders (pyramids, gymnastics); half-time Contests (basketball shoot for a car, dollar-bill contest); BAND (music, UA fight song, movie themes)]*	I. Half-time contests 　A. basketball shoot for a car 　B. dollar-bill contest II. Cheerleaders/ Band 　A. human pyramids 　B. gymnastics 　C. music III. Zippy (the kangaroo mascot)
REVERSE ORDER OF IMPORTANCE Often used: • to explain a topic by analyzing its parts	Describing an Evening at JAR Arena (for a brochure): *[same cluster diagram as above]*	I. Zippy (kangaroo mascot) II. Cheerleaders and Band 　A. human pyramids 　B. gymnastics 　C. music III. Half-time contests 　A. basketball shoot for a car 　B. dollar-bill contest
CAUSE/EFFECT or PROBLEM/ SOLUTION Often used: • to explain the causes and effects of a situation • to describe problems and solutions	Explaining the Causes and Effects of the Loss of the Ozone Layer (for a biology class): *[flow chart: chlorine from CFC's on earth → changes in ozone molecules → loss of ozone layer in the stratosphere → excess ultraviolet rays reach earth → Health Effects (blindness from cataracts, skin cancer, weakened immune systems); Effects on Food Supply (reduction in crops, reduction in marine life)]*	I. Causes 　A. Loss of ozone 　　1. chlorine from CFC's 　　2. changes in molecules 　B. excess UV rays II. Effects 　A. on health 　B. food supply

Chapter 2: Writing for a Campus Brochure

Structure	Sample Data	Outline of Paper
LOGICAL DIVISION Often used: • to explain categories or types	Explaining Psychological Predispositions for Language Learning (for an education class): *Cluster diagram with "Psychological Predispositions" at center connected to: motivation, attitude, learning style, eye-ear learning, tolerance of ambiguity, extroversion, inhibition*	I. Motivation II. Attitude III. Extroversion IV. Inhibition V. Tolerance of Ambiguity VI. Learning Style VII. Eye-Ear Learning

COMPARISON/ CONTRAST
 	
Often used:
• to show similarities and/or differences between topics
• to discuss pros and cons of a topic or issue
	Showing Similarities and/or Differences in the Two Time Zones of the Chuckery (for a brochure):
	
	Cluster diagram with "Chuckery" at center connected to: windows, chairs, tables, food (Zipizza, McDonald's, Creamery), quiet (weekends, after 2:00), 12:00-2:00, crowded, eating, students (all kinds, playing cards, taking naps, talking laughing)
		I. The Crowded Time
		  A. seating
		  B. people
		  C. activities
		II. The Quiet Time
		  A. seating
		  B. people
		  C. activities
		
		OR
		
		I. Seating
		  A. crowded time
		  B. quiet time
		II. People
		  A. crowded time
		  B. quiet time
		III. Activities
		  A. crowded time
		  B. quiet time

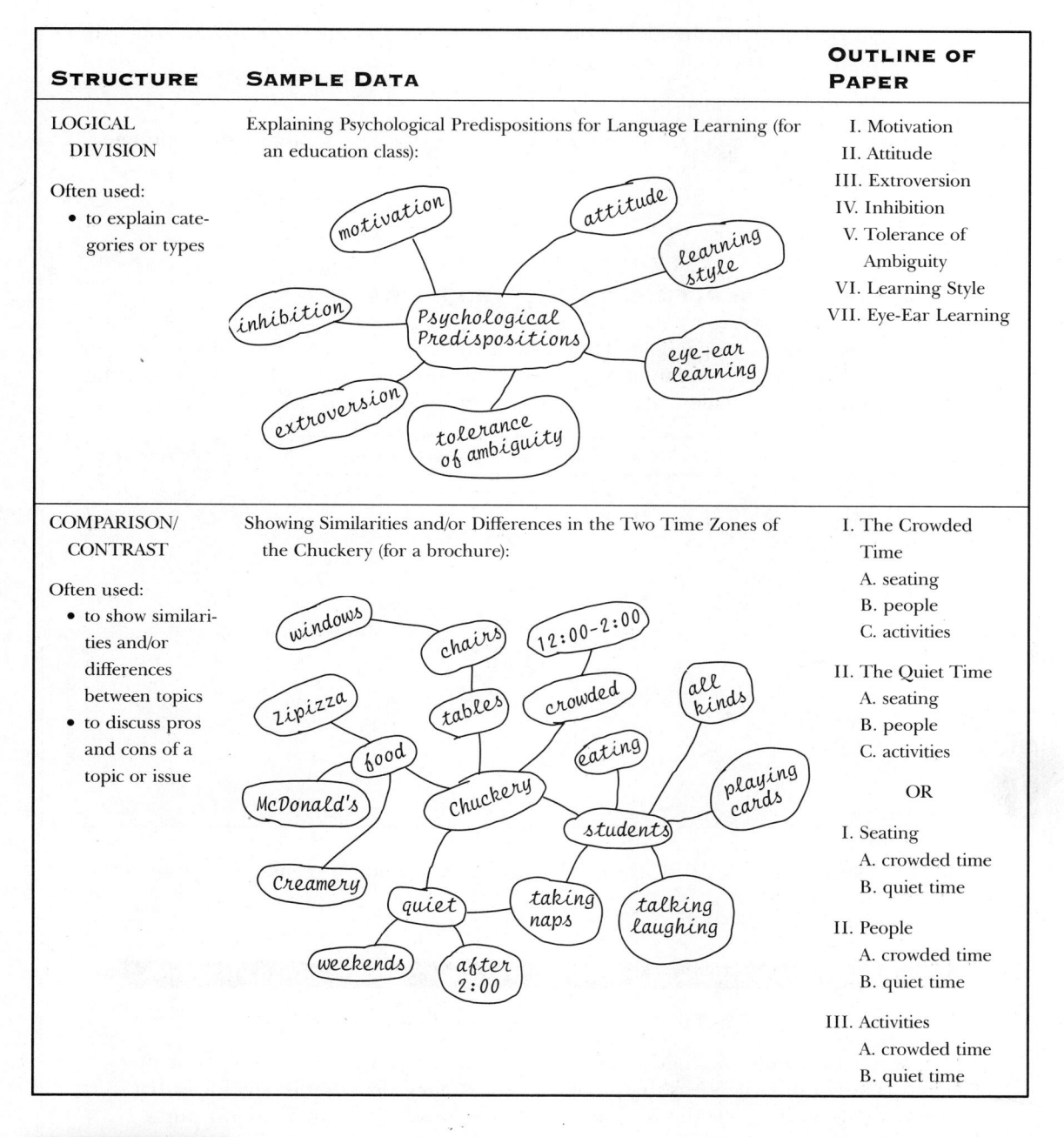

Exercise 2.10 Some writers find outlining to be a useful prewriting strategy; others never use it. For this assignment, try outlining to see if it is useful for you. Go back to your prewriting notes and look at your preliminary thesis statement, your diagram, and your data. What are some possible plans for *your* description?

On the paper where you wrote your preliminary thesis statement:

① Outline at least one possible plan for a description that will match your thesis statement. Feel free to try more than one outline if you think it will help you "see" different possibilities for your essay.

PART I: DRAFTED WORKS IN PROGRESS

② In your outline(s), list the ideas from your notes that you might include in your paper to support your most important message.

③ Use the outlining format provided by the examples above.

When you are finished, read through the outline(s). If you have written more than one, choose the one that you think will work the best for your description.

WRITING YOUR FIRST DRAFT

Reread the assignment on page 38. Think about your topic, your purpose (to recruit new students to your school, college, or university), your main idea, and your audience (international students). Complete the chart below to clarify this information for yourself.

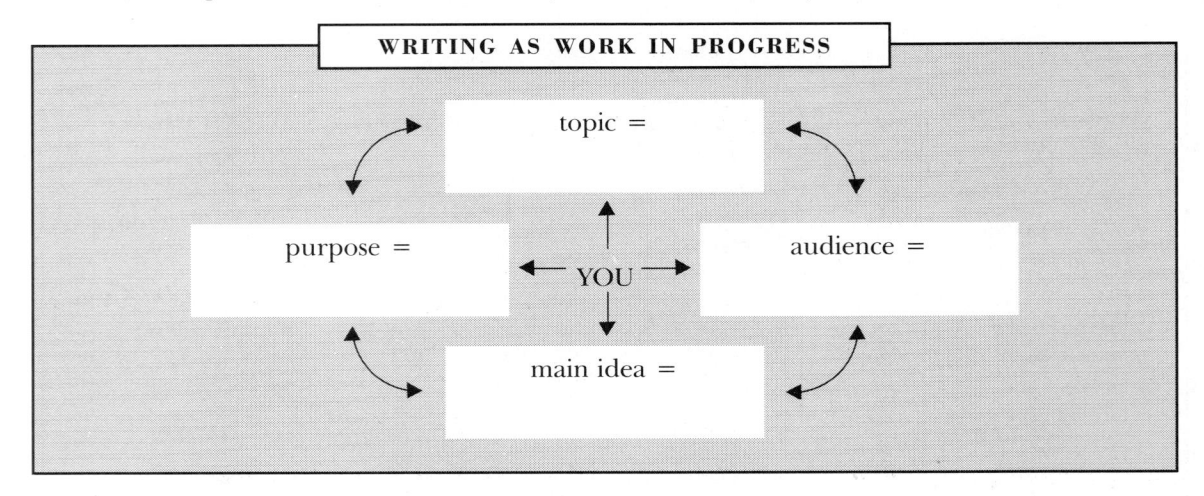

WRITING AS WORK IN PROGRESS

topic =

purpose =   ←YOU→   audience =

main idea =

Scan your prewriting notes and select the ideas that you think you should include in this paper. Write your first draft.

SUGGESTIONS • SUGGESTIONS • SUGGESTIONS • SUGGESTIONS

Here are some suggestions for one way to write your first draft:

1. Look at your list of notes and cross off any ideas that you will not use in your first draft. These would be ideas that do not fit your main idea, that is, any ideas that are not covered by your thesis statement. When crossing out an idea, just put a single line through it; do not cross it out completely and do not erase. (You may find that in a revised version of your description you DO want that information after all.)

2. When you are ready, begin to write your first draft. Write the draft in complete sentences. Include your thesis statement in the essay. Try to follow your organizational plan, but do not feel trapped by it; if you find yourself going off in a different direction, that is o.k.—maybe the new direction is better.

3. If you are using a computer, see Appendix C, page 263, for suggestions about writing your first draft.

CHAPTER 2: WRITING FOR A CAMPUS BROCHURE

REVISING YOUR WRITING

DEVELOPING YOUR IDEAS

LEARNING FROM ANOTHER WRITER Below are two drafts of the description of JAR Arena. Read each draft carefully. Which one do you think is better? Why?

JAR Arena

JAR Physical Education Building looks like a typical gym—a low, large, rectangular building. It is located on the east end of campus. Inside, the basketball court looks like a typical modern basketball court. During a home game, you'll see ten young men running back and forth the length of the court, shooting the ball and scoring points. What might surprise you is that during a home game, you'll see a lot more than just the typical. For a night at JAR Arena is more entertainment than just basketball.

One entertaining sight in JAR is the university mascot. He entertains the fans at all home games. During the pregame warm-up and half-time, he walks around on the court, teasing the players and referees. During the game, he walks through the bleachers.

The cheerleaders provide even more exciting entertainment. The university has a talented and athletic co-ed cheerleading squad. It does gymnastic routines on the court during time-outs in the game. The cheerleaders perform to the music of the Marching Band. The band's members sit in the bleachers and play spirited up-tempo music all evening.

At certain home games in JAR Arena, even the fans provide some entertainment. During half-time, a few lucky fans are selected to participate in contests which are sponsored by local companies. There's a break in the action of the game then. A car dealership might give away a new car to a fan. A super market chain might give away some money. These half-time contests are exciting to watch. All the other spectators cheer for the contestant to win. They all believe that maybe the next time, they'll be a lucky winner.

Even if you don't like basketball, spend a night at JAR Arena. You might not win a car or a hundred dollars; you will have a wonderful time.

JAR Arena

Located on the east end of campus, JAR Physical Education Building looks like a typical gym—a low, large, rectangular building. Inside, JAR Arena, the basketball court, looks like a typical modern basketball court. During a home game, you'll see ten young men running back and forth the length of the court, shooting the ball and scoring points. What might surprise you is that during a home game, you'll see a lot more than just the typical. For a night at JAR Arena is more entertainment than just basketball.

One entertaining sight in JAR is the eight-foot kangaroo you'll see walking around the court and bleachers. Zippy, the university mascot, entertains the fans at all home games. During the pregame warm-up and half-time, he walks around on the court, teasing the players and referees by pulling their shirts, messing up their hair, and untying their shoelaces. During the game, he walks through the bleachers, shaking hands with the adults and posing for pictures with the kids.

53

Part I: Drafted Works in Progress

Sometimes Zippy teams up with the cheerleaders to provide even more exciting entertainment. The university has a talented and athletic co-ed cheerleading squad which does gymnastic routines on the court during time-outs in the game. The squad's members build human pyramids and do flips; the men throw the women high into the air and catch them as they come tumbling back down. The cheerleaders perform to the music of the University Marching Band, whose members sit in the bleachers and play spirited up-tempo music all evening. They play the school fight song, the Blue and Gold, as well as many popular show tunes and contemporary songs. The theme from the movie "Rocky" is always a favorite with the crowd.

At certain home games in JAR Arena, even the fans provide some entertainment. During half-time, when there's a break in the action of the game, a few lucky fans are selected to participate in contests which are sponsored by local companies. A car dealership might give away a new car to the fan who can shoot a basket from the center court line. A supermarket chain might donate one hundred one-dollar bills, which are then scattered across the center court. A randomly selected fan is given 30 seconds to collect as many bills as possible. These half-time contests are exciting to watch because all the other spectators cheer for the contestant to win; they all believe that maybe the next time, they'll be a lucky winner.

Even if you don't like basketball, spend a night at JAR Arena. You might not win a car or a hundred dollars, but you will have a wonderful time.

CHAPTER 2: WRITING FOR A CAMPUS BROCHURE

These two descriptions of JAR Arena illustrate one important characteristic of a good description: An effective description will contain specific, "showing" language and support. If a description has only general language, every reader will "visualize" or imagine something different. If a description is specific, all the readers will "see" just about the same thing.

USING SPECIFIC DETAILS As the chart below illustrates, a description can range from very general to very specific. When you are writing, you will choose the level of generality or specificity that is appropriate for your purpose and audience.

VERY GENERAL	→	VERY SPECIFIC
basketball court	→	JAR Arena
a short time	→	30 seconds
some money	→	100 one-dollar bills
mascot → UA mascot → kangaroo	→	Zippy

USING EXAMPLES Examples are one type of detail. They are specific instances of a general category. Whenever you give an example, you tell your reader that this is one specific type of a general category.

GENERAL CATEGORY	→	EXAMPLES
music	→	the theme from "Rocky" the theme from "Star Wars"
perform gymnastic routines	→	build human pyramids do flips
tease players	→	pull their shirts mess their hair untie their shoelaces

Examples come in different levels of specificity. In other words, you can write fairly general examples, more specific examples, or very specific examples.

The following ladder diagram shows three different levels of examples.

	Category =	Food
General ↓ Specific	Example =	1. fast food
		2. fast food hamburgers
		3. Big Mac Whopper

PART I: DRAFTED WORKS IN PROGRESS

This ladder diagram shows seven different levels of examples.

	Category =	Students
General	Example =	1. international students
		2. international students in the United States
		3. international students in my university in the United States
		4. international students in my English class
		5. Asian international students in my English class
Specific		6. Thai international students in my English class
		7. Malulee, Manop, and Pilaisri

The level of specificity that you choose will depend on your topic, purpose, main idea, and audience.

Exercise 2.11 Turn back to pages 43 to 45. Reread the descriptions of Buchtel Commons, the Chuckery, and Eagle Valley Health Club. Underline places in each description where the writer used specific details and examples.

Exercise 2.12 Below is a list of general words. After each word, fill in the space with a range of specific examples.

VERY GENERAL ───────────▶ VERY SPECIFIC

book ⟶ textbook ⟶ English textbook ⟶ ESL textbook ⟶ ESL writing textbook ⟶ Work in Progress

university _____

library _____

grammar book _____

food _____

class _____

major _____

students _____

movie _____

relaxing _____

preparing for a test _____

Exercise 2.13 Now consider your own writing. Read through your first draft and look for general references and descriptions. Create rough ladder diagrams for each general description that you identify, and fill in different levels of details and/or examples. Choose the appropriate level of specificity to use in your second draft; let your topic, purpose, main idea, and audience guide your decisions.

GIVING AND GETTING FEEDBACK

Share your first draft with a partner (or a small group of readers) from your class.

When you are reading a classmate's first draft, read through the entire paper carefully. If you have trouble with vocabulary or handwriting, ask the writer for clarification. Once you have read and understood the draft, write answers to the following questions. Write your answers on a separate sheet of paper so that you can give them to the writer. (Do not write on your partner's first draft.)

1. What is the writer's topic?
2. What seems to be the writer's main idea? Which sentence do you think is the thesis statement for this paper?
3. Comment on the thesis statement. Is it just right? too broad? too narrow? Explain your comment.
4. Comment on the development of ideas.
    a. Do you see any places in this first draft where the writer used strong specific details or examples to develop ideas? If yes, where?
    b. Where would you like more explanation or more development? Where would you like more specific details or examples? Why?
5. Are there any sentences or ideas that you feel the writer should omit from a later draft? If yes, which ones? Why?
6. Comment on the organization.
    a. What seems to be the global structure of the draft? Comment on its effectiveness.
    b. How many paragraphs does this first draft have?
    c. Are the paragraph divisions effective?
       If yes, what is the focus of each one? If no, what changes would you recommend for the next draft?
    d. Are the ideas within each paragraph grouped properly?
       If no, what changes would you recommend?
7. What part of this first draft do you like the best? Why?

Part I: Drafted Works in Progress

DRAFTING YOUR PAPER: *The Second Draft*

Planning and Writing Your Second Draft

You have written your first draft of a description of one place on campus or in the local community. You have had a little time to get some distance on your first draft. Now reconsider that draft with a fresh eye, and decide how to proceed with your description. Plan and write your second draft.

Suggestions • Suggestions • Suggestions • Suggestions

Here are some suggestions for planning and writing your second draft:

1. Go back to page 38 and reread the writing assignment to be sure that you remember what your "job" is.

2. Reread your first draft and your readers' comments carefully. Then reread your prewriting notes.

3. Reconsider your thesis statement and global structure. Are you satisfied with them? Do they work the way you want them to work? In other words, does your thesis statement express your most important message? Does your plan work well to communicate that message? If you want to make some changes, write them at the end of the first draft or make notes to yourself on a piece of scrap paper.

4. Is there anything from your first draft that doesn't "fit"? If yes, cross it out.

5. Of the ideas in your first draft that you want to keep, are there any that should be reordered or regrouped? If yes, draw arrows or use numbers to show where you would like to move these ideas to.

6. Is there any information that you would like to add? Write that information in note form at the bottom of your first draft.

7. Begin your second draft. Keep and use any of the sentences from your first draft that work well. Make changes and rewrite any of the sentences that you feel should be changed.

8. When you are finished, reread your second draft carefully. If you would like to make any additional changes at this point, just cross off what you want to change and write in the new sentences or ideas neatly.

9. If you are using a computer, see Appendix C, page 263 for suggestions about revising your paper to produce a second draft.

CHAPTER 2: WRITING FOR A CAMPUS BROCHURE

REVISING YOUR WRITING

FOCUSING ON YOUR SENTENCE STRUCTURES

In the draft of your campus brochure that you submit to your readers, you will want all of your ideas to flow smoothly and naturally. You will want your sentences to show the correct balance between ideas, and you will want them to be varied.

LEARNING FROM ANOTHER WRITER Below are several excerpts from another writer's second draft. As you can see, at this point in the work in progress, the writer focused on the sentences in the draft and penciled in revisions so that they flow well and express the ideas clearly.

Exercise 2.14 Read through the original and revised versions of each excerpt carefully. With your classmates, describe each change that the writer made. Then discuss how each change affects the writing. Discuss:

- how the changes help the readers.
- how the changes help the clarity of ideas.
- how the changes help the flow of ideas.

To facilitate the discussion, the revisions are printed for you below each excerpt. Refer to each revision by its number.

Excerpt A: Original

> James A. Rhodes Physical Education Building looks like a typical gym—a low, large, rectangular building. It is located on the east end of campus. Inside, JAR Arena, the basketball court, looks like a typical modern basketball court. During a home game,

Excerpt A: Revision

> ① James A. Rhodes Physical Education Building looks like a typical gym—a low, large, rectangular building. ~~It is~~ *Located* on the east end of campus, Inside, JAR Arena, the basketball court, looks like a typical modern basketball court. During a home game,

1. James A. Rhodes Physical Education Building looks like a typical gym—a low, large, rectangular building. It is located on the east end of campus.
   ↓
   Located on the east end of campus, James A. Rhodes Physical Education Building looks like a typical gym—a low, large, rectangular building.

59

Part I: Drafted Works in Progress

Excerpt B: Original

> One entertaining sight in JAR is an eight-foot kangaroo. You'll see it walking around the court and bleachers. Zippy is the university mascot. He entertains the fans at all home games. During the pregame warm-up and half-time, he walks around on the court,

Excerpt B: Revision

> ② One entertaining sight in JAR is an eight-foot kangaroo~~.~~ *that you'll* ~~You'll~~ see it walking around the court and bleachers. Zippy③, ~~is~~ the university mascot, ~~He~~ entertains the fans at all home games. During the pregame warm-up and half-time, he walks around on the court,

2. One entertaining sight in JAR is an eight-foot kangaroo. You'll see it walking around the court and bleachers.
   ↓
   One entertaining sight in JAR is an eight-foot kangaroo that you'll see walking around the court and bleachers.

3. Zippy is the university mascot. He entertains the fans at all home games.
   ↓
   Zippy, the university mascot, entertains the fans at all home games.

CHAPTER 2: WRITING FOR A CAMPUS BROCHURE

Excerpt C: Original

University has a talented and athletic co-ed cheerleading squad. It does gymnastic routines on the court during time-outs in the game. The squad's members build human pyramids and do flips; the men throw the women into the air and catch them. They come tumbling back down. The cheerleaders perform to the music of the University Marching Band. The band's members sit in the bleachers and play spirited up-tempo music all evening. They play the school fight song, the Blue and Gold, and

Excerpt C: Revision

(4) University has a talented and athletic co-ed cheerleading squad~~.~~ *which* ~~It~~ does gymnastic routines on the court during time-outs in the game. The squad's members build human pyramids and do flips; (5) the men throw the women into the air and catch them~~.~~ *as they* ~~They~~ come tumbling back down. (6) The cheerleaders perform to the music of the University Marching Band, *whose* ~~The band's~~ members sit in the bleachers and play spirited up-tempo music all evening. They play the school fight song, the Blue and Gold, and

4. The University has a talented and athletic co-ed cheerleading squad. It does gymnastic routines on the court during time-outs in the game.
   ↓
   The University has a talented and athletic co-ed cheerleading squad which does gymnastic routines on the court during time-outs in the game.

5. The men throw the women into the air and catch them. They come tumbling back down.
   ↓
   The men throw the women into the air and catch them as they come tumbling back down.

6. The cheerleaders perform to the music of the University Marching Band. The band's members sit in the bleachers and play spirited up-tempo music all evening.
   ↓
   The cheerleaders perform to the music of the University Marching Band, whose members sit in the bleachers and play spirited up-tempo music all evening.

PART I: DRAFTED WORKS IN PROGRESS

Excerpt D: Original

At certain home games in JAR Arena, even the fans provide some entertainment. During half-time, a few lucky fans are selected to participate in contests. There's a long break in the action of the game then. The contests are sponsored by local companies. A car dealership might give away a new car to a fan. That fan has to shoot a basket from the center court line. A supermarket chain might donate one hundred one-dollar bills. They are then scattered across the center court. A randomly selected fan is given 30 seconds to collect as many bills as possible. These half-time contests are exciting to watch. All the other spectators cheer for the contestant to win. They all believe that maybe the next time, they'll be a lucky winner.

Excerpt D: Revision

At certain home games in JAR Arena, even the fans provide some entertainment. ⑦ *when there's a long break in the action of the game,* During half-time, a few lucky fans are selected to participate in contests. ~~There's a long break in the action of the game then. The contests are~~ sponsored by local ⑧ *the who can* companies. A car dealership might give away a new car to ~~a fan.~~ ~~That fan has to~~ ⑨ shoot a basket from the center court line. A supermarket chain might donate one hun- *which* dred one-dollar bills, ~~They~~ are then scattered across the center court. A randomly ⑩ selected fan is given 30 seconds to collect as many bills as possible. These half-time *because all* contests are exciting to watch, ~~All~~ the other spectators cheer for the contestant to win. They all believe that maybe the next time, they'll be a lucky winner.

7. During half-time, a few lucky fans are selected to participate in contests. There's a long break in the action of the game then. The contests are sponsored by local companies.
   ↓
   During half-time, when there's a long break in the action of the game, a few lucky fans are selected to participate in contests sponsored by local companies.

8. A car dealership might give away a new car to a fan. That fan has to shoot a basket from the center court line.
   ↓
   A car dealership might give away a new car to the fan who can shoot a basket from the center court line.

9. A supermarket chain might donate one hundred one-dollar bills. They are then scattered across the center court.
   ↓
   A supermarket chain might donate one hundred one-dollar bills, which are then scattered across the center court.

10. These half-time contests are exciting to watch. All the other spectators cheer for the contestant to win.
    ↓
    These half-time contests are exciting to watch because all the other spectators cheer for the contestant to win.

MODIFYING NOUNS Sentence revisions 1 to 4 and 6 to 9 illustrate the use of **adjective clauses, reduced adjective clauses**, and **appositives**. You can use these structures to *modify* or qualify nouns in English. They help you show the relative importance between ideas, and they add *sentence variety* to your writing.

SUGGESTIONS • SUGGESTIONS • SUGGESTIONS • SUGGESTIONS

If you need more information about the rules of structure and punctuation for adjective clauses, reduced adjective clauses, and appositives or would like to practice these structures, see Part 3 of this book.

Adjective Clauses . . . . see pages 172 to 181.

Adjective Clauses: Reduced . . . . see pages 181 to 183.

Appositives . . . . see pages 193 to 195.

Exercise 2.15 Reread the descriptions of Buchtel Commons, page 43, The Chuckery, page 44, and Eagle Valley Health Club, page 45. Underline the adjective clauses, reduced adjective clauses, and appositives that you find in those descriptions.

PART I: DRAFTED WORKS IN PROGRESS

Exercise 2.15 The following sentences are arranged to form an essay about computer software for language learners.* Combine the sets of lettered sentences. Change the bulleted (•) sentences into adjective clauses, adjective phrases reduced from clauses, or appositives, and combine each one with the sentence before it. (NOTE: Some of these adjective clauses will be restrictive—others will be nonrestrictive. Be careful with punctuation.) Where there are no bullets, combine the sentences with other connecting words that make sense.

1. a. At many colleges and universities, computer programs supplement regular language classes.
   b. • The students interact and do writing assignments in regular language classes.

2. a. With computer programs, the students can control their own lessons.
   b. • The computer programs are used primarily for drills and exercises.
   c. They choose the material to cover.

3. a. During the hours, students can complete their work at their own pace.
   b. • The computer labs are open then.

4. a. In recent years, language educators have developed computer software.
   b. • This software makes language learning even more rewarding.

5. a. Two new programs have been developed for beginning students.
   b. • Their ability in the language is limited.

6. a. These programs help the students develop vocabulary and knowledge of the culture.
   b. • They are offered in French and Spanish.

7. a. The programs allow the learner to visit a village.
   b. • The target language is spoken there.

8. a. The learner is visiting the village.
   b. She learns about family life, meals, education, and travel.

9. a. Both programs received high praise from Katrine Watkins.
   b. • She is an administrator at the French-American School in New York.
   c. • The programs were field-tested there.

10. a. Dartmouth College in New Hampshire is experimenting with other programs.
    b. • The programs are designed to aid students with foreign language study.

11. a. With these programs, the college is creating materials.
    b. • These materials make language learning easier and more efficient.

12. a. One program is called *TextWindow*.
    b. • Learners can use one program to improve their reading.

13. a. It includes authentic foreign language texts.
    b. It includes its own on-line dictionary.

14. a. The learner does not know a word in the text.
    b. He highlights it on the computer screen.
    c. He gets an instant translation.

15. a. In this way, the student learns the new word at the exact moment, not after five minutes of dictionary scanning.
    b. • He needs it then.

16. a. The program saves the learner time and effort.
    b. • The program helps the learner keep the thread of the story.

17. a. Another computer program helps English speakers learn Chinese.
    b. • This program is being developed at Dartmouth.
    c. • Chinese is a tonal language.

18. a. Chinese is very difficult for English speakers to learn.
    b. A change in a word's tone can completely change its meaning.

19. a. To help students understand tones, Dartmouth created the *Hanzi* project.
    b. • The *Hanzi* project is a software package.
    c. • The package uses digitized speech.

(Adapted from Netsel, Tom. 1989. "Speaking in Tongues." *Compute!* Nov.: 109–112.)

DRAFTING YOUR PAPER: *The Third Draft*

PLANNING AND WRITING YOUR THIRD DRAFT

Plan and write the third draft of your essay describing a place on campus or in your local community.

SUGGESTIONS • SUGGESTIONS • SUGGESTIONS • SUGGESTIONS

Here are some suggestions for one way to plan and write your third draft.

1. Reread your second draft carefully.

2. On the second draft, mark any changes that you plan to make in your third draft.
   a. If you plan to reorganize any ideas, try using brackets and arrows to show the new order.
   b. If you plan to omit any ideas, cross them out with one line.
   c. If you plan to add any information, write it in the margin or in a blank space, and somehow indicate to yourself where it will be inserted.
   d. Do you want to make any changes in the sentence structures or sentence variety? If yes, cross out the sentences that you want to change; write in the revised sentences above them.
   e. If you see any corrections that you should make in your grammar, spelling, or punctuation, make them on your second draft.

3. When you are ready, begin to write your third draft. Write it neatly, and skip lines.

4. When you have finished the third draft, reread it carefully. If you see anything that you want to change, mark the change on the paper (i.e., cross out the word(s) you want to change and write in the new word(s) above it).

5. If you are using a computer, see Appendix C, page 264, for suggestions about writing your third draft.

PART I: DRAFTED WORKS IN PROGRESS

EDITING YOUR WRITING

Before you begin to edit your third draft, read pages 31 to 34. If you found a pattern to your errors with Assignment # 1 and you created an editing acronym, write it at the top of your third draft.

Read through the third draft of your essay for the campus brochure several times. Each time that you read, concentrate on looking for and correcting one specific type of error. For example, if one of your common mistakes is with verb tenses, read through one time, focusing on all of the main verb forms. Use the Editing Checklist in Appendix A to guide you. After you have finished reading for your common errors, read the draft several more times focusing on the sentence structures, grammatical forms, and mechanics.

With each reading, when you find an error, cross out the incorrect form and write in the correct form above it.

SUGGESTIONS • SUGGESTIONS • SUGGESTIONS • SUGGESTIONS

When you have finished editing your own paper:

1. Exchange third drafts with another writer in the class.

2. Read each other's third draft carefully.

3. If you see any additional corrections that the writer should make, put a check mark in the margin of the line on which the error appears. Do not correct any errors; that is the writer's job.

4. Discuss each other's paper in turn.

Freewriting Journal Assignment

Take some time out to consider your writing as work in progress. Spend a few minutes looking back over and reflecting on all of the work that you did while drafting your essay for the campus brochure. In your freewriting journal, write a paragraph describing what you like about your work in progress. In other words, celebrate your successes.

Describe:

- what you feel proud of about your work.
- what you have done with this work that you did not think you were capable of doing before you started.
- what you have learned by doing this work.

Write another paragraph describing one aspect of your writing that you want to work on and improve.

Describe:

- why you think that you should work on this aspect.
- what you can do to work on this aspect over the next few weeks.

CHAPTER 3

Sharing Your Knowledge or Expertise

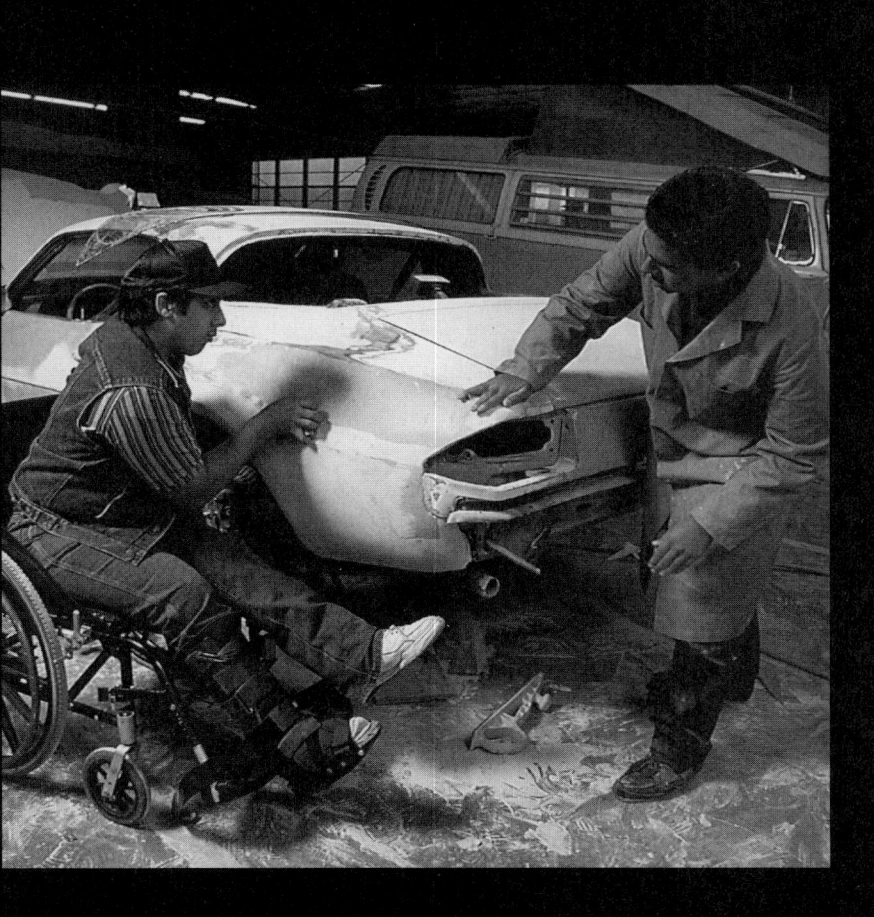

PREWRITING
- Setting the Context
- Understanding the Assignment
- Analyzing the Audience
- Collecting Data

DRAFTING YOUR PAPER: THE FIRST DRAFT
- Planning Your First Draft
- Writing Your First Draft

REVISING YOUR WRITING
- Developing Your Ideas
- Giving and Getting Feedback

DRAFTING YOUR PAPER: THE SECOND DRAFT
- Planning and Writing Your Second Draft
- Adding an Introduction and a Conclusion

REVISING YOUR WRITING
- Focusing on Your Sentence Structures

DRAFTING YOUR PAPER: THE THIRD DRAFT
- Planning and Writing Your Third Draft

EDITING YOUR WRITING

PART I: DRAFTED WORKS IN PROGRESS

PREWRITING

SETTING THE CONTEXT

We all have in-depth knowledge about a variety of subjects or expertise in some skills. Some people know a great deal about astronomy; others know a lot about rock music, or even one rock band in particular. Some people know a lot about a specific sport, for example, baseball or judo; others have detailed knowledge about a traditional custom or cultural phenomenon, for example, a wedding ceremony. Other people have special talents or gifts, abilities that allow them to perform some skill extremely well. For instance, a friend of yours might be a talented learner of new vocabulary; another might give expert haircuts or be especially skilled at packing luggage.

Exercise 3.1 Freewrite answers to the following questions. Then discuss your answers with your classmates.

1. What are some subjects that you know a lot about or skills that you can perform well? List as many as you can think of.
2. How did you acquire your knowledge of each subject or skill?
3. What are the benefits of possessing in-depth knowledge about each subject or the ability to perform each skill?

UNDERSTANDING THE ASSIGNMENT

For this assignment, your topic is either 1) a subject that you have in-depth knowledge about or 2) a skill that you possess. You are going to write an essay in which you share your knowledge or expertise about that subject or skill. Your audience is readers who are *not* familiar with the subject; they have no background knowledge about it.

You are going to determine the purpose and direction of your essay. For example, your purpose might be:

- to inform your readers about something that is new for them.
- to entertain your readers.
- to generate interest in your subject or skill.
- to teach your readers how to do something.

ANALYZING THE AUDIENCE

Your audience is readers with no prior background knowledge about your topic. How might this affect:

- the purpose of your writing?
- the way you develop your topic?
- the depth of explanation?
- the level of vocabulary?

CHAPTER 3 : SHARING YOUR KNOWLEDGE OR EXPERTISE

COLLECTING DATA

You have already identified and freewritten about some possible topics for this paper. Before you make a commitment to one topic, complete the following exercises.

Exercise 3.2 Draw an idea map (see pages 6 to 7) and/or write notes (see pages 39 to 42) about each topic that you listed in the freewriting exercise on page 68. With each of these techniques, write quickly; write whatever comes to mind about each topic.

Exercise 3.3 Exercise 3.2 got you into each topic. Look at and think about the ideas you have generated for each one. Evaluate the appropriateness of each topic for *this* assignment by answering the following questions. Write the answers for each topic in your freewriting notebook or on paper.

TOPIC: _____

(1) How motivated are you to write about this topic? Explain your answer.

```
      1         2         3         4         5
   not very            so-so                very
```

(2) Will you get excited about explaining this topic to others? Bored? Explain your answer.

(3) Will this topic be easy or difficult for you to explain in English? To answer this question, think for a minute and consider questions such as this: Do you know the necessary vocabulary in English to explain this topic?

```
      1         2         3         4         5
   difficult           so-so           easy enough
```

(4) What kind of people do you think would be interested in reading about this topic? Explain your answer.

Exercise 3.4 Now that you have thought about some possible topics, choose the one that you feel is most appropriate for this assignment. Again, be sure it is a topic that you already know well and that you really want to write about. Be sure it is a topic that you will be excited about. Also, be sure it is something that you can successfully explain in English.

CUBING To help you explore your topic and find a purpose and direction for your writing, try another prewriting strategy: *cubing*. A cube is a solid object with six equal sides. This strategy is called cubing because you look at or consider your topic in six different ways or from six different perspectives:

(1) **Describe it** (tell what it looks like).

(2) **Compare/contrast it** (tell what it is similar to or different from).

(3) **Associate it** (tell what it reminds you of or makes you think of).

(4) **Analyze it** (tell what its parts are).

(5) **Apply it** (tell how you can use it).

(6) **Argue for or against it** (tell the pros and/or cons of your topic).

PART I: DRAFTED WORKS IN PROGRESS

Exercise 3.5 In your freewriting notebook or on a piece of paper, spend a few minutes writing about your subject from each of the perspectives listed above. Write quickly and without censorship; try to get your ideas down onto paper as quickly as you can. Below are some of the sentences that one writer freewrote while cubing about her topic, the flute. Study this example before you begin.

The Flute

1. *Describe it*: A flute is about two feet long and weighs about 2 pounds. When you are carrying it, it's divided into 3 pieces, and it can be put in a little bag. Most flutes are silver plated; some extraordinarily expensive ones are made of gold . . . .

2. *Compare/Contrast it*: The flute is like a pipe in that you can control the heights of its sound by opening and closing the combination of holes on its body. A flute has more holes than a pipe, so it is more difficult to learn than a pipe. A flute is easier to learn than a piano because it needs only one melody. Many people who have learned to play the piano since a young age quit, and it seems to be very hard for adults to start to learn the piano. In the case of the flute, it is so easy to learn that many people take it up as adults . . . .

3. *Associate it*: The flute is a beautiful instrument, one that is a joy to see and a pleasure to hear. When I think of the flute I always think of joyful times. In fact, I always think of birthday parties and the "Love Theme from Romeo and Juliet." When I was a child learning how to play the flute, I brought it to one of my friend's birthday parties. I played the love theme for her, and she was so pleased with this gift . . . .

4. *Analyze it*: The flute consists of three parts that fit together. The sound is produced by blowing out through your mouth over the mouth piece. You can change the notes by opening and closing different combination of holes along the body of the flute. The form of the lips and the way to hold the instrument—the carriage—are the most important things to learn about playing the flute; these affect the quality of the notes produced . . . .

5. *Apply it*: You can use the flute for your own pleasure because it makes a gorgeous and elegant lifetime hobby. When you feel bad or bored, this small instrument will lead you to the beautiful world of sound and attract you. It can help you relax and get rid of stress. You can also use the flute to bring pleasure to others . . . .

6. *Argue for or against it*: The flute is a much better instrument to learn than the piano. It is easier to learn because you can produce its primary sound in just 1 or 2 hours of practice. The flute is relatively cheap, and it is a wonderful hobby that you can pick up for 30 minutes a day. You can also take it with you wherever you go . . . .

CHAPTER 3 : SHARING YOUR KNOWLEDGE OR EXPERTISE

DRAFTING YOUR PAPER: *The First Draft*

PLANNING YOUR FIRST DRAFT

FINDING AND EXPRESSING YOUR PURPOSE AND MAIN IDEA You have a collection of notes from which to write the first draft of an essay in which you share your knowledge of a subject or skill. Before you begin the first draft, try to clarify your purpose for writing the essay. Do you want to inform your readers about a topic that is new for them? Do you want to entertain your readers? Do you want to generate interest in a topic that you find interesting? Do you want to provide instructions about a skill so that your readers can try it on their own? Your purpose will affect how you approach your topic, so give this careful thought as you complete the exercises below.

At this point, you might also determine the most important message that you want to communicate to your readers. In other words, try to determine the main idea that you want to focus on in your writing.

Exercise 3.6 Read through all of your notes carefully. What is your purpose in writing this essay? Complete the following sentence:

"My purpose in writing this essay is to _____

_____

What possible main ideas do you see in your notes?

① List the possibilities in your freewriting notebook or on paper.

② Choose the one that you are most interested in pursuing in this essay.

③ What general statement can you make about the subject or skill that you are explaining?

④ Complete the following sentence:
"In this essay, I want to tell my readers that this topic is _____."

Exercise 3.7 Turn to page 47. Read the explanation of what a thesis statement is. Then write a *preliminary* thesis statement for the first draft of your essay. Use the ideas from the sentences in Exercise 3.6 to help you compose this thesis statement. Remember that all of the other sentences in an essay work to support a thesis statement. Remember, too, that you will be able to change your thesis statement later if you want or need to. Do not feel trapped by the sentence that you write today. Consider this sentence an early attempt at focusing your ideas.

PART I: DRAFTED WORKS IN PROGRESS

WRITING YOUR FIRST DRAFT

You know your topic, purpose, main idea, and audience. Complete the chart below to clarify this information for yourself.

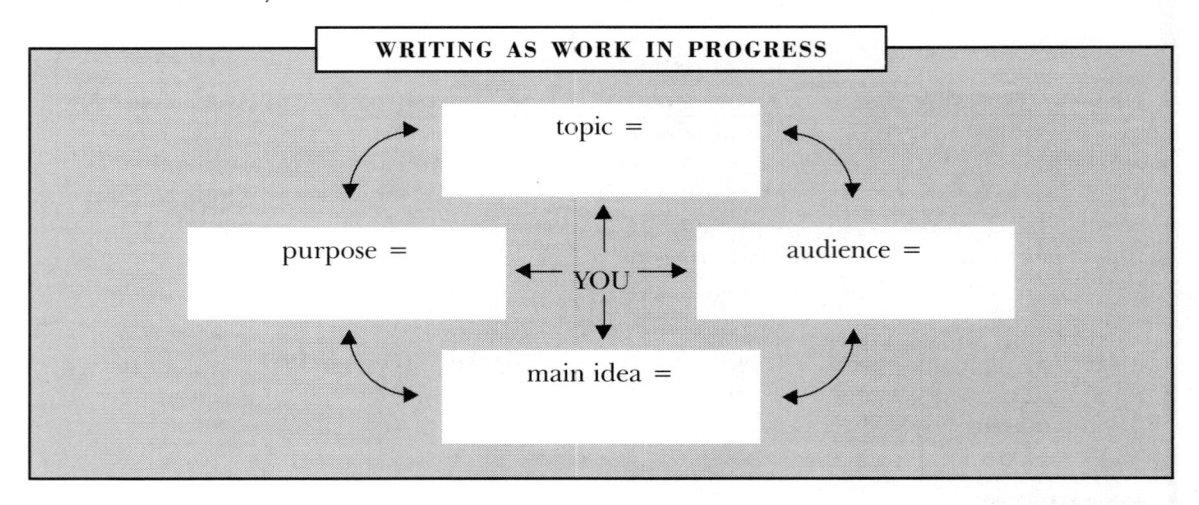

WRITING AS WORK IN PROGRESS

```
              topic =
                ↕
purpose =  ← YOU →  audience =
                ↕
            main idea =
```

Look through your initial collection of data and your preliminary thesis statement. When you are ready, begin to write your first draft. Write the draft in complete sentences.

SUGGESTIONS • SUGGESTIONS • SUGGESTIONS • SUGGESTIONS

Here are some suggestions for writing your first draft:

1. If outlining is a useful planning strategy for you, prepare a rough outline for your first draft. (See pages 48 to 51.)

2. Do not worry about an introduction yet. Instead, use your preliminary thesis statement as the first sentence in your essay. Then begin to develop your ideas in the sentences that follow.

3. If you are using a computer, see Appendix C, page 263, for suggestions about writing your first draft.

REVISING YOUR WRITING

DEVELOPING YOUR IDEAS

LEARNING FROM ANOTHER WRITER Now that you have written a first draft of your paper, let's look at another writer's draft of an essay explaining the preparations for marriage in Japan. The writer has put a lot of ideas down onto paper. He has already found a direction for his paper: He has decided to explain his topic by analyzing it and breaking it into parts. He has also decided to discuss each part in chronological order.

Analyze his essay to see what techniques he might use to develop his ideas. What you learn from analyzing his draft might help you make decisions about your own revision.

Preparations for Marriage in Japan

To make a successful start of a new life, all the preparations for marriage are very complicated. First, the young couple must decide the date and where the wedding ceremony will take place. This step must be done at least 6 months before the wedding day. If the couple wants to have their ceremony on "Taian days," they have to do this step about 1 or 2 years before the wedding date. The main factors that influence this decision are the type of ceremony, how much the wedding will cost approximately, the place of the ceremony, and when the ceremony will take place. Every department store in the big cities has a bridal corner. The couple can meet with bridal consultants there to decide these matters. They will recommend several appropriate places and make pre-reservations for the couple. Then, the couple has to go and see each place and decide which one is better. A reservation should be made within 2 weeks after the pre-reservation; the couple should cancel the pre-reservation for a place they don't like as soon as possible.

The couple chooses the date and place of the ceremony. Then, they have to ask a person to be "Nakoudo." Naturally, the Nakoudo couple must be a happy couple. Once the Nakoudo couple has been determined, the couple must prepare for the engagement ceremony. At this stage, an engagement ring is bought. The cost of the ring depends on the man's budget. At this time, the man's family also prepares some money to spend on the couple. Furthermore, each side must prepare his or her family list, a piece of paper on which the names of his or her family are written, and which is exchanged by both sides at the engagement ceremony. The ceremony usually takes place about 6 months before the wedding ceremony in a restaurant or they go to the house of the woman's family.

Part I: Drafted Works in Progress

After the engagement, the details of the wedding ceremony and the dinner party should be decided. Usually the wedding ceremony and the dinner party take place at the same place on the same day. The couple has to make decisions about the decorations for the dinner party, what kind of dresses and accessories the bride will wear, the clothing of the bridegroom and who will narrate the dinner party. Meanwhile, the invitation letters of the wedding ceremony and dinner party must be prepared and sent. A printer can help the couple with this matter.

After receiving the answers from the invited guests, the couple has to decide the order of seats and ask some of the guests to make speeches at the dinner party. Furthermore, they often have to have meetings with the staff at the place where the dinner party will be held in order to decide the organization of the party. About three weeks before the date of the wedding, the couple has a meeting with the staff of the wedding ceremony and the dinner party to reconfirm everything. "A-party-after-the-party" also takes place on the same day as the wedding ceremony but usually at a different place.

As you can see, the preparations for marriage are very elaborate in Japan, but this process is indispensable for a couple to have their marriage recognized and if they want to make a good start of their new life.

Exercise 3.8 Freewrite answers to the following questions. Then discuss your answers with your classmates.

1. At this point, what seems to be the writer's purpose? Why did he write this essay?
2. At this point, what seems to be the writer's main idea about preparing for a wedding in Japan?
3. At this point, what is the writer's thesis statement? (What sentence covers, or summarizes, all of the ideas in the essay?)
4. How many parts to marriage preparation does this writer discuss?

Exercise 3.9 If you already have background knowledge about this topic, this draft might be clear for you. If you have no background knowledge, you probably need more information in order to understand this new topic well. Where would you like or where do you need more information? In your freewriting notebook or on a piece of paper, list all the questions you would like to ask this writer about his topic. Compare your list of questions with your classmates.

DEVELOPING AND SUPPORTING IDEAS Successful writers try to anticipate where their essays need development and support to make the ideas *clear* and *interesting* for the readers. They choose the type of development and support that will make their main idea clear.

You have already studied how to use specific details (pages 12 and 55) and examples (pages 55 to 56) to develop and support your writing. On page 75, you will see a list of other ways to develop your ideas so that they are clear and interesting for your readers.

CHAPTER 3 : SHARING YOUR KNOWLEDGE OR EXPERTISE

Ways to Develop and Support an Essay

If a Reader Might Ask ↓	Consider Developing and Supporting Your Ideas by ↓
Why?	Providing causes/effects/reasons
What is this?	Defining words
How?	Explaining the way or manner
Can you give some examples?	Illustrating with examples
What does this consist of or involve?	Analyzing the components
What for?	Providing details or examples
Who does this? To whom? For whom? By whom?	Providing details or examples
What are some possible types or categories?	Classifying
How is "X" similar to or different from "Y"?	Comparing/Contrasting
When?	Providing details or examples
Where?	Providing details or examples
What do others say?	Citing published sources or acknowledged experts
How much? How many?	Citing statistics

Exercise 3.10 To see examples of these and other ways to develop and support writing, look at the work of other writers.

Turn to pages 150 and 151 and read the essay, "Remember to Give to the Earth This Holiday Season." In this essay, the writer shares her expertise about how to be kind to the environment during the Christmas and New Year holidays. Then complete the analysis below.

① What is the writer's topic?
② What is the writer's purpose?
③ What is the writer's main idea? Find the thesis statement and underline it.
④ Who is the audience?
⑤ Using the chart on this page as a guide, analyze the development in this writer's essay.
   a. Try to find at least one instance of each type of development. Underline those instances.
   b. Identify and label each type of development.
   c. Did the writer use any other methods of development? If yes, what?

PART I: DRAFTED WORKS IN PROGRESS

Exercise 3.11 Now consider your own writing. Read through your first draft. Try to read it as if you have no background knowledge about the topic at all. Analyze the development in your essay.

Can you identify any ideas in your draft that need more development and support? On a separate sheet of paper, make a list of those ideas. Plan the type of development that you will add for your second draft. Be specific in your planning; write down the information that you will add.

GIVING AND GETTING FEEDBACK

Share your first draft with a partner (or a small group of readers) from your class.

When you are reading a classmate's first draft, read through the entire paper carefully. If you have trouble with vocabulary or handwriting, ask the writer for clarification. Once you have read and understood the draft, write answers to the following questions. Write your answers on a separate sheet of paper so that you can give them to the writer. (Do not write on your partner's first draft.)

1. What is the writer's topic?
2. What seems to be the writer's purpose at this point?
3. What is the writer's main idea?
4. Which sentence do you think is the thesis statement for this paper?
   Comment on the thesis statement. Is it just right? too broad? too narrow? Explain your comment.
5. Comment on the development of ideas.
   a. Do you see any places in this first draft where the writer has developed ideas in an interesting and clear way? If yes, where? What do you like about the development?
   b. Where would you like more explanation or more development? Where would you like more information? What kind of information or development would you like? Why? (Refer to page 75.)
6. Are there any sentences or ideas that you feel the writer should omit from a later draft? If yes, which ones? Why?
7. Comment on the organization.
   a. What seems to be the global structure of the draft? Comment on its effectiveness.
   b. How many paragraphs does this first draft have?
   c. Are the paragraph divisions effective?
      If yes, what is the focus of each one?
      If no, what changes would you recommend for the next draft?
   d. Are the ideas within each paragraph grouped properly?
      If no, what changes would you recommend?
8. What part of this first draft do you like the best? Why?

CHAPTER 3 : SHARING YOUR KNOWLEDGE OR EXPERTISE

DRAFTING YOUR PAPER: *The Second Draft*

PLANNING AND WRITING YOUR SECOND DRAFT

You have seen some different ways for writers to develop their ideas: by providing specific details or examples, by explaining cause/effect, by giving definitions, by analyzing components, by classifying, by comparing and contrasting, by explaining how. You have also received some feedback from your readers.

Go back to your own writing and decide how you would like to develop your ideas. Make any changes that you feel will make your writing better.

SUGGESTIONS • SUGGESTIONS • SUGGESTIONS • SUGGESTIONS

Here are some suggestions for planning and writing your second draft.

1. Reread the sections entitled *Understanding the Assignment* and *Analyzing the Audience* on page 68. Be sure that you clearly understand the writing assignment. Pay special attention to your audience: readers who are not familiar with the topic you are writing about.

2. Reread your first draft carefully.

3. Find and underline your *thesis statement*.

4. Next, ask yourself and answer the following questions. After you have considered each question carefully, note any changes that you will make in your second draft. Note these changes on your first draft or on another sheet of paper, whichever is easier for you.

   a. *About my purpose*: What is the purpose of my essay? Do I want to write an essay that informs my readers about the topic simply because it is interesting? Do I want to entertain my readers? Do I want to teach my readers something new? Or do I have some other purpose in mind? What is it? Does my paper achieve my purpose? If no, what changes should I make?

   b. *About my thesis statement*: Does my thesis statement express my most important message? Do all of my other sentences "match" my thesis? Are there any sentences that contradict my thesis?

   c. *About development*: Do I have enough support for my reader to really understand the topic clearly? Should I define any terms? Should I add examples or details? Should I explain causes, reasons, or effects? Should I analyze any of the ideas by breaking them down into parts? Should I compare or contrast any ideas?

   d. *About organization*: Have I selected the best global structure for presenting my ideas to my readers? Should I try a different global structure?

   e. *About paragraph divisions and structure*: Have I already divided my essay into paragraphs? Are the divisions o.k. at this point, or should I change them? If I have not yet made the divisions, where should they go? Why? Should I rearrange any of the ideas inside the paragraphs?

5. After you have carefully planned your second draft, begin to write it.

6. If you are using a computer, see Appendix C, page 263 for suggestions about revising your paper to produce a second draft.

PART I: DRAFTED WORKS IN PROGRESS

ADDING AN INTRODUCTION AND A CONCLUSION

At this point, focus on writing introductions and conclusions so that you can add these to your second draft.

WRITING INTRODUCTIONS What is the job of an introduction? What do readers expect to learn from an introduction? When you are reading a text, what do you expect to learn from the introduction?

The main jobs of an introduction are:

- to attract the readers' attention and motivate them to continue reading. In this job, the introduction is like a "hook" that grabs the readers.

- to establish a relationship between the readers and the writer. Since the introduction is the readers' first encounter with the writer, it provides them with their first impression.

- to "set the stage" for the essay by giving background information. In this job, the introduction establishes the context for the readers and prepares them for what will happen next.

- to present the writer's most important message or main idea. The writer usually does this in the thesis statement.

For a short piece of writing, the introduction is usually one paragraph. For a longer essay, it may be more than one paragraph.

Exercise 3.12 The introduction below comes from a magazine article describing the importance of waxing cross-country skis. The writer is an expert on this topic; he wrote the article to inform and entertain his readers. After reading the introduction carefully, freewrite answers to the questions that follow. Discuss your answers with your classmates.

"Cross-Country Skiing: The Hows of Wax"*

The U.S. Cross-Country Ski Team will run the entire length of Vermont, a distance of more than 230 miles, in nine straight days to train for the 1984 Winter Games . . . Such training is necessary for races that can last as long as two and a half hours and cover 32 miles, winding through forests, up steep hills, and across broad fields. Conditioning is a top priority for the racers, but the winner among dozens of world-class skiers may not be the one in the best shape. For in competitive cross-country skiing, sometimes it's not who's on top of the ski but what's on the bottom that counts.

1. How does the writer "hook" his readers?
2. How does he "set the stage" for his focus?
3. Where does he state his main idea? (Which sentence is his thesis statement?)
4. What do you expect to read about in this essay? How do you think the writer will develop the essay?
5. What impression do you have of the writer? Why do you have that impression?

*From Chase, Anthony. 1982. "Cross-Country Skiing: The Hows of Wax." *Science 82* Mar.: 90–91.

Exercise 3.13 Now read the following introduction to an essay about sociolinguistics, the study of how language is used in social contexts. The essay comes from a textbook on anthropology, so the authors are experts on the topic. They are writing to inform their readers about a topic that is new for them. After reading the introduction carefully, freewrite answers to the questions that follow. Discuss your answers with your classmates.

> Linguists have traditionally concentrated on studying language as a system of rules governing what is considered acceptable speech in a particular society. Recently, however, some linguists have begun to study predictable variations in the ways people actually use their language when speaking. On the one hand, we may deal with language as a socially shared system of symbols, generated by a similarly shared system of rules; and on the other we may consider how people customarily speak differently in different social contexts. This second type of linguistic study, called *sociolinguistics*, is concerned with the ethnography of speaking—that is, with cultural and subcultural patterns of speaking in different social contexts.*

1. How do the writers "hook" their readers?
2. How do they "set the stage" for their focus?
3. Where do they state their main idea? (Which sentence is the thesis statement?)
4. What do you expect to read about in this essay? How do you think the writers will develop the essay?
5. What impression do you have of the writers? Why do you have that impression?

These are just two examples of ways to introduce a text; as stated above, there are many ways for writers to "hook" and establish a relationship with their readers, and "set the stage." The way that you choose to introduce your texts will always depend on your readers, your purpose, and the topic that you are writing about.

WRITING CONCLUSIONS What is the job of a conclusion? What do readers expect from a conclusion? When you are reading a text, what do you expect from the conclusion?

The main jobs of a conclusion are:

- to *restate* the main idea. By restating the main idea, the writer brings the readers "full circle" on the topic and keeps them focused.

- to provide closure for the readers. This relates to the idea of coming "full circle." When they finish reading a text, readers want to feel that the essay is complete, without any loose ends.

Just as there are many ways to introduce an essay, there are many ways to conclude a text. Among the more common ways to conclude a text are:

1. To summarize the main ideas.
2. To discuss the significance of the ideas or their implications for other situations or the future.

---

*From page 238 of Ember, Carol R., and Melvin Ember. 1981. *Anthropology* 3rd Ed. Englewood Cliffs, NJ: Prentice-Hall.

PART I: DRAFTED WORKS IN PROGRESS

Exercise 3.14 Below is the conclusion to the magazine article describing the importance of waxing cross-country skis. Reread the introduction (page 78) and then read this conclusion. Freewrite answers to the questions that follow. Discuss your answers with your classmates.

> For those recreational skiers who don't want to spend more time waxing than skiing, there is a whole new market of waxless skis that perform well in almost all types of snow. Most have a fish-scale or wedge-shaped pattern stamped into the polyethylene itself so that the ski grips when the skier pushes off and then glides forward. Some companies have begun experimenting with interchangeable ski bases so that a whole new bottom can be snapped on when the snow conditions change. Most racers, however, will stick to wax. Its infinite variety allows them to literally tune the ski to the snow, making the bottom of the ski as unique as each snow crystal on which it glides.*

(1) In which sentence does the writer restate his main idea?
(2) How do the other sentences in this conclusion provide closure for the readers?

Exercise 3.15 Below is the conclusion to the textbook selection about sociolinguistics. Reread the introduction (page 79) and then read this conclusion. Freewrite answers to the questions that follow. Discuss your answers with your classmates.

> The field of sociolinguistics has only recently emerged. At the present time, sociolinguists seem to be interested primarily in describing variation in the use of language. Eventually, however, sociolinguistic research may enable us to understand why such variation exists. Why, for example, do some societies use many different status terms in address? Why do other societies use modes of speaking that vary with the sex of the speaker? If we can understand why language varies in different contexts, this might also suggest why structural aspects of language change over time. For as social contexts in a society change, the structure of the language might also tend to change.†

(1) In which sentence do the writers restate their main idea?
(2) How do the other sentences in this conclusion provide closure for the readers?

Exercise 3.16 Look at the introductions and the conclusions of several texts written in English. Look at magazine and newspaper articles and textbook sections. For each introduction that you read, try to answer these questions:

(1) How does the writer "hook" the readers?
(2) How does the writer "set the stage" for the focus?
(3) Where does the writer state the main idea? (Which sentence is the thesis statement?)
(4) What do you expect to read about in this essay? How do you think the writer will develop the essay?
(5) What impression do you have of the writer? Why do you have that impression?

---

*From Chase, Anthony. 1982. "Cross-Country Skiing: The Hows of Wax." *Science 82* Mar.: 90–91.
†From page 240 of Ember, Carol R., and Melvin Ember. 1981. *Anthropology* 3rd Ed. Englewood Cliffs, NJ: Prentice-Hall.

For each conclusion that you read, try to answer these questions:

① Does the writer restate the main idea? In which sentence?

② How do the other sentences in this conclusion provide closure for the readers?

Exercise 3.17 Go back to your second draft now. If you have already written an introduction and a conclusion, reread them and evaluate their effectiveness. Consider these questions:

① Do the introduction and conclusion work well for your purpose?

② Do they work well for your audience?

③ Does your introduction have a "hook"? If yes, what is it? Evaluate its effectiveness. If not, what can you add to grab your readers' attention?

④ Does your introduction "set the stage" for your paper? If yes, how does it achieve this? Evaluate its effectiveness. If not, what can you add to provide background knowledge for your readers?

⑤ Does your introduction contain your thesis statement? If yes, underline it. Evaluate its effectiveness. If not, add one.

⑥ Does your conclusion summarize your main points?

⑦ Does your conclusion provide closure for your reader? If yes, how does it achieve this? If not, what can you add to make it do so.

If you have not yet written an introduction and a conclusion, write them now. Be sure that the introduction includes a "hook" and that you successfully "set the stage" for your readers. Write a conclusion that restates your main idea and provides closure for your readers.

REVISING YOUR WRITING

FOCUSING ON YOUR SENTENCE STRUCTURES

In the draft that you submit to your readers, your ideas should flow smoothly and naturally. Your sentences should show the correct balance between ideas; they should also be varied.

LEARNING FROM ANOTHER WRITER Below are some excerpts from the second draft of the essay explaining the different aspects of wedding customs in Japan. After the writer developed and organized his ideas, he turned his attention to his sentence structures to make sure that all of his sentences flowed well and were properly balanced and varied.

Exercise 3.18 Read through the original and revised versions of each excerpt carefully. With your classmates, describe each change that the writer made. Then discuss how each change affects the writing. Discuss:

- how the changes help the readers.
- how the changes help the clarity and balance of ideas.
- how the changes help the flow of ideas.

To facilitate the discussion, the revisions are printed for you below each excerpt. Refer to each revision by its number.

Part I: Drafted Works in Progress

Excerpt A: Original

> Marriage is one of the most important once-in-a-lifetime events. It means the beginning of a new life. In Japan, it entails lots of events. All of these events are definitely necessary. These events include an engagement ceremony, a wedding ceremony, a

Excerpt A: Revision

> ①   *which*
> Marriage, is one of the most important once-in-a-lifetime events., ~~It~~ means the beginning of a new life. In Japan, it entails lots of events , ② ~~All~~ *all* of ~~these events~~ *which* are definitely necessary. These events include an engagement ceremony, a wedding ceremony, a

1. Marriage is one of the most important once-in-a-lifetime events. It means the beginning of a new life.
   ↓
   Marriage, which is one of the most important once-in-a-lifetime events, means the beginning of a new life.

2. In Japan, it entails a lot of events. All of these events are definitely necessary.
   ↓
   In Japan, it entails a lot of events, all of which are definitely necessary.

Excerpt B: Original

> First, the young couple must decide the date and where the wedding ceremony will take place. This step must be done at least 6 months before the wedding day. If the

Excerpt B: Revision

> ③ First, the young couple must decide the date and ~~where~~ *place of* the wedding ceremony ~~will take place~~. This step must be done at least 6 months before the wedding day. If the

3. First, the young couple must decide the date and where the wedding ceremony will take place.
   ↓
   First, the young couple must decide the date and place of the wedding ceremony.

Excerpt C: Original

> to do this step about 1 or 2 years before the wedding date. The main factors that influence this decision are the type of ceremony—Buddhist, Shinto or Christian- how much the wedding will cost approximately, the place of the ceremony, and when the ceremony will take place. Every department store in the big cities has a bridal corner. The couple can meet with bridal consultants there to decide these matters. They will recommend several appropriate places and pre-reservations will be made for the couple. Then, the couple has to go and see each place to decide which one is better.

Part I: Drafted Works in Progress

Excerpt C: Revision

---

to do this step about 1 or 2 years before the wedding date. ④ The main factors that influ-
ence this decision are the ~~type of ceremony—Buddhist, Shinto or Christian- how much~~ *place, the date, the approximate cost, and the type of ceremony — Buddhist, Shinto, or Christian.*
~~the wedding will cost approximately, the place of the ceremony, and when the ceremony will take place.~~ ⑤ Every department store in the big cities has a bridal corner✗ *where the* ~~The~~ couple can meet with ~~bridal~~ consultants ~~there~~ to decide these matters. ⑥ They will recommend several appropriate places and *make* pre-reservations ~~will be made~~ for the couple. Then, the couple has to go and see each place to decide which one is better.

---

4. The main factors that influence this decision are the type of ceremony—Buddhist, Shinto, or Christian- how much the wedding will cost approximately, the place of the ceremony, and when the ceremony will take place.
   ↓
   The main factors that influence this decision are the place, the date, the approximate cost, and the type of ceremony—Buddhist, Shinto, or Christian.

5. Every department store in the big cities has a bridal corner. The couple can meet with bridal consultants there to decide these matters.
   ↓
   Every department store in the big cities has a bridal corner where the couple can meet with consultants to decide these matters.

6. They will recommend several appropriate places and pre-reservations will be made for the couple.
   ↓
   They will recommend several appropriate places and make pre-reservations for the couple.

CHAPTER 3 : SHARING YOUR KNOWLEDGE OR EXPERTISE

Excerpt D: Original

> The couple chooses the date and place of the ceremony. Then they have to ask a person such as a teacher at school or they might ask a superior at work to be "Nakoudo," a go-between who arranges the engagement ceremony and wedding ceremony. Traditionally, the Nakoudo, who must be accompanied by his wife, acts as a guarantor

Excerpt D: Revision

> ⑦ ~~The~~ After the couple chooses the date and place of the ceremony~~.~~, ~~Then~~ they ~~have to ask a person such as a teacher at school or they might ask a superior at work to be~~ select the "Nakoudo," a go-between who arranges the engagement and wedding ceremonies. They ~~ceremony and wedding ceremony.~~ usually ask a person such as a teacher or a superior at work.
>
> Traditionally, the Nakoudo, who must be accompanied by his wife, acts as a guarantor

7. The couple chooses the date and place of the ceremony. Then they have to ask a person such as a teacher at school or they might ask a superior at work to be "Nakoudo," a go-between who arranges the engagement ceremony and wedding ceremony.
   ↓
   After the couple chooses the date and place of the ceremony, they have to select the "Nakoudo," a go-between who arranges the engagement and wedding ceremonies. They usually ask a person such as a teacher or a superior at work.

Part I: Drafted Works in Progress

Excerpt E: Original

> At this stage, an engagement ring is bought. Normally, engagement rings are diamond rings, but pearls or rubies are also currently popular. The cost of the ring depends

Excerpt E: Revision

> At this stage, an engagement ring is bought. Normally, engagement rings are ~~diamond rings~~ *diamonds*, but pearls or rubies are also currently popular. The cost of the ring depends

8. Normally, engagement rings are diamond rings, but pearls or rubies are also currently popular.
 ↓
 Normally, engagement rings are diamonds, but pearls or rubies are also currently popular.

Excerpt F: Original

> clothing, kitchen items, beds, and furniture. This amount is usually about $3,000. Furthermore, each side must prepare the family list, a piece of paper on which the names of family members are written, and which is exchanged by both sides at the engagement ceremony. The ceremony usually takes place about 6 months before the wedding ceremony in a restaurant or they go to the house of the woman's family. Present

Excerpt F: Revision

> clothing, kitchen items, beds, and furniture. This amount is usually about $3,000. ⑨ Further-
> more, each side must prepare the family list, a piece of paper on which the names of
> family members are written~~,~~ *These ~~list~~ lists are* ~~and which is~~ exchanged by both sides at the engagement
> ceremony. ⑩ The ceremony usually takes place about 6 months before the wedding ~~cere-~~
> ~~mony~~ in a restaurant or ~~they go to~~ *in* the house of the woman's family. Present

9. Furthermore, each side must prepare the family list, a piece of paper on which the names of family members are written, and which is exchanged by both sides at the engagement ceremony.
   ↓
   Furthermore, each side must prepare the family list, a piece of paper on which the names of family members are written. These lists are exchanged at the engagement ceremony.

10. The ceremony usually takes place about 6 months before the wedding ceremony in a restaurant or they go to the house of the woman's family.
    ↓
    The ceremony usually takes place about 6 months before the wedding in a restaurant or in the house of the woman's family.

Excerpt G: Original

> wedding ceremony and the dinner party take place at the same place on the same day.
> The couple has to make decisions about the decorations for the dinner party, what kind
> of dresses and accessories the bride will wear, the clothing of bridegroom and who will
> narrate the dinner party.

PART I: DRAFTED WORKS IN PROGRESS

Excerpt G: Revision

> wedding ceremony and the dinner party take place at the same place on the same day.
> ⑪
> The couple has to make decisions about the decorations for the dinner party, ~~what kind~~
> *the bride's dresses*   *bridegroom's*
> ~~of dresses~~ and accessories ~~the bride will wear~~, the ∧ clothing ~~of bridegroom~~, and ~~who will~~
> *the narrator for*
> ~~narrate~~ the dinner party.

11. The couple has to make decisions about the decorations for the dinner party, what kind of dresses and accessories the bride will wear, the clothing of bridegroom and who will narrate the dinner party.
    ↓
    The couple has to make decisions about the decorations for the dinner party, the bride's dresses and accessories, the bridegroom's clothing, and the narrator for the dinner party.

Excerpt H: Original

> As you can see, the preparations for marriage are very elaborate in Japan, but this process is indispensable for a young couple to have their marriage recognized and if they want to make a good start of their new life.

Excerpt H: Revision

> ⑫
> As you can see, the preparations for marriage are very elaborate in Japan~~, but~~.
> *Nonetheless,*
> this process is indispensable for a young couple to have their marriage recognized and
> ~~if they want~~ to make a good start of their new life.

12. As you can see, the preparations for marriage are very elaborate in Japan, but this process is indispensable for a young couple to have their marriage recognized and if they want to make a good start of their new life.
    ↓
    As you can see, the preparations for marriage are very elaborate in Japan. Nonetheless, this process is indispensable for a young couple to have their marriage recognized and to make a good start of their new life.

PARALLELISM Parallelism is a structure of written English that helps maintain the flow of ideas within a sentence. According to the principle of parallelism, when a writer makes a list or presents two or more ideas in a series, those ideas should be presented in similar grammatical structures. By using the same structures, the writer keeps the readers on track and helps them clearly understand the relationship between ideas.

Example:

(not parallel)

The couple must decide the date and where the ceremony will take place.
          1 = noun phrase   2 = clause

(parallel)

The couple must decide the date and the place of the ceremony.
          1 = noun phrase   2 = noun phrase

Sentence revisions 3, 4, 6, 7, 8, 10, 11, 12 on pages 83 to 88 illustrate changes to make non-parallel sentences parallel.

SUGGESTIONS • SUGGESTIONS • SUGGESTIONS • SUGGESTIONS

If you would like more information about parallelism or would like additional practice writing parallel structures or the other structures listed below, consult Part 3 of this book.

Coordination and parallelism .... see pages 212 to 217
Passive constructions .... see pages 228 to 233
Conditionals .... see pages 196 to 211
Noun clauses .... see pages 223 to 227
Discourse threads .... see pages 217 to 222

Exercise 3.19 The following essay describes wedding customs in the United States. Read through all of the sentences. Determine how many paragraphs you think the essay should have. Then rewrite the sentences in paragraphs, combining each set of lettered sentences. NOTE: With each of the bulleted (•) sentences, be careful with parallelism.

- ① a. It is difficult to characterize wedding customs in the United States.
    b. They vary a great deal depending on the wishes of the couple and what their families desire.

  ② a. Wedding customs can vary in many ways.
    b. I am going to focus on only three.

- ③ a. Wedding customs can vary in how many guests are invited.
    b. They can vary in the financial arrangements for the wedding.
    c. They can vary in the type and cost of the gifts.
    d. Family and friends give these gifts.

- ④ a. Some couples have large ceremonies.
    b. Family members attend these ceremonies.
    c. These ceremonies are attended by all of their friends.

  ⑤ a. For example, my older sister and her husband invited 200 guests to their wedding.
    b. Their wedding was in August three years ago.

Part I: Drafted Works in Progress

- **6.** a. Other couples prefer a simpler wedding.
  b. They invite just the immediate family and friends who are the closest.

7. a. My younger sister got married last year.
b. Only 20 guests attended the wedding and reception.

8. a. Still other couples go alone to a justice of the peace.
b. They have a ceremony that lasts five minutes.

- **9.** a. Typically, these couples do not care about tradition.
  b. These couples want to get married quickly. (use *either . . . or*)

10. a. Another variation is in terms of who pays for the wedding.
b. You'll find this variation in the United States.

- **11.** a. According to the traditional custom, the parents of the woman pay for the ceremony.
  b. They pay for the wedding dress.
  c. They pay to receive the guests at the party after the ceremony.

12. a. The wedding is quite large.
b. The costs are extremely high.

- **13.** a. In other cases, the bride and groom break with tradition.
  b. The expenses for their wedding are shared between them.

- **14.** a. The parents of the bride or the groom's parents might help out by giving some money.
  b. Most of the bills are taken care of by the young couple.

15. a. A third variation in wedding customs has to do with gift-giving.
b. Gift-giving is a custom that affects the guests.

- **16.** a. In some cases, weddings are very expensive for the couple.
  b. Weddings are very expensive for the guests. (use *not only . . . but also*)

17. a. Some guests feel obligated to buy gifts.
b. These gifts cost hundreds of dollars.

18. a. In other situations, the amount is much lower.
b. The amount is spent on gifts.

19. a. It is appropriate to give a nice practical gift.
b. The gift is worth $15 to $20.

- **20.** a. These variations in wedding customs reflect differences in people's lifestyles.
  b. These variations in wedding customs reflect differences in people's economic situations. (use *not only . . . but also*)
  c. These variations can be found in all parts of the United States.

CHAPTER 3 : SHARING YOUR KNOWLEDGE OR EXPERTISE

DRAFTING YOUR PAPER: *The Third Draft*

PLANNING AND WRITING YOUR THIRD DRAFT

Plan and write the third draft of your essay in which you share your expertise. The list below provides some suggestions.

> **SUGGESTIONS • SUGGESTIONS • SUGGESTIONS • SUGGESTIONS**
>
> Here are some suggestions for one way to plan and write your third draft.
>
> 1. Reread your second draft carefully.
> 2. Plan any additions, deletions, or reorganization that you would like to make for the third draft.
> 3. Do you want to make any changes in sentence structures, variety, or length? If yes, cross out the sentences or sentence parts that you want to change. Write in the revised sentences above them.
> 4. When you are ready, begin to write the third draft. Write neatly; skip lines.
> 5. When you have finished the third draft, reread it carefully. If you see anything that you want to change, mark the change on the paper (i.e., cross out the words you want to change and write in the new words above them).
> 6. If you are using a computer, see Appendix C, page 264, for suggestions about writing your third draft.

EDITING YOUR WRITING

Before you begin to edit your third draft, read pages 31 to 34. If you found a pattern to your errors when editing previous assignments and you created an editing acronym, write it at the top of your third draft.

Read through your third draft of this assignment several times. Each time that you read, concentrate on looking for and correcting one specific type of error. For example, if one of your common mistakes is with verb tenses, read through one time, focusing on all of the main verb forms. Use the Editing Checklist in Appendix A to guide you. After you have finished reading for your common errors, read the draft several more times, focusing on the sentence structures, grammatical forms, and mechanics.

With each reading, when you find an error, cross out the incorrect form and write in the correct form above it.

PART I: DRAFTED WORKS IN PROGRESS

> **SUGGESTIONS • SUGGESTIONS • SUGGESTIONS • SUGGESTIONS**
>
> When you have finished editing your own paper:
>
> 1. Exchange third drafts with another writer in the class.
> 2. Read each other's third draft carefully.
> 3. If you see any additional corrections that the writer should make, put a check mark in the margin of the line on which the error appears. Do not correct any errors; that is the writer's job.
> 4. Discuss each other's paper in turn.

Freewriting Journal Assignment

Take some time to consider your writing as work in progress. Spend a few minutes looking back over and reflecting on all of the work that you did while drafting your essay sharing your expertise. In your freewriting journal, write a paragraph describing what *you* like about your work in progress. In other words, celebrate your successes.

Describe:

- what you feel proud of about your work.
- what you have done with this work that you did not think you were capable of doing before you started.
- what you have learned by doing this work.

Write another paragraph describing one aspect of your writing that you want to work on and improve.

Describe:

- why you think that you should work on this aspect.
- what you can do to work on this aspect over the next few weeks.

CHAPTER 4

Taking a Stand

PREWRITING
- Setting the Context
- Understanding the Assignment
- Analyzing the Audience
- Collecting Data

DRAFTING YOUR PAPER: THE FIRST DRAFT
- Planning Your First Draft
- Writing Your First Draft

REVISING YOUR WRITING
- Developing Your Ideas
- Documenting the Use of Borrowed Material
- Focusing on Your Sentence Structures

DRAFTING YOUR PAPER: THE SECOND DRAFT
- Planning and Writing Your Second Draft

REVISING YOUR WRITING
- Giving and Getting Feedback

DRAFTING YOUR PAPER: THE THIRD DRAFT
- Planning and Writing Your Third Draft

EDITING YOUR WRITING

PART I: DRAFTED WORKS IN PROGRESS

PREWRITING

SETTING THE CONTEXT

Some universities in the United States have different tuition fees for different categories of students. For example, many state universities charge one fee for state residents and another, higher fee for non-residents. Most universities charge different fees for graduate and undergraduate students.

Imagine this situation: The state in which you are studying is considering raising tuition for all international students who attend state universities or colleges. If approved, this policy would affect F-1 students, those who enter the United States to study. Supporters of this policy claim that because F-1 students are not permanent residents or citizens, they should pay the complete cost of their tuition and not receive subsidies from the state government or from the institution itself.

Exercise 4.1 Freewrite answers to the following questions.

1. What do you think about the current tuition fees for international students?
2. What is your initial reaction to the suggestion that tuition for international students at state colleges and universities should be increased?
3. What are the reasons behind your initial reaction? Try to analyze your thinking at this time.

UNDERSTANDING THE ASSIGNMENT

For this assignment you are going to explore the issue of whether or not state institutions of higher education should raise tuition for international students.

The purpose of your paper is to express your opinion about this issue and to show the validity of that opinion. In other words, you will construct and support an argument. In order to learn about the topic, you will read some articles about it. In your paper, you can use ideas from other writers to support and develop the ideas that you assert.

The polished draft that you submit to your readers will include support from authorities on the topic, that is, material "borrowed" from published sources and a Works Cited page, a list of the published sources that you borrowed from. (To see an example of an essay that uses support from published sources and includes a Works Cited page, see pages 111 to 113.)

ANALYZING THE AUDIENCE

Your paper will be of interest to state legislators, university and college officials, faculty, staff, students, and state residents who pay taxes. Your audience is quite diverse and may have differing opinions about this question. As you begin to collect data for your essay and to sort out your own opinion, you will be in a better position to address the concerns of your audience.

CHAPTER 4: TAKING A STAND

Exercise 4.2 Right now, freewrite about the following questions:

How do you think each of the following groups of people would feel about a special tuition increase for international students? How would each group be affected by such an increase? Try to consider positive and negative consequences for each group.

1. You.
2. Your friends who are on student visas.
3. International students in general.
4. State-resident students.
5. University administration, faculty, and staff.
6. State taxpayers.
7. Your local community.

COLLECTING DATA

For this paper, you are considering the issue of a tuition increase for international students at state institutions of higher education. In your paper, you are going to present your opinion about the topic, an opinion that has been developed as a result of your investigation and analysis of the issue.

You have already done some freewriting about this topic. Reread what you have written. Then reflect on:

1. What you already know and think about your topic.
2. What kind of information you have to find out or learn.

Continue to explore your thoughts on this topic and collect more ideas by using whatever data collection strategies work well for you. Try:

- making notes.
- freewriting.
- idea maps.

Exercise 4.3 To help you explore your topic further, try cubing (see page 69). In your freewriting notebook or on a piece of paper, spend a few minutes writing about the subject from each of the perspectives listed below. Write quickly and without censorship; try to get your ideas down onto paper as quickly as you can.

1. Describe the issue in your own words.
2. Compare/contrast it to other issues.
3. Associate it. What other topics or issues does it remind you of?
4. Analyze it by discussing its parts.
5. Apply it by discussing how it impacts your life and the life of other people affected by it.
6. Argue for or against it by writing about the pros and cons.

PART I: DRAFTED WORKS IN PROGRESS

Exercise 4.4 To get other perspectives about your topic, discuss it with at least two other people, one who agrees with your point of view at this time and one who does not. Take notes during the discussions.

USING WRITTEN SOURCES In addition to the data collection strategies mentioned above, you will also collect information by reading about the topic. Through your reading, you can learn what some authorities on this topic have to say and evaluate the strengths and weaknesses of their ideas. You can then show the validity of your opinion by citing some of these authorities in your paper. You can also use other types of support: examples, your experience, statistics, facts, historical details, etc.

To identify written sources that are relevant for this topic, you will have to do some library research. Use your library's catalog system and periodical indexes. If you are unfamiliar with the reference materials available in your library, ask a librarian or your instructor for help.

PREPARING BIBLIOGRAPHY CARDS Preliminary bibliography cards are a way to keep a record of all the written sources that you *might* consult while preparing a paper. This record will include information such as the author's name, the title of the book or article, the date of publication, the publisher if a book, and the periodical title if an article.

Whenever you identify source material that you think *might* be related to your topic and, therefore, useful for your paper, you should prepare a bibliography card. Then, you can go find the source material and decide if you want to consult it or not.

One method for preparing bibliography cards is to write the information on index cards. Prepare a separate index card for each source. (If you are using a computer, you might want to enter the information about each source directly into your computer.)

To save you time when you are preparing your Works Cited page, the order and presentation of information on these cards should follow the documentation style that you will use on that page in your paper. (See pages 116 and 117 for an explanation of documentation style.) The works cited entry is slightly different for each type of source (e.g., book, weekly magazine, monthly magazine, journal).

The examples below illustrate the forms to use with several different sources when you are following the MLA (Modern Language Association) Author-Date system, one of many documentation styles. (NOTE: The MLA Author-Date system is the documentation style that is used in the examples and exercises throughout this chapter. If your instructor prefers that you use another documentation style in your own writing, he or she will explain it to you.)

Use this Form for a Book:

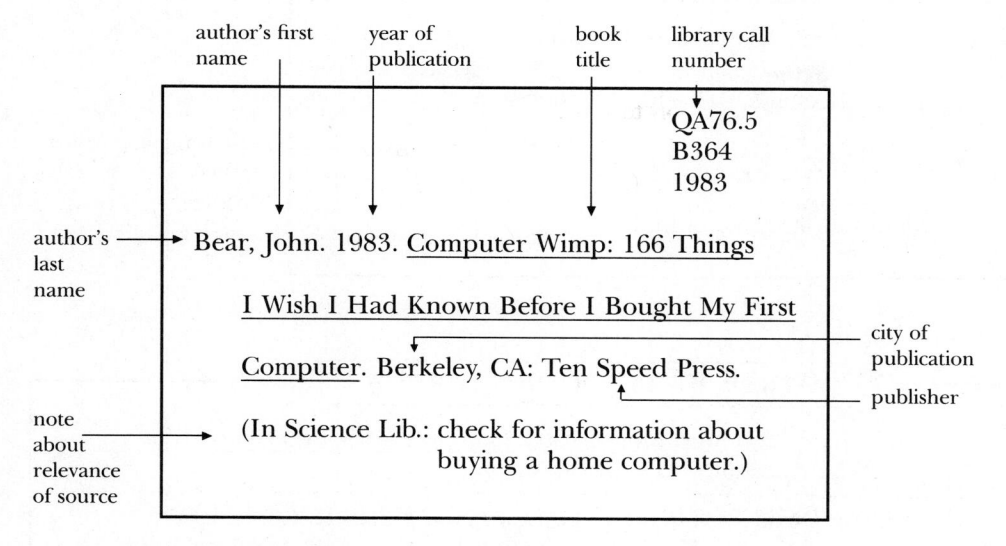

labels pointing to the entry:
- author's last name
- author's first name
- year of publication
- book title
- library call number: QA76.5 B364 1983
- city of publication
- publisher
- note about relevance of source

Bear, John. 1983. <u>Computer Wimp: 166 Things I Wish I Had Known Before I Bought My First Computer</u>. Berkeley, CA: Ten Speed Press.

(In Science Lib.: check for information about buying a home computer.)

Use this Form for a Monthly Magazine:

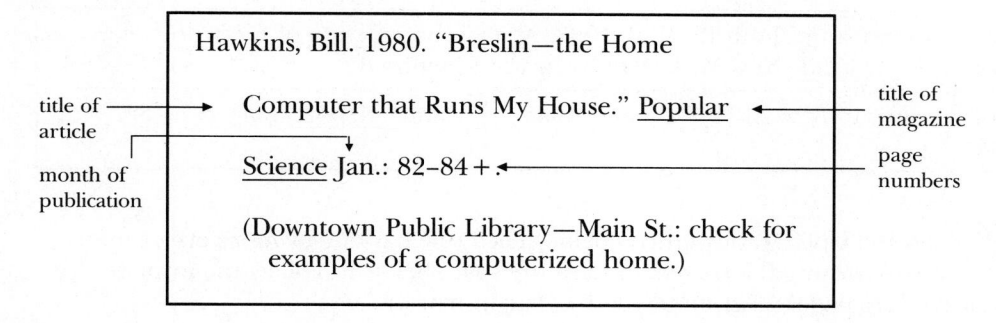

labels:
- title of article
- month of publication
- title of magazine
- page numbers

Hawkins, Bill. 1980. "Breslin—the Home Computer that Runs My House." <u>Popular Science</u> Jan.: 82–84+.

(Downtown Public Library—Main St.: check for examples of a computerized home.)

Use this Form for a Weekly Magazine:

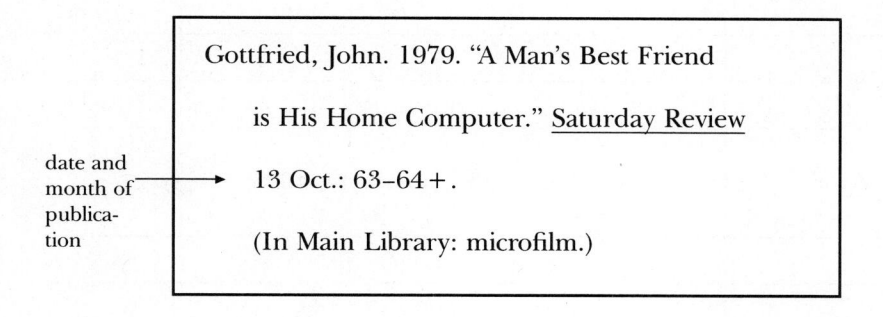

label: date and month of publication

Gottfried, John. 1979. "A Man's Best Friend is His Home Computer." <u>Saturday Review</u> 13 Oct.: 63–64+.

(In Main Library: microfilm.)

PART I: DRAFTED WORKS IN PROGRESS

Use this Form for a Newspaper:

> Grady, Sandy. 1982. "Costly 20th Century Electronic Geegaws." <u>The Kansas City Star</u> 29 Dec.: 11A. ← *page number and section of newspaper*
>
> (In Main Library: microfilm.)

OTHER BIBLIOGRAPHY FORMS

TWO AUTHORS	Willis, Jerry, and Merl Miller. 1982. <u>Computers for Everybody</u>. Blue Ridge Summit, PA: TAB Books.
THREE AUTHORS	Sullivan, David R., Theodore G. Lewis, and Curtis R. Cook. 1985. <u>Computing Today: Microcomputer Concepts and Applications</u>. Boston: Houghton.
MORE THAN THREE AUTHORS	Greenbaum, John R., et al. 1988. <u>Analysis and Design of Electronic Circuits</u>. New York: Van Nostrand Rheinhold.
ANONYMOUS AUTHOR	"How to Buy an IBM Clone." 1988. <u>Consumer Reports</u> Mar.: 179–84.

Exercise 4.5 Read the bibliography entries below. Each one has one or more errors in form. Revise each entry by writing the correct form in the space below it. Follow the formats illustrated on the preceding pages or given to you by your instructor.

Joan Rubin and Irene Thompson, "How to Be a More Successful Language Learner" 1982. Heinle & Heinle Publishers, Boston, MA.

_____
_____
_____

<u>Beacon Can Be a Lifesaver</u>. "The Denver Post." Page B6. January 14, 1993.

_____
_____
_____

Clark, Matt. "The Cultures of Medicine." 1988. <u>Newsweek</u>. Sept. 19.: 83.

_____
_____
_____

Barbara Perris. Excuses, Excuses. Northern Ohio Live. Sept. 1989, pages 88 and 85.

___

___

___

Exercise 4.6 Prepare bibliography cards for these four articles. Follow the formats illustrated in the examples above or given to you by your instructor.

"Foreign Students under Fire" by James Baker. Newsweek, Oct. 19, 1987, pages 73 and 74.

"Diplomats in Our Backyard" by Mark D. Rentz. Newsweek, February 16, 1987, page 10.

"Foreign Students Still Flock to the U.S." by Craufurd D. Goodwin and Michael Nacht. Wall Street Journal, July 21, 1983, p. 26, column 3.

"Foreign Students Are a Burden to America" by Georgie Anne Geyer. The Plain Dealer, July 8, 1981, page 21A.

READING AND ANALYSIS

After you identify and locate written sources that discuss aspects of your topic, you should carefully read and analyze the ideas presented in those sources.

Exercise 4.7 Read the articles cited in *Exercise 4.6*; they will give you some historical perspective on the issue. You can find copies of those articles and worksheets in Appendix D on pages 265 to 276.

Exercise 4.8 Collect more data for your paper by reading additional written sources. To do this:

① Use indexes and other reference materials in the library to help you identify relevant sources.

② Prepare a bibliography card for each source that seems relevant to your topic and paper.

③ After you identify likely sources, find them in the library.

④ Pre-read them to see if they are directly related to your topic.

⑤ Photocopy sources that seem especially relevant.

⑥ Read the articles carefully. While you are reading, relate the ideas to the context of your paper. Ask yourself: How do the ideas in this article relate to universities and students in my state? As you read, evaluate the ideas carefully and apply them to your own situation.

BORROWING FROM PUBLISHED SOURCES: NOTE-TAKING
In your paper, you will express an opinion, your thesis, and you will have to develop and support it. Your support can come from a variety of sources: your experience, the experience of friends, interview material, ideas from your reading, etc.

PART I: DRAFTED WORKS IN PROGRESS

When you use someone else's words or ideas in your own writing, you are *borrowing information*. *Every* piece of borrowed material that you use in your paper *must* be documented. The documentation tells the reader *what* ideas are borrowed, *who* the author of the borrowed material is, and *where* that borrowed material comes from.

A convenient way to borrow material is to use note cards. Write each idea that you might use in your draft on an index card. Write only one note per card. (If you are using a computer, you might want to enter each note into a file on the computer.)

There are three ways to borrow ideas: by summarizing, by paraphrasing, and by quoting.

SUMMARY	• *Restate* the main ideas of the original writer.
	• Present the original writer's ideas accurately.
	• Document the source.

PARAPHRASE	• *Restate* specific details or sentences from the original writer.
	• Present the original writer's ideas accurately.
	• Document the source.

QUOTE	• *Copy* specific details or sentences from the original writer.
	• Present the original writer's exact words.
	• Use quotation marks (". . .").
	• Document the source.

SAMPLE NOTECARDS:

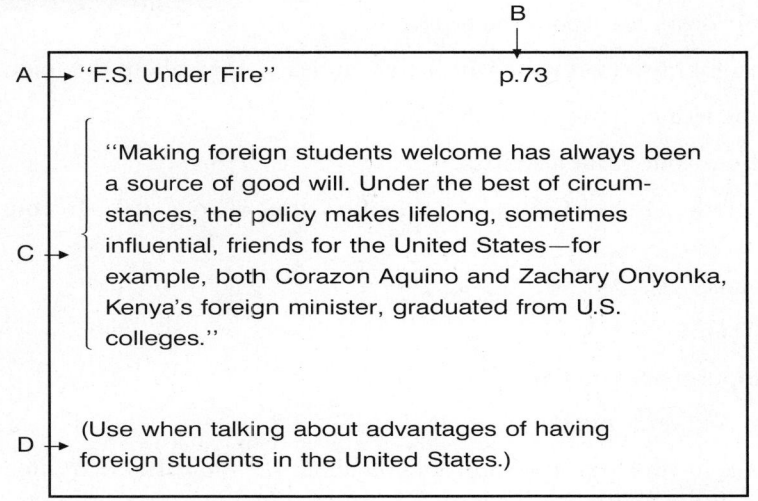

```
                                    B
                                    ↓
A → "F.S. Under Fire"             p.73

    "Making foreign students welcome has always been
    a source of good will. Under the best of circum-
    stances, the policy makes lifelong, sometimes
C → influential, friends for the United States—for
    example, both Corazon Aquino and Zachary Onyonka,
    Kenya's foreign minister, graduated from U.S.
    colleges."

D → (Use when talking about advantages of having
    foreign students in the United States.)
```

Your notecards should include the following information:

(A) Write the title of the source material in abbreviated form. (The complete title is not necessary because you have that information on your bibliography card.)

(B) Write the page number of the borrowed information.

(C) Write the note, either a summary, a paraphrase, or a quote.

(D) Write a note to yourself, explaining *why* you borrowed the information.

Here's an example of a notecard with a paraphrase.

```
                        p. 73

"F. S. Under Fire"

Welcoming foreign students has always helped build
good relations between the United States and other
countries.

        (Use when talking about advantages of having
        foreign students in the United States.)
```

Exercise 4.9 While you are reading your sources, prepare notecards for any information that you think might be useful for your paper.

Part I: Drafted Works in Progress

DRAFTING YOUR PAPER: *The First Draft*

Planning Your First Draft

CONSTRUCTING AN ARGUMENT At this point in your work in progress, you have:

- started to consider your own ideas about the topic.
- compiled a preliminary list of sources from which you can learn more about the topic.
- read and analyzed some written sources on the topic.
- started to take notes from your written sources.

You have a collection of ideas from which to write the first draft of your essay. In your paper, you will:

- make one or more claims.
- give reasons for your claims.
- marshal evidence to support your reasons.
- anticipate and address counterarguments to your claims.

The *claim* that you make in your paper is your opinion about the topic. In an argument paper, the claim is debatable; some readers will agree with your claim, but others will not.

In order to show the wisdom or validity of your claim, you must give *reasons* for it and *evidence* to support those reasons. A claim without reasons and evidence is weak and liable to be quickly rejected by readers.

Because a claim is debatable and some readers will disagree with it, you should address the *counterarguments* made by opponents. By anticipating and writing about these counterarguments, you show yourself to be knowledgeable, thoughtful, and fair.

LEARNING FROM OTHER WRITERS Reread the article by Craufurd Goodwin and Michael Nacht. (See pages 269 and 270). An analysis of these writers' argument shows the following parts:

ANALYSIS OF "FOREIGN STUDENTS STILL FLOCK TO THE U.S."	
By Craufurd Goodwin and Michael Nacht	
MAKING CLAIMS:	The writers believe that foreign students should be welcomed to the United States.
GIVING REASONS:	1. Higher education is a depression-proof export. 2. Foreign students benefit the United States.
MARSHALING EVIDENCE:	1. Foreign students add billions of dollars to the economy. 2. They contribute to research and classes. 3. They educate American students on global issues.
PROVIDING ADDITIONAL SUPPORT AND DEVELOPMENT:	The writers provide background information about foreign students: statistics, some historical information, and an explanation of why they come to study in the United States. They also give advice to policymakers.
ANTICIPATING AND ADDRESSING COUNTERARGUMENTS:	Others might argue that foreign students are a threat to the national security and economic competitiveness of the United States. The writers assert that there is no strong evidence to support these fears.

EVALUATING THE STRENGTH OF THE REASONING AND EVIDENCE When taking a stand, you must use strong reasoning and marshal adequate evidence. An argument based on faulty reasoning and/or insufficient evidence will be dismissed by your readers immediately. Everyone can fall victim to faulty reasoning and providing inadequate evidence. When writing, you must have strategies to evaluate the strength of your reasoning and evidence. The chart below gives you some guidelines.

PART I: DRAFTED WORKS IN PROGRESS

EVALUATING THE STRENGTH OF YOUR REASONING AND EVIDENCE

DO'S	DON'TS	EXAMPLES OF WEAK REASONING AND EVIDENCE
Do reason clearly and analyze your topic thoroughly.	Don't look at your topic in either-or terms.	Students in ESL programs in the United States should speak only English or return to their home countries.
Do make your claims and your reasons clear and distinct.	Don't use circular reasoning.	Claim: People should not smoke. Circular Reason: Smoking is bad.
Do provide sufficient, clear, relevant, and generalizable evidence.	Don't ignore or withhold important information or counterevidence.	Claim: Mary should be charged with aggravated murder. Reason: She killed her husband John. Evidence: She was found standing over the body holding the gun. She admitted shooting him. Ignored Counterevidence: John had physically abused Mary for 20 years. The night of the murder, he pulled a gun and threatened to kill her. She grabbed the gun and shot him dead.
	Don't make faulty cause-effect relationships.	Claim: Foreign students take jobs away from Americans. Reason: The number of foreign students in the United States has been increasing every year. Unemployment in the United States has been increasing every year. Faulty Cause-Effect: Therefore, foreign students cause higher unemployment.
	Don't overgeneralize from atypical or anecdotal evidence.	Claim: Americans are inconsiderate. Reason: They are difficult to live with. Anecdotal Evidence: I lived with two Americans last semester. They played loud music all night and never cleaned up after themselves.
	Don't provide irrelevant evidence	Claim: McDonald's are the most nutritious fast-food hamburgers. Reason: Famous people eat McDonald's hamburgers. Irrelevant Evidence: Michael Jordan and Larry Bird eat McDonald's hamburgers.
	Don't provide ambiguous evidence.	Claim: Model Y is the most popular car among young people. Reason: Many young people drive this car. Ambiguous Evidence: Nine out of ten college-aged students responding to a nation-wide survey prefer this car to others.

Exercise 4.10 Read each of the following short arguments. Evaluate the weaknesses in each one. Discuss your analyses with your classmates.

1. The university must solve the parking problem on campus. First of all, there are not enough spaces available now. The university has 28,000 students but only about 20 student parking lots. When I come to campus for my 10:00 A.M. classes, I have to look around in three or four lots before I can find an empty space. Often I am late for class because of this.

2. The menus in the university cafeterias need to be changed. If you walk through the cafeterias, you see a lot of food left behind on the plates.

3. In order to better meet the needs of the students on our campus, the main library should be open 24 hours. The libraries at other major universities in the state are open 24 hours.

4. If we computerize our campus and do all of our lessons on line, people will not talk to each other anymore.

5. The campus dorms went co-ed last year. The number of thefts in my dorm increased last year. This increase must be attributable to the fact that the dorms are now co-ed.

6. The university should either lower the required TOEFL score from 550 to 500 or eliminate the requirement altogether.

7. The university should lower the tuition fees because they are too high.

8. Smoking should be banned in all public places because it increases health risks for non-smokers. Whenever I am near smokers, I start to cough.

9. Universities and colleges in the United States should not raise tuition for international students. In many other countries tuition for higher education is free; this policy extends to citizens as well as international students.

DISCOVERING AND EXPRESSING YOUR MAIN IDEA AND THE PARTS OF YOUR ARGUMENT Before you begin the first draft, clarify your opinion about the topic and the points that you want to make in your paper.

Exercise 4.11 Go back to your freewriting notes. Read through them carefully, trying to discover which points or ideas seem the most valid and supportable to you. When doing this, consider what you learned from the readings and from discussions with your classmates or others.

Circle the ideas or points that you think you would like to discuss in *your* paper. (Keep in mind that you will be able to add new ideas or change these ideas at any point in your process.)

Exercise 4.12 In your freewriting notebook or on a piece of paper, write the answers to these questions:

1. What seems to be your **claim** or opinion about this topic?

2. What **reasons** lead you to that opinion? Evaluate the strength of your reasoning. Use the chart on page 104 to guide this evaluation.

3. What **evidence** do you have to support your reasons? Evaluate the strength of your evidence. Use the chart on page 104 to guide this evaluation.

4. What **other development or support** might you present in this paper?

5. What **counterarguments** do you anticipate? How will you address them?

PART I: DRAFTED WORKS IN PROGRESS

Exercise 4.13 Turn to page 47 to review what a thesis statement is. Then write a preliminary thesis statement for your essay. Use your claim to help you compose this thesis statement. Remember that all of the other sentences in your essay will work to develop and support this statement. Remember, too, that you will be able to change your thesis statement later if you want to or need to.

Exercise 4.14 Under the thesis statement, list the points that you think you will discuss in your paper. List them in the order in which you think you might present them. Remember, this plan is subject to change. (See page 108 for an example of a preliminary outline.)

After you have listed each point, read through your notecards carefully. Each notecard contains one piece of borrowed support from a published source. Match the borrowed support on the notecards to the relevant points in your outline. Code the notecards to your outline by writing the outline numbers on each card. (See page 108 for an example of how one writer coded his notecards to his outline.)

◆ WRITING YOUR FIRST DRAFT ◆

Look through your initial collection of data, your preliminary thesis statement, and your outline. Fill in the chart below to clarify your topic, purpose, main idea, and audience.

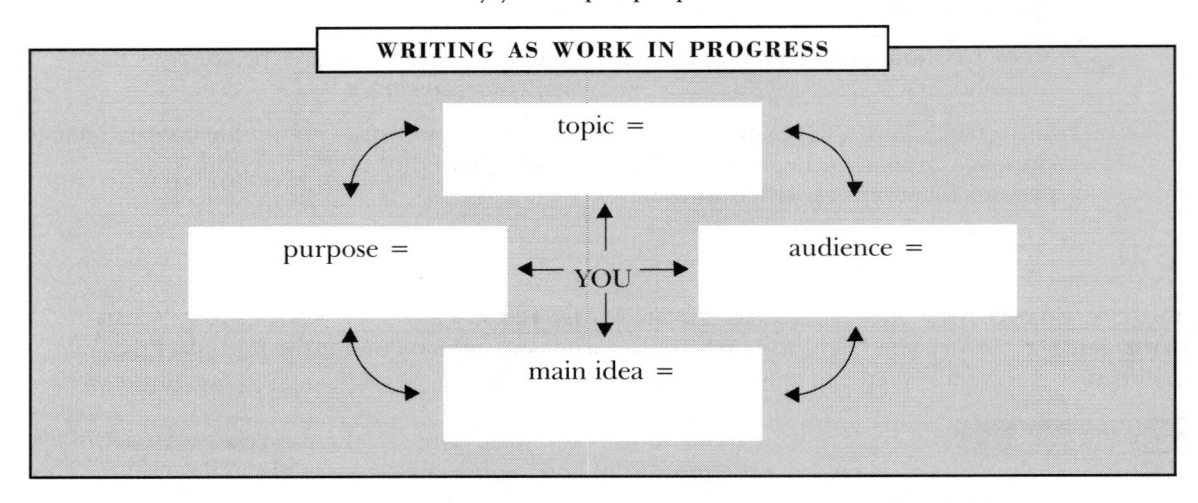

WRITING AS WORK IN PROGRESS

topic =

purpose =   ← YOU →   audience =

main idea =

When you are ready, begin to write your first draft.

CHAPTER 4: TAKING A STAND

> **SUGGESTIONS • SUGGESTIONS • SUGGESTIONS • SUGGESTIONS**
>
> These suggestions can help you work efficiently and avoid plagiarism. (See page 113 for a discussion of plagiarism.)
>
> 1. For your first draft, write the sections of your paper that express *your* ideas. Write the parts of your paper where you explain *your* interpretation of what you have learned through your reading and analysis.
>
> 2. Do *not* use any borrowed material in your first draft. Instead, keep the borrowed material on the notecards. Code each notecard to the place in your draft where you will use that borrowed support. While it might be useful to code the cards to your draft by using your outline numbers, you can do this coding anyway that you like. Use numbers, letters, or whatever code works well for you.
>
> 3. Do not worry about an introduction yet. Instead, use your preliminary thesis statement as the first sentence in your essay.
>
> 4. If you are using a computer, see Appendix C, page 263, for suggestions about writing your first draft.

On the next pages, you will see the steps that were followed by the writer of a documented essay, "The Home of the 1990's." This writer followed the suggestions above.

On page 108, you see two of the note cards that this writer prepared. The writer coded these cards to his preliminary outline, which appears on the same page.

On page 109, you see the first page of the writer's first draft. In the right-hand margin, you see an analysis of the draft. This analysis shows you what the writer's first draft consists of.

PART I: DRAFTED WORKS IN PROGRESS

Preliminary Outline

Thesis Statement: The time has come to equip all new homes with built-in computer systems.

I. Maintain pleasant and efficient environment
   A. Pleasant environment
      1. temperature control
      2. health
   B. Efficiency
      1. appliances
      2. utilities
      3. energy costs
II. Provide and process information
   A. Access databanks
      1. access home shopping networks
      2. link with electronic bulletin boards
   B. Facilitate record-keeping
      1. keep medical records
      2. keep vital statistics
   C. Calculate
      1. balance checkbook
      2. project investment earnings
      3. figure taxes
      4. track bills

Sample Note Cards

"Computers: At the Crossroads . . ."   p. 98.

"Today, Ohio Scientific's C8P home computer can monitor home temperatures and electric and gas consumption, turn lights off and on, operate security and fire alarms and warn police or firemen of breakdowns in heating or plumbing while you are away."

(Use when talking about maintaining a pleasant environment.)

I. A. 1. ← (code that refers to the writer's outline)

"Home Computers: Life in . . ."   p. 23.

"Home appliances may include self-diagnostic systems that tell your computer what is wrong and what sort of repair is required. Some may even be able to fix themselves."

(Use when talking about appliances.)

I. B. 1. ← (code that refers to the writer's outline)

CHAPTER 4: TAKING A STAND

First Draft

The time has come to equip all new homes with built-in computer systems. A built-in system could control the appliances and utilities in the house.

— Claim → thesis statement

— First reason

(Card I. A. 1.)

— Evidence from published source (code to refer to borrowed material)

The ability to control the temperature in a house is extremely important for comfort and health reasons. This is especially true in the parts of the country where outside temperatures vary a lot from season to season. In the Midwest, for instance, the temperature can range from the 60's to the 30's. This kind of vartiation outside makes it difficult to keep the inside temperature comfortable. Furthermore, sudden temperature changes in the house can cause more colds and flus. A computer system could control the temperature 24 hours a day, thereby guaranteeing round-the-clock comfort.

— Development of reason → interpretation and application

— Evidence from the writer's experience

— Summarizing generalization

In addition to comfort, a computerized home would be more efficient.

— Paragraph link
— Another reason

(Card I. B. 1.)

— Evidence from published source (code to refer to borrowed support)

Imagine the efficiency that could be attained in a house where the washing machine signals that it is broken and then fixes itself, or the hot water . . .

— Development

PART I: DRAFTED WORKS IN PROGRESS

REVISING YOUR WRITING

DEVELOPING YOUR IDEAS

LEARNING FROM ANOTHER WRITER Below are the first pages of the second draft of the essay in which the writer expressed his opinion about computerized homes. Analyze this essay to see some ways to develop a paper by citing published sources. Note the techniques that the writer used to present his ideas to his readers. What you learn from analyzing this essay might help you make decisions about ways to revise your own essay.

Read the paper carefully. Then analyze it for the following:

① Find the thesis statement.

② Identify the kind of support and development that the writer used.

③ Look at the techniques that the writer used to move from one point or idea to the next.

④ Examine the Works Cited page to see how the writer organized it.

Yin 1

Li Yin

Professor Deane

English 104

8 May 1992

The Home of the 1990's: Should It Be Computerized?

Today, a computerized home is still looked upon as a unique example of high-tech gadgetry, a luxury "toy" for the wealthy. Should it be? If we consider some of the benefits of a computerized home, we can see that all new homes should be equipped with built-in computer systems for at least two reasons: the maintenance of a pleasant and efficient environment and the processing of great amounts of information.

A built-in system can maintain a pleasant and efficient environment by controlling the major appliances and utilities in the house. According to Robert L. Perry, a writer for <u>Mechanics Illustrated</u>, Ohio Scientific's C8P home computer can monitor the temperature in a house (1981, 98). This control of the temperature is extremely important for comfort and health reasons, especially in the parts of the country where outside temperatures vary widely from season to season or even from day to day. In the Midwest, for instance, in the fall and spring seasons, the temperatures can range from the 60's during the day to the 30's at night. This amount of variation outdoors makes it difficult to manually maintain a comfortable temperature inside the house. Furthermore, sudden temperature changes inside the house can cause health problems such as colds and flus, particularly for small children and older people. A computer system could automatically control the temperature at an appropriate level in the house 24 hours a day, thereby guaranteeing round-the-clock comfort.

In addition to comfort, a computer system would make a home more efficient and contribute to energy conservation. Writing in Ms, Barry Stein and Jane Covey Brown report that home appliances could be linked to computerized networks in the house in such a way that the appliances could self-diagnose breakdowns and tell the main computer what kind of repairs were needed. They go on to say that "some [appliances] may even be able to fix themselves" (1982, 23). Imagine the efficiency that could be attained in a house where the washing machine immediately signals that it is broken and then fixes itself, or the hot water heater lets the home owner know that it is getting old and less efficient and needs to be retired. Moreover, Perry points out that a computerized system can keep track of the use of gas and electricity and even switch the lights on and off (1981, 98). This automatic control means that no source of energy would be used unless needed. Lights would never be left on needlessly; hot water heaters and furnaces would never run unnecessarily. Perry also reports that "experiments show that a computer-controlled house uses one-third the electricity of a regular house" (1981, 98). This degree of efficiency demonstrates that a computerized home would help conserve energy at a time when it is a major concern for individuals and governments. And if, as Perry states, the predicted cost for computerizing a home is less than $1,000 (1981, 98), this alternative to energy conservation could prove less expensive than others such as nuclear power or solar energy.

Overall, then, we can see that a computerized home is a well-controlled, efficient home that conserves energy and, therefore, saves money. These facts alone should convince us that newly-constructed homes should be computer-

Chapter 4: Taking a Stand

> Yin 3
>
> ized. However, there are other compelling reasons for making computer systems standard equipment in all new homes. One of these reasons relates to the amount of information that a built-in computer system can provide and process . . .

> Yin 6
>
> Works Cited
>
> Gottfried, John. 1979. "A Man's Best Friend Is His Home Computer." <u>Saturday Review</u> 13 Oct.: 63–64+.
>
> Hawkins, Bill. 1980. "Breslin - the Home Computer that Runs My House." <u>Popular Science</u> Jan.: 82–84+.
>
> Perry, Robert L. 1981. "Computers: At the Crossroads and Beyond." <u>Mechanics Illustrated</u> Jan.: 63+.
>
> Stein, Barry, and Jane Covey Brown. 1982. "Home Computers: Life in the 'Electronic Cottage.'" <u>Ms</u> Dec.: 22–24.

AVOIDING PLAGIARISM All borrowed material—be it a quote, summary, or a paraphrase—*must* be properly acknowledged. This means that you must tell the readers where the original information comes from.

Plagiarism is the act of taking someone else's words or ideas and presenting them in your own writing without proper documentation. In the academic community it is considered "stealing;" it is not tolerated. Sometimes writers knowingly commit plagiarism, but often it happens by accident. Whether it is done on purpose or by accident, it is considered a very serious offense. In a university or college, the consequences for plagiarism can range from a warning, to an F for the paper or the class, to dismissal from the institution.

Part I: Drafted Works in Progress

INCORPORATING BORROWED MATERIAL You must present the ideas that you borrow accurately. You cannot change or misrepresent in any way the ideas of the original writer.

There must be clarity and explicit logical connections between *your* ideas and the borrowed support. Also, the borrowed support *must* be grammatically integrated into the style and "flow" of your text. To achieve this "flow" of text, you will have to decide if the borrowed support should be quoted or restated in your text.

Here is an example to illustrate how to and how NOT to incorporate borrowed support into your text. Below, you will find part of the *first* draft of one writer's paper. This writer is arguing that his state should not raise foreign student tuition because the state universities need international students. Read through this small section of his paper and the borrowed material on his note card. That material is from an article entitled "Faculty Member Relates Experience as 'Let's Talk' Conversation Partner." Written by Jeanne Cebulla, the article appeared in a university newsletter entitled <u>International Notes</u> (published by the University of Akron, Spring 1990, Volume 3, Issue 2, p. 4).

Foreign students make another contribution to our state universities in that they share their cultures, customs, and ways of thinking. They bring the world to the campuses and provide American students and faculty with the chance to learn about other languages and countries from primary sources. Many Americans seem eager for this exchange of cultures and they welcome the opportunity.

(Card # 5)

> "Faculty Member Relates . . . "   p. 4
>
> " 'It's been great,' says John Lanshe, UA academic adviser. 'Before meeting my Chinese partner, Du Feng, I didn't have much sustained exposure to people from other cultures. I think I'm learning more than he is! I'd recommend it for anybody.'
>
> Lanshe and Du Feng meet every Thursday at noon for an hour. Sometimes they just chat over brown-bag lunches in Lanshe's office or go to a restaurant for lunch. Sometimes they stop for a quick snack on the way to a place of interest to give Du Feng an insight into American life. . . ."
>
> (use when discussing cultural benefits of f.s.)
>
> (Card #5)

Another advantage of having foreign students on our state campuses is . . .

CHAPTER 4: TAKING A STAND

The writer of this paper would *not* want to quote all of this borrowed support into the text of his paper. Why not?

Below is one attempt at the second draft of this section of the writer's paper. In the second draft, the writer moved the borrowed support from the note card to the text of his paper. In this case, he paraphrased just part of the borrowed material. Read through the text now.

> Foreign students make another contribution to our state universities in that they share their cultures, customs, and ways of thinking. They bring the world to the campuses and provide American students and faculty with the chance to learn about other languages and countries from primary sources. Americans seem eager for this exchange of cultures and they welcome the opportunity. According to Jean Cebulla, John Lanshe didn't have many chances to meet people from other countries until he joined the "Let's Talk" program.
>
> Another advantage of having foreign students on our state campuses is . . .

In this example, did the writer successfully integrate the borrowed material into the text of his paper? What are the problems? Discuss them with your classmates.

Now, read this version:

PART I: DRAFTED WORKS IN PROGRESS

> Foreign students make another contribution to our state universities in that they share their cultures, customs, and ways of thinking. They bring the world to the campuses and provide American students and faculty with the chance to learn about other languages and countries from primary sources. Americans seem eager for this exchange of cultures. In <u>International Notes</u>, the newsletter from the Office of International Programs at the University of Akron, Jean Cebulla, the university's foreign student advisor, described their conversation partner program, "Let's Talk" (1990,4). One American partner, John Lanshe, joined the program because he hadn't had many chances to meet people from other countries. Lanshe reported that he felt he was learning more than his Chinese partner was. Furthermore, he recommended the program to others (qtd. in Cebulla 1990, 4). This example indicates that some Americans seek out and take advantage of the opportunity to broaden their knowledge of the world. They recognize that foreign students are a valuable resource on their campuses.
>
> Another advantage of having foreign students on our state campuses is . . .

Here, the writer successfully *wove* the borrowed material into his text. How did he achieve this success?

DOCUMENTING THE USE OF BORROWED MATERIAL

To document a paper means that you acknowledge the authors of the ideas that you borrow by telling your readers who those authors are and where and when their ideas were published. Conventions for documenting a paper are an agreed upon set of rules or standards that writers follow so that the readers can understand the paper easily.

The conventions for documentation are explained in style sheets. There are several different style sheets used in American English because different disciplines or fields of study have adopted different sets of conventions. For example, the MLA (Modern Language Association) documentation style is often used by writers in the humanities. The conventions for this style are explained in the *MLA Handbook for Writers of Research Papers*. The A.P.A. (American Psychological Association) style, explained in the *Publication Manual of the American Psychological Association*, is used by writers in the social sciences. The American Chemical Society style, used by chemists and other scientists, is explained in the *Handbook for Authors of Papers in American Chemical Society Publications*.

Below you will find explanations and examples of some of the conventions for documentation using the author-date system of the MLA style sheet. (See pages 111 to 113 for an example of a paper that uses this style.) If your instructor wants you to use a different documentation style in your paper, he or she will explain the conventions to you.

INTRODUCING THE BORROWED MATERIAL You should tell your reader where the borrowed material (that is, quote, summary, or paraphrase) begins. There are several ways to do this. Some of the more common ways are illustrated below.

To signal the *start* of the borrowed material, you might:

(1) Identify the author in an introductory clause or phrase.

   a. **First Use of an Expert**: The first time you use borrowed material, you might want to introduce it by explaining who the author is:

   Example:

   According to Craufurd Goodwin, the dean of the Graduate School at Duke University, and Michael Nacht, an associate professor of public policy at Harvard, foreign students, "by their mere presence, help to educate American students at a time when sophisticated understanding of the world is crucial" (1983, 26).

   b. **Subsequent Use of an Expert**: If you borrow from the same author again, later in your paper, use just the last name.

   Example:

   Goodwin and Nacht report that there were 327,000 foreign students here in 1981–82 (1983, 26).

(2) Identify the source in an introductory phrase or clause.

   Example:

   Newsweek reported that Massachusetts had passed legislation to raise tuition for international students attending state universities (Baker 1987, 73).

MARKING THE END OF THE BORROWED MATERIAL With the MLA author-date system, use in-text documentation. In parentheses (. . .) at the end of the borrowed material, you write the date of publication of the source and the page number on which the borrowed material appears in the original text. If the author's name is not included in the introduction to the borrowed material, you should include the last name inside the parentheses.

Part I: Drafted Works in Progress

SPECIAL RULES WITH QUOTES

1. The quote must flow along within the context of your sentence and your paper.

   a. Capitalize the first word of the quotation if it follows a comma and the quote is a complete clause.

   Example:

   As Mark Rentz acknowledges, "Making a foreign friend is easy, but turning a foreigner into an enemy is apparently easier still" (1987, 10).

   b. Do *not* capitalize the first word of a quotation if it is worked into the sentence as part of a clause.

   Example:

   Mark Rentz acknowledges that "making a foreign friend is easy, but turning a foreigner into an enemy is apparently easier still" (1987, 10).

2. The quote must be *exact*. The only times you can alter a quote are through the use of ellipsis for omissions or through the use of brackets for additions.

   a. **Ellipsis:** Use ellipsis if you want to omit information from the MIDDLE or the END of a quote. You can only omit information that is NOT necessary for your context.

   Example with ellipsis in the middle:

   Here is the original sentence from Goodwin and Nacht's article:

   The education of foreign students, like banking and insurance, is the sale abroad of a valuable service.

   Here is the borrowed quote with ellipsis:

   As Goodwin and Nacht point out, "The education of foreign students . . . is the sale abroad of a valuable service" (1983, 26).

   Example with ellipsis at the end:

   Here is the original sentence:

   Costly advisory services must be provided and the foreign student may create a host of challenges for an institution, from admissions and housing to record-keeping and community relations.

   Here is the borrowed quote with ellipsis:

   Goodwin and Nacht point out that "costly advisory services must be provided and the foreign student may create a host of challenges for an institution . . ." (1983, 26).

b. **Brackets:** When you need to add a brief explanatory note to a quotation, do it with brackets.

Example:

Here is the original sentence:

For a few, of course, an American education can be a first step to permanent U.S. residence or citizenship.

Here is the borrowed quotation:

When discussing the reasons why students come to study, Goodwin and Nacht acknowledge that "for a few [foreign students] . . . an American education can be a first step to permanent U.S residence or citizenship" (1983, 26).

(3) *A Quote Within a Quote:* If you borrow a sentence that has quotation marks within it, use single quotation marks, that is '. . .'

Example:

Here is the original sentence:

Massachusetts likes to call its capital city "the cradle of liberty" and compare it to ancient Athens.

Here is the borrowed quote:

Newsweek reporter, James Baker, points out the irony of a state like Massachusetts raising foreign student tuition when he says, "Massachusetts likes to call its capital city 'the cradle of liberty' and compare it to ancient Athens" (1987, 73).

(4) *LONG Quotations:* If a quote is more than four lines long, set it off from the text by indenting all of it (ten spaces on a typewriter or computer). Do *not* use quotation marks. Introduce the long quote with a colon (:).

Example:

> Goodwin and Nacht express dismay over the fact that the few people in the state governments who are making decisions about foreign students are ill-informed:
>
> > What is most surprising about the foreign student scene is that so few people are paying serious attention to it. And those who are manifest a negative attitude inconsistent with the facts. State legislators demand quotas or differential pricing which bear little relationship to the costs and benefits (1983, 26).
>
> It seems that the politicians should turn to the educators on this matter and find out what really is in the best interests of the United States.

Part I: Drafted Works in Progress

(5) *Indirect Quotes (double references):* Sometimes you might want to borrow some borrowed material. For example, James Baker borrowed Robert Weatherall's statement about the important role that foreign students play in universities in the United States. Suppose you want to borrow Weatherall's quote from Baker. You must indicate that this is an indirect quote. You do so by putting extra information in the in-text documentation. Add the abbreviation "qtd. in," which means "quoted in." Use it whether you quote or paraphrase the indirect quote. Study the example below.

Example:

> Robert Weatherall, the job-placement director at MIT, feels that "we [the U.S.] are shooting ourselves in the foot if we send foreigners home" (qtd. in Baker 1987, 74). If this state wants to avoid hurting itself, it should make its foreign students feel welcome and perhaps even recruit more.

SPECIAL RULES WITH PARAPHRASES AND SUMMARIES When you paraphrase or summarize, you must *restate* the original text. You keep the original author's ideas, *but* you state them in your own way. A paraphrased sentence must look different from the original. You can combine quotes and paraphrases, *but* be sure to use quotation marks with the quoted parts.

WORKS CITED PAGE The Works Cited or reference page is the last page of the paper. (See page 113 for an example.) On this page, you list all of the sources that you borrowed information from and used as support in your paper. These sources are listed in alphabetical order, by the author's last name. The information should be in the exact order as you wrote it on your bibliography card.

See pages 97 and 98 for examples of the conventions to use when preparing each entry for your Works Cited page. If you have used a source other than those illustrated, consult the *MLA Handbook for Writers of Research Papers*, 3rd Edition for the correct form to use.

FOCUSING ON YOUR SENTENCE STRUCTURES

As you incorporate the borrowed material into your second draft, you want your ideas to flow smoothly and naturally. Because you will be reporting the words and ideas of other writers, you will use quotations, paraphrases, and summaries. Pages 118 to 120 explain some of the conventions for presenting quotes in your writing. To present ideas through paraphrase and summary, you can use reported speech.

CHAPTER 4: TAKING A STAND

> **SUGGESTIONS • SUGGESTIONS • SUGGESTIONS • SUGGESTIONS**
>
> If you need more information about the rules of structure for reported speech or would like to practice these structures, see Part 3 of this book.
>
> Reported speech . . . . see pages 233 to 237
> Noun clauses . . . . see pages 223 to 227

Exercise 4.15 In each of the short texts below, the writer states a general idea and provides evidence from published sources to support it. In each case, the writer's idea and the borrowed idea are not integrated properly.

Practice correctly incorporating and documenting borrowed material by revising the excerpts below. Integrate the borrowed material so that it flows with the writer's text. Add what is necessary to properly document each use of borrowed material. Use a separate sheet of paper for your answers.

① In addition to absorbing some of the cost of educating foreign students, the state and the institutions of higher education have other expenses to budget for. Foreign students have special needs and problems that must be attended to. Costly advising services must be made available and the foreign student may create many challenges for an institution, from admissions and housing to record-keeping and community relations.

(Refer to "Foreign Students Still Flock to the U.S.," pages 269 and 270.)

② Foreign students enhance the cultural diversity of a campus by bringing a global perspective to the classroom and campus community. They "help to educate American students at a time when sophisticated understanding of the world is crucial" (1983).

(Refer to "Foreign Students Still Flock to the U.S.," pages 269 and 270.)

③ At this point, many graduate programs need foreign students in order to survive. James Baker reports that we're shooting ourselves in the foot if we send foreigners home.

(Refer to "Foreign Students Under Fire," pages 265 to 267.)

DRAFTING YOUR PAPER: *The Second Draft*

PLANNING AND WRITING YOUR SECOND DRAFT

In your second draft, incorporate the borrowed material into your text. The list of suggestions below remind you of some things to consider while you are planning and writing your next draft. Keep and use any of the sentences from your first draft that work well. When you are integrating borrowed material into your second draft, be sure to weave it into the flow of your text. Also, remember to mark the beginning and the end of every borrowed idea.

PART I: DRAFTED WORKS IN PROGRESS

SUGGESTIONS • SUGGESTIONS • SUGGESTIONS • SUGGESTIONS

Here are some suggestions for one way to proceed with planning your second draft.

1. Reread your first draft and any readers' comments carefully.
2. Determine whether or not you need to make any changes in your thesis statement. Does it need to be more specific? less specific?
3. Determine whether or not you need to make any changes in the global structure of your paper. Are the ideas in a good order? Are the different ideas distinct? Do your paragraph divisions reflect the shifts in focus within your paper? Note any changes that you want to make for your second draft.
4. Reevaluate the strength of your evidence. Reconsider the support and logical development that came from your own analysis and interpretation of the topic. Reconsider each piece of borrowed support. Use the support that is the strongest and most convincing for your readers.
5. Are there any ideas that do not fit your thesis statement or for which you do not have convincing evidence? If yes, throw them away.
6. Are there any ideas that you still want to add to your second draft? If yes, write those ideas down on scrap paper.
7. If you have already written an introduction and a conclusion, reread them and evaluate their effectiveness. Consider these questions:
    a. Do the introduction and conclusion work well for your purpose and audience?
    b. Does your introduction have a "hook"? If yes, what is it? Evaluate its effectiveness. If not, what can you add to grab your readers' attention?
    c. Does your introduction "set the stage" for your paper? If yes, how does it achieve this? Evaluate its effectiveness. If not, what can you add to provide background knowledge for your readers?
    d. Does your introduction contain your thesis statement?
    e. Does your conclusion summarize your main points?
    f. Does your conclusion provide closure for your readers? If yes, how does it achieve this? If not, what can you add to make it do so.
8. If you have not yet written an introduction and a conclusion, write them now. Be sure that the introduction includes a "hook" and that you successfully "set the stage" for your readers. Write a conclusion that restates your main idea and provides closure for your readers.
9. When you have finished, reread the entire draft. Feel free to make any adjustments or revisions.
10. If you are using a computer, see Appendix C, page 263, for suggestions about revising your paper to produce a second draft.

PREPARING YOUR WORKS CITED PAGE Prepare a Works Cited page to submit with your second draft.

- Use the correct forms as illustrated on pages 97 to 98 and 113.
- Arrange the list in alphabetical order by author's last name.

REVISING YOUR WRITING

GIVING AND GETTING FEEDBACK

Share your second draft with another writer (or a small group) from your class.

When you are reading another writer's second draft, read through the entire paper carefully. If you have trouble with vocabulary or handwriting, ask the writer for clarification. Once you have read and understood the draft, discuss or write answers to the following questions. (If you write your answers, put them on a separate sheet of paper so that you can give them to the writer. Do not write on your partner's draft.)

1. What is the writer's main idea?

2. Which sentence do you think is the thesis statement for this paper?
   Comment on the thesis statement. Is it just right? too broad? too narrow? Explain your comment.

3. Analyze the writer's argument by making a chart like the one on page 103. List the writer's claims, reasons, and evidence. How did the writer address counterarguments?

4. Comment on the development of ideas.
   a. Do you see any places in this first draft where the writer used strong support?
   b. Where would you like more explanation or more development? Why?
   c. Comment on the writer's use of borrowed material. Is it successfully woven into the text? If not, why not?
   d. Is the borrowed material properly documented? If not, why not?

5. Are there any sentences or ideas that you feel the writer should omit from a later draft? If yes, which ones? Why?

6. Comment on the organization.
   a. What seems to be the global structure of the draft? Comment on its effectiveness.
   b. How many paragraphs does this first draft have?
   c. Are the paragraph divisions effective?
      If yes, what is the focus of each one?
      If no, what changes would you recommend for the next draft?
   d. Are the ideas within each paragraph grouped and sequenced effectively?
      If no, what changes would you recommend?

7. Comment on the introduction and the conclusion.
   a. What is the "hook?"
   b. How does the writer "set the stage?"
   c. Does the conclusion provide closure? If not, what can you suggest?

8. Comment on the sentence structures and grammar.
   a. Do you see any sentences that the writer should revise? If yes, which ones and why?
   b. Do you see any errors that the writer should correct? If yes, what?

9. What part of this draft do you like the best? Why?

PART I: DRAFTED WORKS IN PROGRESS

DRAFTING YOUR PAPER: *The Third Draft*

PLANNING AND WRITING YOUR THIRD DRAFT

Prepare the third draft of your essay in which you express your opinion about a tuition increase for international students. The list below provides some suggestions.

SUGGESTIONS • SUGGESTIONS • SUGGESTIONS • SUGGESTIONS

Here are some suggestions for one way to plan and write your third draft.

1. Reread your second draft carefully.
2. Consider your readers' comments carefully.
3. Plan any changes that you would like to make for the third draft.
4. When you are ready, begin to write the third draft. Write neatly; skip lines.
5. When you have finished the third draft, reread it carefully. If you see anything that you want to change, mark the change on the paper (i.e., cross out the words you want to change and write in the new words above them).
6. If you are using a computer, see Appendix C, page 264, for suggestions about writing your third draft.

EDITING YOUR WRITING

Before you begin to edit your third draft, reread pages 31 to 34. If you found a pattern to your errors when editing previous assignments and you created an editing acronym, write it at the top of your third draft.

Read through your third draft of this essay several times. Each time that you read, concentrate on looking for and correcting one specific type of error. For example, if one of your common mistakes is with verb tenses, read through one time, focusing on all of the main verb forms. Use the Editing Checklist in Appendix A to guide you. After you have finished reading for your common errors, read the draft several more times focusing on the sentence structures, grammatical forms, and mechanics.

With each reading, when you find an error, cross out the incorrect form and write in the correct form above it.

SUGGESTIONS • SUGGESTIONS • SUGGESTIONS • SUGGESTIONS

When you have finished editing your own paper:

1. Exchange third drafts with another writer in the class.

2. Read each other's third draft carefully.

3. If you see any additional corrections that the writer should make, put a check mark in the margin of the line on which the error appears. Do not correct any errors; that is the writer's job.

4. Discuss each other's paper in turn.

Freewriting Journal Assignment

Take a few minutes to consider your accomplishments in writing in English. Look back over all of the work that you did while drafting your essay about a tuition increase for international students. In your freewriting journal, write a paragraph describing what you like about your work in progress to date. Describe:

- what you feel proud of about your work.
- what you have learned about writing from your work in progress to date.
- what you learned about your capabilities in English while doing this work.

Write another paragraph describing one aspect of your writing that you want to work on and improve.

Describe:

- why you think that you should work on this aspect.
- what you can do to work on this aspect over the next few weeks.

PART 2
Summary Writing and Essay Exams as Works in Progress

CHAPTER 5   **129**

Summary/Comment Writing

CHAPTER 6   **157**

Writing Essay Exams

CHAPTER 5

Summary/ Comment Writing

PREWRITING
- Setting the Context
- Understanding the Assignment

WRITING SUMMARIES AND COMMENTS
- Pre-reading
- Reading
- Post-Reading
- Writing the Summary
- Writing a Comment

TEXTS TO SUMMARIZE AND COMMENT ON
- Text #1: "Miss Manners"
- Text #2: "The Cultures of Medicine"
- Text #3: "The Jeaning of America—and the World"
- Text #4: "Remember to Give to the Earth This Holiday Season"
- Text #5: "Excuses, Excuses"

PART 2: SUMMARY WRITING AND ESSAY EXAMS AS WORKS IN PROGRESS

PREWRITING

SETTING THE CONTEXT

Freewrite answers to the following questions. Then discuss your answers with your classmates.

① What is a summary? Write a short definition.

② For what reasons do people write summaries? Think of as many as you can.

③ How much experience have you had with summary writing in your first language? in English? Briefly describe your experience.

UNDERSTANDING THE ASSIGNMENT

WHAT IS A SUMMARY? A summary is a restatement of the main ideas of a text. When you write a summary, you:

- accurately present the original writer's ideas, whether you agree with them or not.
- condense the original text by presenting only the main ideas.
- restate the original writer's ideas in your own words.
- acknowledge the original writer.

WHAT ARE THE PURPOSES OF WRITING SUMMARIES?

You might write a summary for yourself:

- as a comprehension strategy to help you understand a text while you are reading.
- as a study skills strategy to help you organize and learn material after you have read the text.

You might write a summary for other readers:

- to demonstrate your knowledge of a text (for example, for an instructor).
- to present and respond to or analyze the ideas of another writer.
- to present the ideas of another writer in your own writing. In this case, you are borrowing the ideas of an expert and using them to support an idea that you assert in your paper.
- as an abstract, to preview for the readers the main ideas of a long paper you have written.

WRITING SUMMARIES AND COMMENTS

In order to write an effective summary, you have to read and comprehend the text, identify the main ideas, identify the ideas that you will exclude, reorganize and restate the information to be included, ensure that the summary accurately presents the original writer's ideas, and acknowledge the original writer.

STEPS TO EFFECTIVE SUMMARY WRITING

I. Pre-Reading
   A. Easing into the Text: Getting Your Feet Wet
   B. Tapping Prior Knowledge
   C. Getting in Deeper
   D. Forming Hypotheses about the Text
II. Reading
III. Post-Reading
IV. Writing the Summary
V. Writing the Comment

Pre-Reading*

To write a good summary, you must have an understanding of the "big picture" of the text. You must have a sense of the text as a whole. To help you get this sense before you even start to read, pre-read the text.

EASING INTO THE TEXT: GETTING YOUR FEET WET

① **Read the title and subtitle.** The title and subtitle will give you a general idea about the text and sometimes even the writer's approach to or opinion about the topic.

② **Note the author(s).** If you are familiar with the author, you may be able to anticipate the subject to be discussed and the type and style of writing.

③ **Note the source and date of publication.** If they are given, always note the source and date of the text. The date will tell you how current the information is; the source might give a clue about the type and style of writing and about how the topic will be treated.

④ **Study any charts, graphs, pictures, or diagrams.** Pictures or visual aids usually emphasize important ideas that are discussed within the text.

---

*This material is adapted from pages 8 and 9 of McWhorter, Kathleen T. and Candalene J. McCombs. 1983. *Write to Read, Read to Write*. Little, Brown and Co.

PART 2: SUMMARY WRITING AND ESSAY EXAMS AS WORKS IN PROGRESS

LEARNING FROM ANOTHER WRITER

Below are the title and subtitle of a text along with information about the source and the author. You also see the marginal notes that the summary writer made while pre-reading this text.

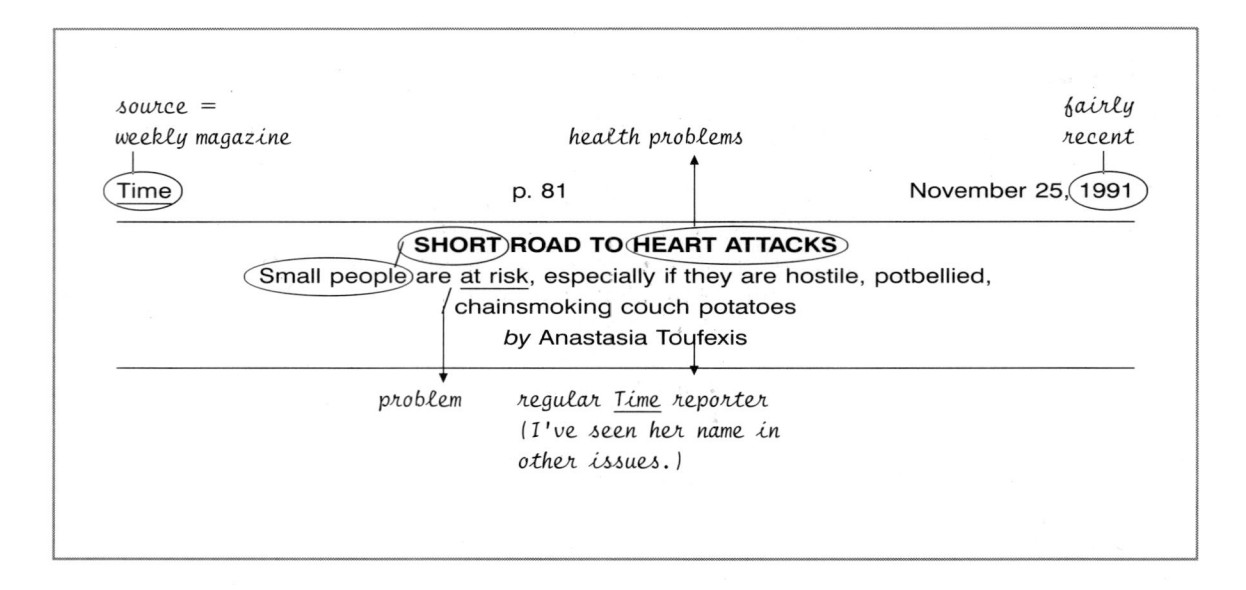

---

source = weekly magazine — (Time)   *health problems* ↑   *fairly recent*

p. 81   November 25, (1991)

SHORT ROAD TO HEART ATTACKS
Small people are at risk, especially if they are hostile, potbellied, chainsmoking couch potatoes
by Anastasia Toufexis

↓ *problem*   *regular Time reporter (I've seen her name in other issues.)*

TAPPING PRIOR KNOWLEDGE Once you have a preliminary idea about the topic of the text and the direction that the author might take in the text, you should stop and consider what you already know about that topic. Think about other texts you have read or t.v. shows you have seen that dealt with the topic. Think about conversations you may have had about the topic or your own personal experience with it.

LEARNING FROM ANOTHER WRITER

Below are notes that the summary writer made to himself in order to tap his prior knowledge of the topic.

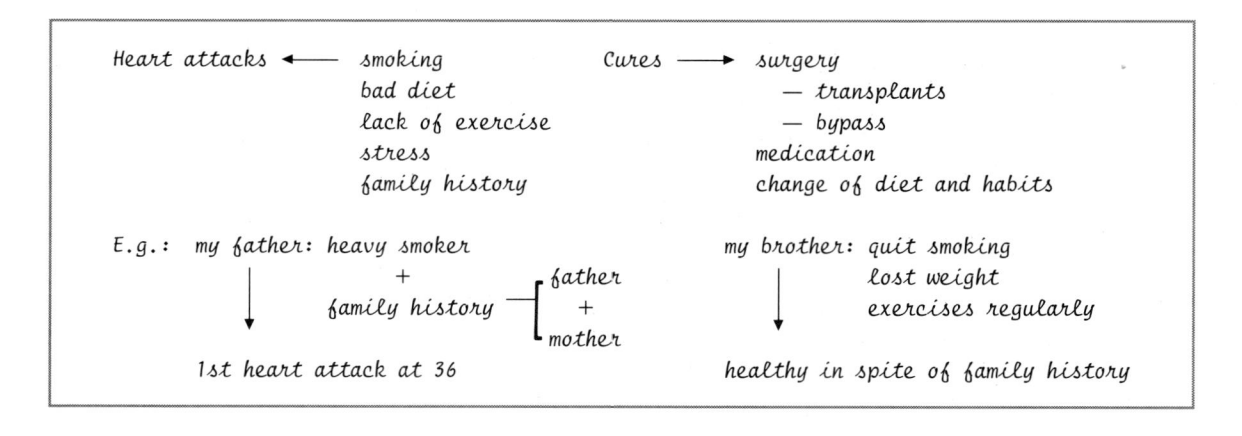

Heart attacks ← smoking   Cures → surgery
              bad diet   — transplants
              lack of exercise   — bypass
              stress   medication
              family history   change of diet and habits

E.g.: my father: heavy smoker   my brother: quit smoking
                   +   lost weight
           family history ⎡ father   exercises regularly
                          ⎣ + ↓
             1st heart attack at 36   mother   healthy in spite of family history

GETTING IN DEEPER   These next four steps give you an overview of the text. While you are completing these steps, you are dealing with a smaller piece of the whole text. At the same time, you are getting a sense of the big picture of the text.

① **Read the first paragraph.** The first paragraph often (but not always) tells you the topic and the main idea of the text. If you know the topic and what the writer is going to say about that topic, it will make your reading a lot easier.

② **Read any subheadings.** If the text is divided into parts and has subheadings, read each one carefully. These subheadings provide a sense of the "big picture" (global) structure of the text.

③ **With a short text (1–2 pages), read the first and last sentence of each paragraph.** The first sentence of a paragraph often (but not always) tells you what the paragraph is about. The last sentence often tells you how its paragraph is connected to the next one. By reading each first and last sentence, you will get a sense of the organization and content of the text. You can also try to predict what you think will appear in the middle of each paragraph.

With a long text, skim the pages quickly and break the text into sections. Read the first and last sentence of each section.

④ **Read the last paragraph completely.** Often, the last paragraph summarizes the main ideas of the text.

As you are completing these four steps, relate what you are reading to the ideas that you thought about while tapping your prior knowledge.

PART 2: SUMMARY WRITING AND ESSAY EXAMS AS WORKS IN PROGRESS

LEARNING FROM ANOTHER WRITER

Below you see the first paragraph, the first and last sentences of paragraphs 2 and 3, and the final paragraph of this short text.

Time   p. 81   November 25, 1991

SHORT ROAD TO HEART ATTACKS
Small people are at risk, especially if they are hostile, potbellied, chainsmoking couch potatoes
by *Anastasia Toufexis*

Good luck to anyone who tries to keep up with the research on heart disease. Rarely does a month go by without new revelations of environmental, physical and even psychological factors that are supposedly linked to an increased risk of heart attack. Among the suspected culprits: feeling hostile or stressed; drinking too much coffee; living with a smoker; being exposed to car exhaust; having high levels of the kidney protein renin; being bald; and having a body shape that puts excess weight around the belly rather than the hips and thighs.

Now researchers have added another item to the list: being short.

↓

Researchers speculate that smaller people have smaller coronary vessels that are more vulnerable to blockage.

How upset should anyone be by the entire jumble of findings concerning heart attacks? Not very.

↓

These can be offset by changes in diet and behavior.

Americans are still best advised to stop smoking, cut their consumption of foods high in cholesterol and fats, especially the saturated kind, and start exercising. "I wouldn't want to see an overweight, short, bald smoker with high cholesterol saying, 'Well, I'm short and bald. I guess I'll just have to accept that I'm at risk,'" says Dr. Charles Hennekens of Harvard Medical School, co-author of last week's report regarding the impact of height. "And a man who is 6 ft. 1 in. and smokes has a far greater risk of heart attack than someone who is short." All people, regardless of their height or other factors, should be making the recommended life-style changes. When it comes to heart attacks, that's the long and short of it.

FORMING HYPOTHESES ABOUT THE TEXT After you have pre-read the text, try to predict:

- the writer's topic.
- the writer's purpose.
- the writer's main idea.
- the writer's audience.

Also, try to predict the global structure of the text. (See pages 48 to 51 for more information about global structure.) To do this, ask yourself: Is the writer presenting the ideas according to:

- chronological order?
- cause/effect order?
- comparison/contrast?
- logical division?
- pros/cons?

- spatial order?
- problem/solution order?
- order of importance?
- reverse order of importance?
- a combination of structures?

LEARNING FROM ANOTHER WRITER

Below are the hypotheses that the summary writer formed about the text after he completed the pre-reading.

> At this point, I think:
> ① the writer's topic = the relationship between height and heart attacks.
> ② the writer's purpose = to report the results of recent research.
> ③ the writer's main idea = that diet and lifestyle are more important risk factors for heart disease than hereditary factors such as height.
> ④ the global structure = problem/solution

READING

Read the entire text one time to get a sense of the whole. Reread the text a second time; if you find it helpful, take notes while you read. You can take notes by:

- highlighting and/or underlining (if you own the text). Highlight or underline only main ideas.
- writing one sentence to summarize each paragraph.
- labeling each paragraph or section in the margin (if you own the text).

PART 2: SUMMARY WRITING AND ESSAY EXAMS AS WORKS IN PROGRESS

LEARNING FROM ANOTHER WRITER

Below is the complete text with the marginal notes that the summary writer made while reading. As you can see, he underlined main ideas and labeled sections of the text. Read through the text and notes carefully.

Time   p. 81   November 25, 1991

SHORT ROAD TO HEART ATTACKS

Small people are at risk, especially if they are hostile, potbellied, chainsmoking couch potatoes

by **Anastasia Toufexis**

---

background information to set the stage

Good luck to anyone who tries to keep up with the research on heart disease. Rarely does a month go by without new revelations of environmental, physical and even psychological factors that are supposedly linked to an increased risk of heart attack. Among the suspected culprits: feeling hostile or stressed; drinking too much coffee; living with a smoker; being exposed to car exhaust; having high levels of the kidney protein renin; being bald; and having a body shape that puts excess weight around the belly rather than the hips and thighs.

★ *site of research*

Now researchers have added another item to the list: being short. Men who are 5 ft. 7 in. and under appear to be up to 70% more likely to have a heart attack than those who stand 6 ft. 1 in. and above, according to a report by Boston scientists at a meeting of the American Heart Association last week. The taller the man, the less the risk, they found. For every inch above 5 ft. 7 in., chances dropped by about 3%. The findings are drawn from an ongoing study at Brigham and Women's Hospital on the health of 20,000 male physicians. The results are similar to those from a previous study that found a higher risk of heart attacks in shorter women than in taller ones. Researchers speculate that smaller people have smaller coronary vessels that are more vulnerable to blockage.

possible explanation

How upset should anyone be by the entire jumble of findings concerning heart attacks? Not very. Yes, innumerable factors can influence cardiovascular disease, and many of them are hereditary and, taken by themselves, are beyond a person's control. But the bewildering research has not undermined the essential facts: by far the most important risk factors remain smoking, high cholesterol and high blood pressure. These can be offset by changes in diet and behavior.

Americans are still best advised to stop smoking, cut their consumption of foods high in cholesterol and fats, especially the saturated kind, and start exercising. "I wouldn't want to see an overweight, short, bald smoker with high cholesterol saying, 'Well, I'm short and bald. I guess I'll just have to accept that I'm at risk,'" says Dr. Charles Hennekens of Harvard Medical School, co-author of last week's report regarding the impact of height. "And a man who is 6 ft. 1 in. and smokes has a far greater risk of heart attack than someone who is short." All people, regardless of their height or other factors, should be making the recommended life-style changes. When it comes to heart attacks, that's the long and short of it.

advice

solution

136

CHAPTER 5: SUMMARY/COMMENT WRITING

POST-READING

Check your pre-reading hypotheses with your knowledge of the whole text. If necessary, revise your assessment of the writer's topic, purpose, and main idea.

To help you see the "big picture" of the text, you might also find it useful to construct a graphic representation of the global structure of the text. A graphic representation is a drawing or a picture of the text; it outlines the main points and shows the relationships between them.

LEARNING FROM ANOTHER WRITER

Below is the summary writer's graphic representation of the global structure of this text.

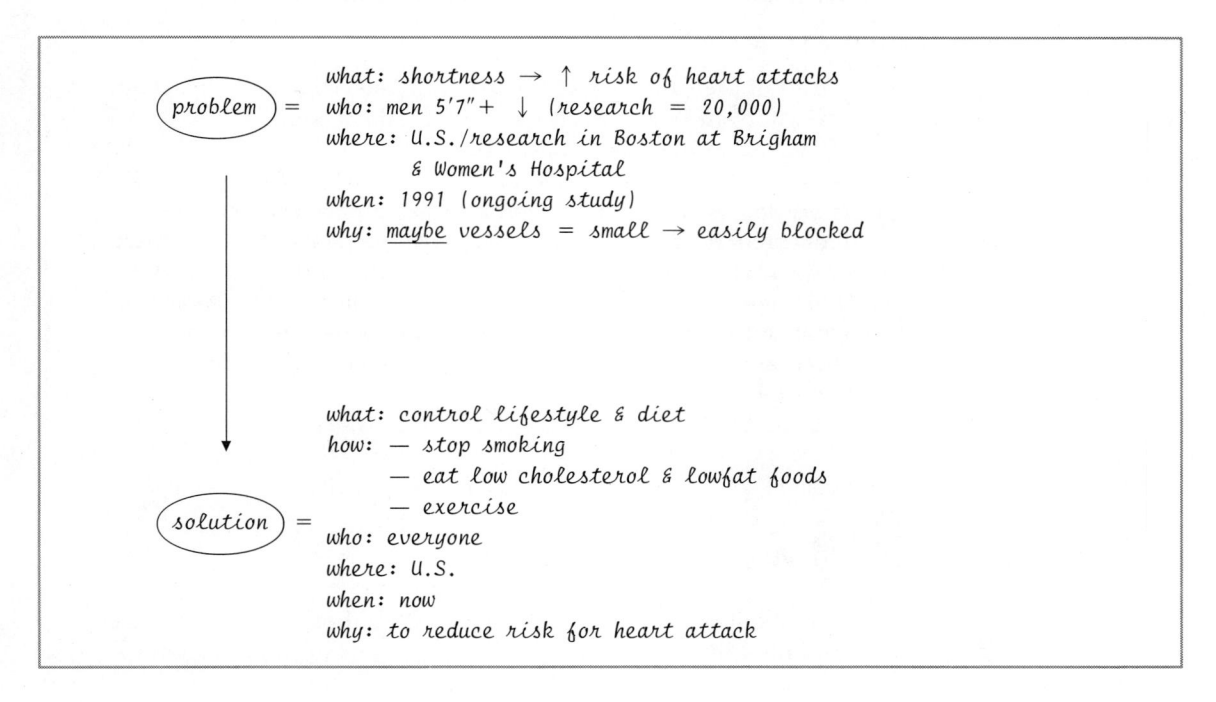

(problem) =
- what: shortness → ↑ risk of heart attacks
- who: men 5'7"+ ↓ (research = 20,000)
- where: U.S./research in Boston at Brigham & Women's Hospital
- when: 1991 (ongoing study)
- why: <u>maybe</u> vessels = small → easily blocked

↓

(solution) =
- what: control lifestyle & diet
- how: — stop smoking
  — eat low cholesterol & lowfat foods
  — exercise
- who: everyone
- where: U.S.
- when: now
- why: to reduce risk for heart attack

WRITING THE SUMMARY

Using your graphic representation of the text and the text itself for reference, reorganize and restate the ideas to be included in your summary. Be sure to write them in your own words. Begin your summary by acknowledging the writer and the source:

PART 2: SUMMARY WRITING AND ESSAY EXAMS AS WORKS IN PROGRESS

In [his / her / their] [article / book / chapter], ["title in quotes" / title underlined / "title in quotes"], [John Smith states that . . . / Mary Johnson maintains that . . . / Smith and Johnson state that . . .]

OR

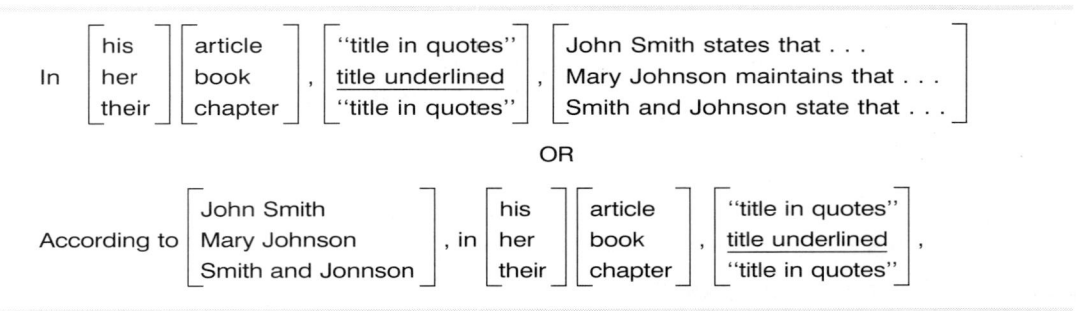

According to [John Smith / Mary Johnson / Smith and Jonnson], in [his / her / their] [article / book / chapter], ["title in quotes" / title underlined / "title in quotes"],

When you finish the summary, reread it carefully. Check each of your sentences for accuracy.

LEARNING FROM ANOTHER WRITER

Here is the writer's final draft of the summary of the article about height and heart attacks. (The writer worked through several drafts before producing this final version.)

> In her Time magazine article, "Short Road to Heart Attacks," Anastasia Toufexis reports that according to researchers at Brigham and Women's Hospital in Boston, short men are at greater risk for heart attacks than tall men. Scientists guess that this might be due to the smaller size of the heart vessels of smaller people. In spite of these findings, the researchers maintain that since diet and life style are more important risk factors for heart disease than hereditary factors such as height, everyone should make necessary changes in their diet or behavior.

WRITING A COMMENT

When you write a comment about or response to the work of another writer, you should react to or analyze the ideas presented by that writer. Here are some possible approaches to a comment:

- **Compare/Contrast** the ideas presented by the writer with those of other writers or authorities on the topic. How are this writer's ideas similar to or different from those of others?

- **Associate** the ideas presented by this writer with other ideas. What do the ideas remind you of or make you think of?

- **Analyze** the ideas presented by this writer. Break them into parts and discuss each part.

- **Apply** the ideas presented by this writer to another situation, one from your own experience or one that you have read or heard about.

- **Argue for or against** the ideas presented by this writer. Do you agree or disagree with the writer? Why?

The way you comment will depend on the nature of the text you are responding to and on your background knowledge about the material. Draft your response carefully. Be sure it is supported and well-organized.

CHAPTER 5: SUMMARY/COMMENT WRITING

LEARNING FROM ANOTHER WRITER

Here is the final draft of one writer's summary and comment about the article about height and heart attacks. (The writer worked through several drafts before producing this final version.)

In her *Time* magazine article, "Short Road to Heart Attacks," Anastasia Toufexis reports that according to researchers at Brigham and Women's Hospital in Boston, short men are at greater risk for heart attacks than tall men. Scientists guess that this might be due to the smaller size of the heart vessels of smaller people. In spite of these findings, the researchers maintain that since diet and life style are more important risk factors for heart disease than hereditary factors such as height, everyone should make necessary changes in their diet or behavior.

I agree with these researchers' recommendation. Because genetic factors cannot be controlled for or changed, people should concentrate on living in a healthy way. Changes in diet and behavior are relatively easy to make, and as I have seen in my own family, the results can be dramatic. My father is predisposed to heart attacks because of family history: both of his parents suffered heart attacks and passed away at young ages. In addition to being 5'6", my father was a heavy smoker for years and never exercised. He also has a very stressful job. Given his lifestyle and genetic makeup, his doctors were not surprised when he suffered a heart attack at 36. They advised him to stop smoking and to start an exercise program. Now, at 42, (and still at 5'6") he is in excellent health.

TEXTS TO SUMMARIZE AND COMMENT ON

Titles	Pages
Text 1: "Miss Manners"	139 to 141
Text 2: "The Cultures of Medicine"	142 to 145
Text 3: "The Jeaning of America—and the World"	145 to 149
Text 4: "Remember to Give to the Earth This Holiday Season"	149 to 151
Text 5: "Excuses, Excuses"	152 to 155

TEXT # 1: "MISS MANNERS"

Many newspapers in the United States carry a syndicated advice column called "Miss Manners." The column, written by Judith Martin, provides answers to readers' questions about the rules of etiquette. On the next page you will find a short text from Miss Manners' column. Follow the steps below to write a summary of that text.

PART 2: SUMMARY WRITING AND ESSAY EXAMS AS WORKS IN PROGRESS

PRE-READING

(A) *Easing into the Text and Tapping Prior Knowledge*
1. Have you ever read "Miss Manners"? If yes, what do you know about her writing?
2. What are "rules of etiquette"? Why might people have questions about them?
3. Read the subtitle below. What situation is discussed in this column? What rules of etiquette might be associated with the situation?

(B) *Getting in Deeper and Forming Hypotheses about the Text*
1. Read the bold print in the text below.
2. How is the text organized?
3. How many writers are involved? Who are they?
4. Can you predict the topic, purpose, and main idea of each writer?
5. Can you predict the global structure of the entire text? What is it?

READING Read the entire text one time to get a sense of the whole. Reread the text a second time.

Go back through the first letter and underline the sentence that clearly and directly states the reader's problem. Go through Miss Manners' letter and underline the two clauses that clearly and directly state the solution.

Miss Manners*

Speaking Through an Interpreter

Dear Miss Manners: As a graduate-student coordinator at a large university, I deal constantly with the International Student Office and many students from foreign countries. Can you tell me the proper protocol for speaking through an interpreter?

I know that when speaking to a hearing-impaired person who uses an interpreter, one looks directly at the hearing-impaired individual. At whom does one look when oral translation of a foreign language is involved?

Looking directly at an individual who obviously does not understand a word I am saying makes me feel uncomfortable, but ignoring that person and looking at the interpreter appears, and makes me feel, rude.

Gentle Reader: Conversation is almost as much a matter of tone and looks as it is of words. Miss Manners imagines that the students—who in any event must be learning English, to study at an American university—are picking up more of your gist than you think. They will be able to do this better if they can see your eyes, and will feel less foolish than if they are merely standing there, being talked about.

Provided you remember that the interpreter is not a machine but a skilled human being, to be looked at occasionally as well (and thanked), you should address your speech to the student. When the interpreter is translating what the student says, nod at the interpreter to show that you understand, but direct your looks of reaction at the student with whom you are, however cumbersomely, conversing.

---

*MISS MANNERS reprinted by permission of UFS, Inc.

CHAPTER 5: SUMMARY/COMMENT WRITING

POST-READING Make a graphic representation of the text by filling in the chart below.

problem =

what:	
who:	
where:	
when:	
why:	

solution =

what:	
who:	
where:	
when:	
why:	

WRITING THE SUMMARY Write a summary of the text. Begin your summary as follows:

In her column "Miss Manners," Judith Martin recommends that . . .

OR

According to Judith Martin, in her column "Miss Manners," . . .

WRITING A COMMENT Write a short response to the ideas presented in Miss Manners' column.

PART 2: SUMMARY WRITING AND ESSAY EXAMS AS WORKS IN PROGRESS

TEXT # 2: "THE CULTURES OF MEDICINE"

On the next two pages you will find a short magazine article. Follow the steps below to write a summary of that text.

PRE-READING

(A) *Easing into the Text and Tapping Prior Knowledge:* Read the title and subtitle. Now answer these questions.
1. What are the source and date of the article? _____
2. Who is the writer of this article? _____
3. What do you think the topic of this article is? _____
4. What do you already know about this topic? Freewrite some notes.

(B) *Getting in Deeper and Forming Hypotheses about the Text*
1. Read the bold print in the article.
2. How is the text organized?
3. Read the first paragraph, the first and last sentences of paragraphs 2 through 6, and the last paragraph.
4. What do you think the writer's topic is?
5. What are the writer's purpose and main idea?
6. What do you think the global structure of the entire text is?

READING Read the entire text one time to get a sense of the whole. Reread the text a second time. Highlight or underline main ideas.

The Cultures of Medicine*

Why doctors and treatments differ the world over

It isn't how sick you are but where you are when you get sick that determines how you're treated by a doctor. Thousands of Americans undergo coronary-bypass surgery every year for narrowing in the arteries of the heart; an Englishman suffering chest pain would get more antiangina drugs. In the United States a simple sinus condition warrants a prescription for penicillin; a German wouldn't receive an antibiotic unless he was sick enough to be hospitalized. An American suffering from prostate cancer would undergo major surgery; a Frenchman would receive less drastic radiation therapy.

The citizens of the United States, Great Britain, France and West Germany are equally healthy and can expect to live to the same respectable old ages. Yet their physicians treat them in vastly different ways, notes Lynn Payer, an American who spent eight years as a medical journalist in Europe. In her recent book, "Medicine & Culture" *(204 pages. Holt. $18.95)*, Payer concludes that the way doctors deal with patients and their ailments is largely determined by attitudes acquired from their national heritage. "In seeing how another country's cultural prejudices affected its medicine, I found it easier to perceive how our own prejudices affect our own practice of medicine," she writes. Some highlights:

United States. American medicine owes a lot to the aggressive, "can do" spirit of the frontier. "American doctors want to *do* something, preferably as much as possible," Payer says. They order up more diagnostic tests than most of their colleagues in Europe, prescribe drugs frequently and at relatively high doses and seem to resort to surgery whenever possible. American women are far more likely to undergo radical mastectomies, deliver their babies by Caesarean and undergo routine hysterectomies while still in their 40s. Americans and their physicians regard the body as a machine, like a car, which helps explain their enthusiasm for annual checkups and devices like the artificial heart. Americans like to think of diseases as enemies to be "conquered"; doctors are quick to prescribe antibiotics—preferably in massive doses—for even minor infections. They expect their patients to be aggressive, too. Those who undergo drastic treatments in order to "beat" cancer are held in higher regard than patients who resign themselves to the disease.

Great Britain. By comparison, British medicine is low key. English physicians don't go in for routine physical exams, seldom prescribe drugs and order only half as many X-rays as American doctors do. The British patient is only one-sixth as likely to have coronary-bypass surgery and will probably never get a CAT scan. Such economy of practice reflects a certain amount of rationing under the state-funded National Health Service. But British doctors have always been conservative—when in doubt they don't treat. Medical attitudes also reflect the British stiff upper lip. Psychiatrists, for example, tend to regard people who are quiet and withdrawn as normal, while quickly prescribing tranquilizers to anyone who seems unsuitably overactive.

---

*Clark, Matt. 1988. *Newsweek* 19 Sept.: 83

France. Like many Frenchmen, physicians follow in the intellectual footsteps of Descartes. They put more stock in the theory that underlies a treatment than any experimental evidence that it actually works. Doctors routinely prescribe the yogurt derivative lactobacillus along with antibiotics to prevent the stomach upsets that sometimes occur from those drugs, yet there is no proof that it actually helps normalize the intestinal tract. The French are keenly sensitive to bodily esthetics, a major reason why doctors treat breast and other types of cancer by radiotherapy rather than surgery. French physicians show great respect for a woman's childbearing ability, consequently performing hysterectomies only for cancer and other serious conditions. While American doctors focus on the role of external agents, including bacteria, as a cause of disease, the French believe that the patient's constitution, or *terrain,* plays an equally important part in disease. That's why doctors prescribe tonics and vitamins to bolster the terrain more often than antibiotics to fight germs.

West Germany. Medicine here is an unlikely blend of 19th-century romanticism, which puts emotion ahead of thought, and 20th-century technology. There are more doctors per capita than in either of the three other countries Payer studied, and a German patient sees a doctor an average of 12 times a year, compared with 4.7 in the United States. More than 120,000 kinds of drugs are on the market. Doctors use CAT scans, electrocardiograms and other devices with abandon. German medicine reveals its romantic side in the emphasis doctors place on the heart. They frequently diagnose *Herzinsuffizienz,* a mild cardiac disorder which is virtually unrecognized by doctors anywhere else, and prescribe low doses of digitalis to prevent full-blown heart failure.

Not long ago, American doctors weren't considered well trained unless they spent some time in the hallowed clinics of Great Britain or Europe. And Payer concludes that they could still learn some lessons from their colleagues abroad. Among them: to prescribe lower doses of drugs, rely less on radical surgery and put more faith in the ability of the body to heal itself. But her most important conclusion is that "the choice of diagnoses and treatments is *not* a science." The practice of medicine, finally, is an art. And like painting and sculpture, it reflects the culture from which it comes.

POST-READING Make a graphic representation of the text by filling in the chart below.

COMPARISON/CONTRAST: "THE CULTURES OF MEDICINE"

Country	Cultural Characteristics that Affect Medical Practices (according to Lynn Payer)

CHAPTER 5: SUMMARY/COMMENT WRITING

WRITING THE SUMMARY   Write a summary of the text. Begin your summary as follows

In his article "The Cultures of Medicine," Matt Clark reports on . . .
or
According to Matt Clark, in his article, "The Cultures of Medicine," . . .

WRITING A COMMENT   Write a reaction to the ideas presented in this article.

SUGGESTIONS • SUGGESTIONS • SUGGESTIONS • SUGGESTIONS

See pages 184 to 186 in Part 3 of this book for sentence structure practice related to "The Cultures of Medicine."

TEXT #3: "THE JEANING OF AMERICA—AND THE WORLD"

On the next three pages you will find a magazine article. Follow the steps below to write a summary of that text.

PRE-READING

Ⓐ *Easing into the Text and Tapping Prior Knowledge*: Read the title. Now answer these questions.

1. What are the source and date of the article? _____
   _____

   What do you think a magazine entitled *American Heritage* is probably about?
2. Who is the writer of this article? _____
   _____

3. In the title, what could the word "Jeaning" refer to?
   _____

4. What do you already know about this topic? Freewrite some notes.

Ⓑ *Getting in Deeper and Forming Hypotheses about the Text*
1. Read the first paragraph, the first and last sentences of paragraphs 2 through 8, and the last paragraph.
2. What do you think the writer's topic is?
3. What are the writer's purpose and main idea?
4. What do you think the global structure of the entire text is?

READING   Read the entire text one time to get a sense of the whole. Reread the text a second time. Highlight or underline main ideas.

The Jeaning of America—and the World*

This is the story of a sturdy American symbol which has now spread throughout most of the world. The symbol is not the dollar. It is not even Coca-Cola. It is a simple pair of pants called blue jeans, and what the pants symbolize is what Alexis de Tocqueville called "a manly and legitimate passion for equality...." Blue jeans are favored equally by bureaucrats and cowboys; bankers and deadbeats; fashion designers and beer drinkers. They draw no distinctions and recognize no classes; they are merely American. Yet they are sought after almost everywhere in the world—including Russia, where authorities recently broke up a teen-aged gang that was selling them on the black market for two hundred dollars a pair. They have been around for a long time, and it seems likely that they will outlive even the necktie.

This ubiquitous American symbol was the invention of a German immigrant. His name was Levi Strauss.

He was born in Bad Ocheim, Germany, in 1829, and during the European political turmoil of 1848 decided to take his chances in New York, to which his two brothers already had emigrated. Upon arrival, Levi soon found that his two brothers

---

*Quinn, Carin C. 1978. *American Heritage* April/May: 14–21.

had exaggerated their tales of an easy life in the land of the main chance. They were landowners, they had told him; instead, he found them pushing needles, thread, pots, pans, ribbons, yarn, scissors, and buttons to housewives. For two years he was a lowly peddler, hauling some 180 pounds of sundries door-to-door to eke out a marginal living. When a married sister in San Francisco offered to pay his way West in 1850, he jumped at the opportunity, taking with him bolts of canvas he hoped to sell for tenting.

It was the wrong kind of canvas for that purpose, but while talking with a miner down from the mother lode, he learned that pants—sturdy pants that would stand up to the rigors of the diggings—were almost impossible to find. Opportunity beckoned. On the spot, Strauss measured the man's girth and inseam with a piece of string and, for six dollars in gold dust, had them tailored into a pair of stiff but rugged pants. The miner was delighted with the result, word got around about "those pants of Levi's," and Strauss was in business. The company has been in business ever since.

When Strauss ran out of canvas, he wrote his two brothers to send more. He received instead a tough, brown cotton cloth made in Nîmes, France—called **serge de Nîmes** and swiftly shortened to "denim" (the word "jeans" derives from **Gênes**, the French word for Genoa, where a similar cloth was produced). Almost from the first, Strauss had his cloth dyed the distinctive indigo that gave blue jeans their name, but it was not until the 1870's that he added the copper rivets which have long since become a company trademark. The rivets were the idea of a Virginia City, Nevada, tailor, Jacob W. Davis, who added them to pacify a mean-tempered miner called Alkali Ike. Alkali, the story goes, complained that the pockets of his jeans always tore when he stuffed them with ore samples and demanded that Davis do something about it. As a kind of joke, Davis took the pants to a blacksmith and had the pockets riveted; once again, the idea worked so well that the word got around; in 1873 Strauss appropriated and patented the gimmick—and hired Davis as a regional manager.

By this time, Strauss had taken both his brothers and two brothers-in-law into the company and was ready for his third San Francisco store. Over the ensuing years the company prospered locally, and by the time of his death in 1902, Strauss had become a man of prominence in California. For three decades thereafter the business remained profitable though small, with sales largely confined to the working people of the West—cowboys, lumberjacks, railroad workers, and the like. Levi's jeans were first introduced to the East, apparently, during the dude-ranch craze of the 1930s, when vacationing Easterners returned and spread the word about the wonderful pants with rivets. Another boost came in World War II, when blue jeans were declared an essential commodity and were sold only to people engaged in defense work. From a company with fifteen salespeople, two plants, and almost no business east of the Mississippi in 1946, the organization grew in thirty years to include a sales force of more than twenty-two thousand, with fifty plants and offices in thirty-five countries. Each year, more than 250,000,000 items of Levi's clothing are sold—including more than 83,000,000 pairs of riveted blue jeans. They have become, through marketing, word of mouth, and demonstrable reliability, the common pants of America. They can be purchased pre-washed, pre-faded, and pre-shrunk for the suitably proletarian look. They adapt themselves to any sort of idiosyncratic use; women slit them at the inseams and convert them into long skirts, men chop them off above the knees and turn them into something to be worn while challenging the surf. Decorations and ornamentations abound.

PART 2: SUMMARY WRITING AND ESSAY EXAMS AS WORKS IN PROGRESS

The pants have become a tradition, and along the way have acquired a history of their own—so much so that the company has opened a museum in San Francisco. There was, for example, the turn-of-the-century trainman who replaced a faulty coupling with a pair of jeans; the Wyoming man who used his jeans as a towrope to haul his car out of a ditch; the Californian who found several pairs in an abandoned mine, wore them, then discovered they were sixty-three years old and still as good as new and turned them over to the Smithsonian as a tribute to their toughness. And then there is the particularly terrifying story of the careless construction worker who dangled fifty-two stories above the street until rescued, his sole support the Levi's belt loop through which his rope was hooked.

Today "those pants of Levi's" have gone across the seas—although the company has learned that marketing abroad is an arcane art. The conservative-dress jeans favored in northern France do not move on the Cote d'Azur; Sta-Prest sells well in Switzerland but dies in Scandinavia; button fronts are popular in France, zippers in Britain.

Though Levi Strauss & Co. has since become Levi Strauss International, with all that the corporate name implies, it still retains a suitably fond regard for its beginnings. Through what it calls its "Western Image Program," employing Western magazine advertisements, local radio and television, and the promotion of rodeos, the company still pursues the working people of the West who first inspired Levi Strauss to make pants to fit the world.

POST-READING Make a graphic representation of the text by filling in the time line below.

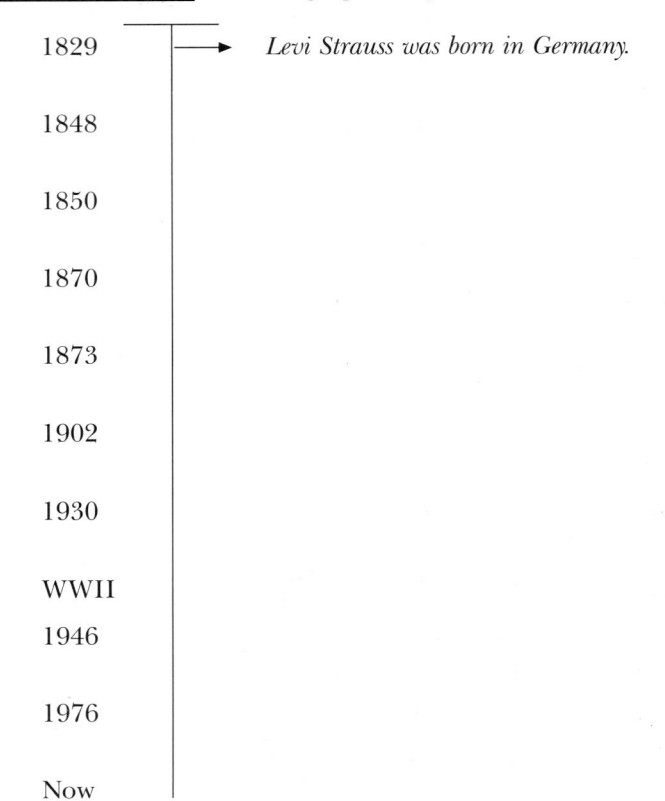

1829 ⟶ *Levi Strauss was born in Germany.*

1848

1850

1870

1873

1902

1930

WWII

1946

1976

Now

CHAPTER 5: SUMMARY/COMMENT WRITING

WRITING THE SUMMARY Write a summary of the text. Begin your summary as follows:

In her article "The Jeaning of America—and the World," Carin Quinn . . .

or

According to Carin Quinn, in her article, "The Jeaning of America—and the World," . . .

WRITING A COMMENT Write a response to the ideas presented in this article.

> **SUGGESTIONS • SUGGESTIONS • SUGGESTIONS • SUGGESTIONS**
>
> See pages 193 to 195, 203 to 205, and 217 to 219 in Part 3 of the book for sentence structure practice related to "The Jeaning of America—and the World."

TEXT # 4: "REMEMBER TO GIVE TO THE EARTH THIS HOLIDAY SEASON"

On the next two pages you will find a short magazine article. Follow the steps below to write a summary of that text.

PRE-READING

A. *Easing into the Text and Tapping Prior Knowledge*: Read the title. Now answer these questions.

1. What are the source and date of the article? _____

2. Who is the writer of this article? _____
_____

3. What do you think the topic of this article is? _____
_____

4. What do you already know about this topic? Freewrite some notes.

B. *Getting in Deeper and Forming Hypotheses about the Text*

1. Read the first paragraph, the first and last sentences of paragraphs 2 through 7, and the last paragraph.
2. What do you think the writer's topic is?
3. What are the writer's purpose and main idea?
4. What do you think the global structure of the entire text is?

READING Read the entire text one time to get a sense of the whole. Reread the text a second time. Highlight or underline main ideas.

Remember to Give to the Earth This Holiday Season*

Earth Day was months ago and now the holiday season is upon us—replete with shopping, parties and increased consumption. With all the commercial hype encouraging us to spend, use and waste, it could be easy to set aside our commitments to the Earth. However, with a little planning, it can be just as easy to stick to them. Starting with a list—and checking it twice—decide right away what you will need for holiday decorating, entertaining, card mailing and gifts. Then, examine your list to see where you can make Earth-conscious choices.

Are your decorations easy on energy and the environment? Instead of outdoor lights, consider luminarias—sand-filled paper bags with small candles inside. Indoors, try decorating with candles and strings of popcorn, or cranberries, which can later be left outside for birds. Planning a party? Conserve resources by using only reusable utensils, plates and napkins. At potluck gatherings, have your visitors bring their own place settings along with vegetarian food that is easier on the environment (not to mention the turkeys!).

When you get ready to send your annual greeting cards, look for cards printed on recycled paper. Many stationery stores now carry them. Some cards now also use soybased inks, though you will be more likely to find those in mail order catalogs.

The most challenging experience—even when you're not trying to conserve resources—is gift shopping. Deciding what to get each person on your list takes plenty of thought, especially when you want the gift to be meaningful and Earth-friendly. For example, almost everyone likes books that teach them something about our world and its inhabitants. Magazine subscriptions also make nice gifts—to periodicals such as *Kind News* for children, for example, or to *E Magazine* for adults. And gift memberships to environmental groups often include magazines or calendars. Or, your gifts could simply invite your loved ones to enjoy the outdoors. Wildflower seeds, plants, hiking boots or a bird feeder will help them feel connected to the Earth.

Although you can conserve your time and energy shopping by mail (many excellent catalogs offer Earth-caring products), a few items may remain which you can only get by car. Plan your route to save time and gas. Can you get most things in one or two stops? Maybe the nearest mall has most of the shops that you need to visit. Can you carpool with a friend or take public transportation? The holiday season is one for sharing; so share your shopping trips as well!

When it comes time to wrap these gifts, consider alternatives to wrapping paper, or at least use the recycled kind. Some options include tote bags, boxes, baskets, fabric, scarves, decorative tins, or even T-shirts. Decorate your packages with useful items like hair ribbons, belts, or suspenders. Use paper ribbon or colored string; avoid resin-coated plastic ribbon.

Will you be putting these treasures under a Christmas tree? If so, consider using a live tree this year. Enough trees are cut down each Christmas to cover the state of Rhode Island. And, according to the

---

*Roberts, Paula Clark. 1990. *E Magazine* Nov./Dec.: 52.

National Christmas Tree Association, enough are left in landfills to circle the globe twice, if stretched from end to end. Instead, live trees can be planted in pots to be used year after year or planted outside where they can help clean the air. The key is to move the live tree outside before it becomes too acclimated to the indoor warmth and "wakes up" (usually this happens in three weeks). After Christmas, leave it in its burlap in your garage or on your fire escape until spring, when the ground is soft enough to plant the tree.

With a little imagination, you can probably come up with a dozen or more ideas of your own. Then relax and enjoy the holidays and the warm feeling you'll get from knowing that you've given the Earth a holiday gift this year.

Helpful Resources

- *Earth Care Paper Company,* P.O. Box 14140, Madison, WI 53714/(608) 256-5522.

- *The First Green Christmas: How To Make This Holiday An Ecological Celebration,* Evergreen Alliance, Halo Books, P.O. Box 2529, San Francisco, CA 94126/(415) 981-5144.

- *Kind News,* National Association for Humane and Environmental Education, Box 362, East Haddam, CT 06423/(203) 434-8666.

- *Nature Company,* P.O. Box 2310, Berkeley, CA 94702/(800) 227-1114.

- *Paperchoice,* 303 East 6th Avenue, Vancouver, BC V5T 1J9/(604) 873-5700.

- *Recycled Paper Products,* 3636 North Broadway, Chicago, IL 60613/(800) 777-9494.

- *Seventh Generation,* Colchester, VT 05446-1672/(800) 441-2538.

- *Widget Factory Cards,* 11 North Hancock Street, Lexington, MA 02173/(617) 863-5365.

POST-READING Make a graphic representation of the text by filling in the chart below.

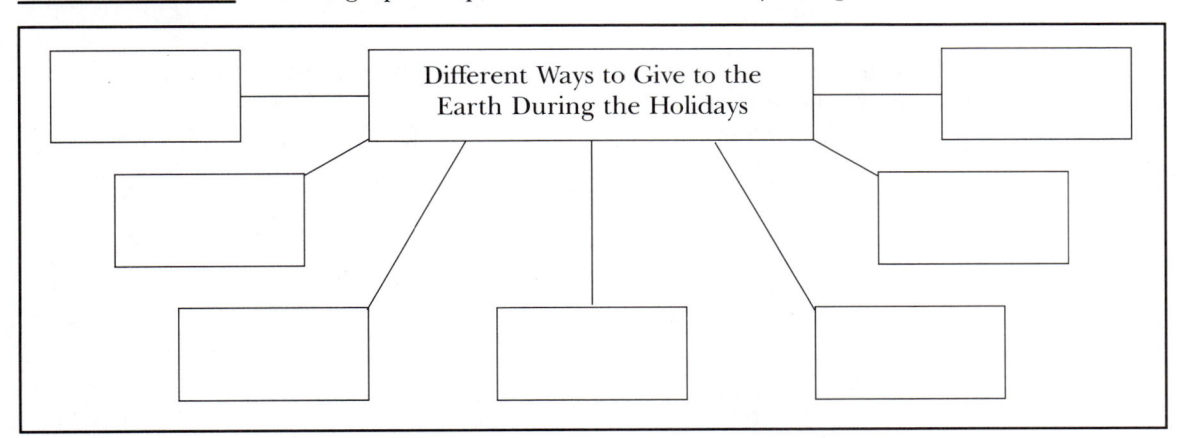

[Chart: Different Ways to Give to the Earth During the Holidays — center node with six empty boxes branching out]

WRITING THE SUMMARY Write a summary of the text. Begin your summary as follows:

In her article "Remember to Give to the Earth This Holiday Season," Paula Clark Roberts . . .

or

According to Paula Clark Roberts, in her article, "Remember to Give to the Earth This Holiday Season," . . .

WRITING A COMMENT Write a comment about the ideas presented in this article.

PART 2: SUMMARY WRITING AND ESSAY EXAMS AS WORKS IN PROGRESS

TEXT # 5: "EXCUSES, EXCUSES"

On the next three pages you will find a short magazine article. Follow the steps below to write a summary of that text.

PRE-READING

Ⓐ *Easing into the Text and Tapping Prior Knowledge*: Read the title and subtitle. Now answer these questions.

1. What are the source and date of the article? _____
   _____

2. Who is the writer of this article? _____
   _____

3. What do you think the topic of this article is? _____
   _____

4. What do you already know about this topic? Freewrite some notes.

Ⓑ *Getting in Deeper and Forming Hypotheses about the Text*

1. Read the first paragraph, the first and last sentences of paragraphs 2 through 12, and the last paragraph.
2. What do you think the writer's topic is?
3. What are the writer's purpose and main idea?
4. What do you think the global structure of the entire text is?

READING
Read the entire text one time to get a sense of the whole. Reread the text a second time. Highlight or underline main ideas.

Excuses, Excuses*

Heard any good ones lately? With the start of a new school year, college professors will be getting an exculpatory earful.

Heard any good excuses lately? If you teach college, you have. I don't profess, myself, but I live with someone who does, and he has amassed quite an album of tall tales—as well as some that are notably short of stature. If you ever worry about the resourcefulness of the younger generation, the explanations they offer for failing to fork over their assignments or for neglecting to show up in class should put your mind at rest. After collecting a few corkers from my companion, I took an informal poll among colleagues at his southern university, and among some academics I know in Northern Ohio. There might be a book here—or maybe there already is one that college kids across the country consult, since their excuses tend to fall into a severely limited number of types.

Let's start with the simplest: the updated classic. You remember the one that goes "My dog ate it," right? Well, how about this variation, proffered to a studio-art professor: "My dog had a heart attack." Kids still kill off their relatives without turning a hair, of course: That same teacher had a student afflicted with three dead grandmothers in one term. When the teacher suggested that three somewhat exceeded the usual number, the student sputtered that there'd been a divorce in his family. One divorce, and three funerals in a single semester.

Then there's the freak-accident excuse. From a student in another art teacher's class: "My roommate threw a Frisbee across the room and it ricocheted off the wall and destroyed my sculpture." Or maybe that one belongs in the My Roommate Did It category, along with "I stayed up all night and did the assignment, and then I went out for breakfast and my roommate locked me out and never came back." (*Never*? Have they sent out a search party?)

More freak accidents: "I'd done all the work and I had it in my car and then I got in a car wreck with a petroleum truck and petroleum got all over my work." Now, wouldn't you figure she'd claim she had whiplash and couldn't finish the work before she'd say petroleum got all over it? And what *is* a petroleum truck, exactly? Are we talking Exxon, here, or Vaseline?

On to the ever-popular medical excuse. "All the work is in my car," a student told her teacher, "and it's all the way across campus." Why didn't she, the teacher casually inquired, go and get it? "Because I'm pregnant and I can't really walk that far." The teacher remarks that if the student was pregnant, it wasn't visible and had never been mentioned before the assignment came due. Another student announced to a professor of psychology about to hand out exam papers, "I can't take your test because I have a boil on my rear end and I can't sit down." Back to the art department for one more medical mishap: "I almost cut my thumb off with an X-Acto knife, and I bled all over my drawings."

Occasionally students make a play for pedagogical sympathy by emphasizing

---

Perris, Barbara. 1989. "The Looking Glass." *Northern Ohio LIVE* Sept.: 88, 85.

the burden their other classes put on them. A young man who turned up missing from the last session of a semester (one of a number of classes from which he'd been conspicuously absent), during which he was to hand in his term project, called the professor at home at midnight and whined that he'd forgotten about the class because he'd been so caught up in typing his philosophy paper. Could he meet the professor at seven-thirty the next morning to deliver the work? The professor said no, which is more than they say in general; my poll indicates a lot of eye-rolling before the teacher silently repairs to the gradebook.

In another plea of temporary amnesia, made to an English professor, a student asserted that he'd swept his term-paper-in-progress off the dining-room table when unexpected company arrived, stashing it in—of all places—the oven. Then he forgot it was there, turned on the broiler and burned his work to a crisp.

In most cases, you'll have noticed, the work is all finished, or almost, before catastrophe befalls, establishing the student as a righteous citizen of the academic world who's been buffeted by an uncaring universe, or at least an uncaring roommate. Sometimes, though, kids simply disappear from class for two or three weeks. That calls for the I Dare You Not to Believe Me genre of excuse. "Why haven't you been in class?" asked a professor of a student she finally bumped into in the grocery store. The student looked her right in the eye and said, "I was committed to a mental institution."

A refinement of this form is what one graphic-design teacher calls the Greek Tragedy type, a compound complex amalgamation of misfortune, usually to the student's extended family, that defies response. "Why haven't you done the assignment?" "My uncle committed suicide, my mother's in the hospital and my sister's anorexic." The polar opposite of this grand effort, the same professor notes, is the pitiful "My marker ran out of ink."

The computer age, not surprisingly, has opened up a whole new field of excuses. "I had just finished my paper when the system went down and I lost the whole thing." "Someone got into my file and deleted my paper when I wasn't looking." "My paper has been finished for two days but I can't get the printer to work." "I had my paper on the computer disk but when I came through the airport security system I lost everything on the disk."

There are twists, too, on the I Lost Everything in the Crash excuse: "Everything on my floppy was garbaged when I left it in the sun (or left it on top of the TV, or left it on the table during a pizza party, or used it for a Frisbee)." As the one beleaguered professor who'd been subjected to all these wearily observes, "No one ever has saved backup copies or even draft versions, of course, though they have them for love letters and job applications."

It would make you tired, wouldn't it? The photography faculty at my companion's university, in fact, got so sick of listening to their kids' justifications that they typeset a list under the heading "Common Excuses of Photo Students" and posted it in the department, presumably to drive the kids, if not actually to do their work, to think up some new explanations for why they hadn't.

Here's the list in all its blame-shifting glory:

They were out of film

My film messed up

It's been too cloudy (remember, these kids attend school in the Sunshine State)

My prints stuck together

Someone threw my negatives away

The enlarger was messed up

No one would model for me

I'm waiting for my photo paper

Chemistry screwed up my film

My camera was broken

My car broke down

I was sick

I was out of town

I went to the beach

Oh, it was due today?!?

There you are. Today's students, I conclude, show a degree of energy, inventiveness and sheer chutzpah that, if harnessed in the service of their schoolwork, could be truly awesome. I hope you enjoyed reading their creative efforts. Oh, and David? I'm sorry I turned in this story so late—I had it all finished, but then the cat got on top of the computer, and every time I went to take the disk out, she tried to bite me.

POST-READING Make a graphic representation of the text by filling in the chart below.

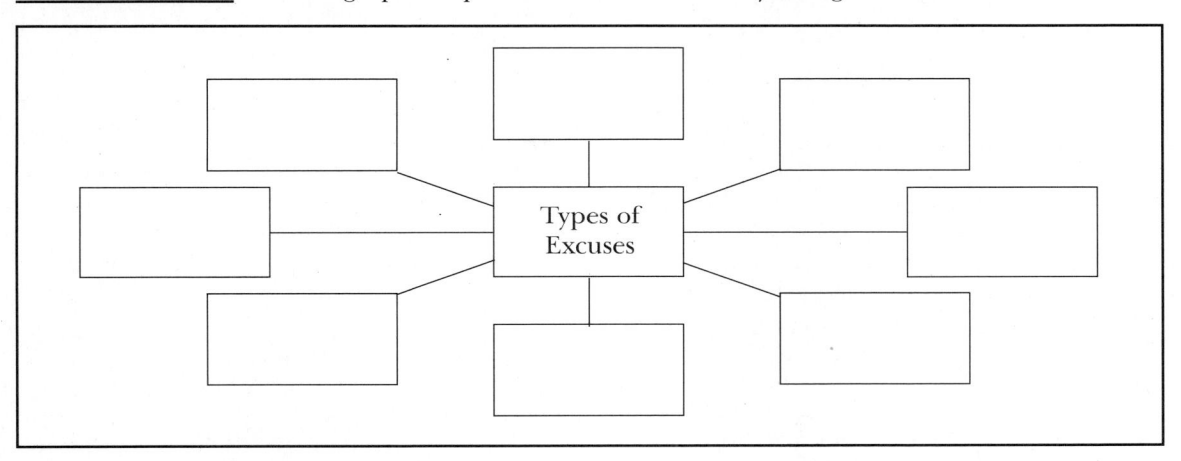

[Chart with "Types of Excuses" in center, connected to eight empty boxes arranged around it]

WRITING THE SUMMARY Write a summary of the text. Begin your summary as follows:

In her article "Excuses, Excuses," Barbara Perris . . .

or

According to Barbara Perris, in her article, "Excuses, Excuses," . . .

WRITING A COMMENT Write a comment about the ideas presented in this article.

Freewriting Journal Assignment

Freewrite about the process of writing summaries.

- What step in the process of writing a summary seems to be the easiest for you? Why?
- What step in the process of writing a summary seems to be the most difficult for you? Why?
- What strategies will you use the next time that you prepare a summary? In other words, what strategies work well for you? Why?
- What will you try to do differently the next time that you write a summary? Why?

CHAPTER 6

Writing Essay Exams

PREWRITING
- Setting the Context
- Understanding the Assignment

WRITING ESSAY EXAMS
- Prewriting BEFORE Test Day
- Prewriting ON Test Day
- Test Day: Writing Your Answer

TAKING A PRACTICE ESSAY EXAM
- Prewriting BEFORE Test Day
- Prewriting ON Test Day
- Test Day: Writing Your Essay Exam

A SECOND CHANCE

PART II: SUMMARY WRITING AND ESSAY EXAMS AS WORK IN PROGRESS

PREWRITING

SETTING THE CONTEXT

Freewrite answers to the following questions. Then discuss your answers with your classmates.

1. What are some different types of test formats? Which test formats do you prefer? Why?
2. How do you usually prepare for a test?
3. How do you usually feel before a test? Why?
4. Why do instructors give tests?

UNDERSTANDING THE ASSIGNMENT

WHAT ARE ESSAY EXAMS? Essay exams are tests for which you write an essay in response to a question. To answer an essay exam question, you use the content and ideas that you have learned from class notes, lectures, discussions, and readings. The purpose of these exams is to assess your knowledge of a topic by measuring your recall and understanding and your ability to use the material covered in class. These exams also help your instructors assess their success in presenting the course material.

For this assignment, you are going to learn and practice some useful strategies for preparing for and taking essay exams. In order to do that, you need some course content to learn and then be tested on.

Imagine that you are taking a psychology course. During part of the semester, your instructor focuses on language learning. One of the books that you must read is entitled *How to Be a More Successful Language Learner* by Joan Rubin and Irene Thompson. On pages 277 and 278, you will find a section from Chapter 1 of their book. Read it now.

TYPES OF ESSAY EXAM QUESTIONS If your instructor wanted to test your knowledge of some or all of this content, she might give you an essay exam test. Essay exam questions fall into three basic types: *restatement* questions, *analysis* questions and *application* questions.

1. *Restatement questions* To successfully answer these questions, you must *restate* ideas, concepts, or materials that you have studied. In essence, you are giving back to the instructor what she gave to you through the course readings and lectures.

    Example:

    According to Rubin and Thompson, in addition to motivation, there are six psychological traits related to language learning. What are these six traits? Explain the significance of each one.

2. *Analysis question*: To successfully answer these questions, you must do more than merely restate the information that you have acquired from the course. You must evaluate or interpret what you have learned and make an original statement about it.

Example:

According to Rubin and Thompson, in addition to motivation, there are six psychological traits related to language learning. Describe these six traits. Of these six, which one do you think is the most important for success? Why? Refer to the course material to help explain your reasons.

③ *Application questions*: To successfully answer these questions, you must apply or extend what you have learned to a new situation. You have to *use* the knowledge that you have gained through the course in a new context, one that you did not study about.

Example:

According to Rubin and Thompson, in addition to motivation, there are six psychological traits related to language learning. Describe yourself as a language learner by explaining how each of these traits does or does not characterize you. Use specific examples from your language learning experience to support your description.

WRITING ESSAY EXAMS

STEPS TO WRITING SUCCESSFUL ESSAY EXAMS

I. Prewriting BEFORE Test Day
   A. Reviewing the Course Material
   B. Anticipating the Questions
   C. Studying and Rehearsing
II. Prewriting ON Test Day
   A. Reading the Question
   B. Brainstorming on Paper
   C. Rereading the Question
   D. Focusing Your Answer
   E. Planning a Global Structure
   F. Writing a Thesis Statement
III. Test Day: Writing Your Answer
   A. Writing
   B. Rereading
   C. Editing

PREWRITING BEFORE TEST DAY

To do well on any test, you have to prepare. The steps below will help you prepare for an essay exam. You might find it useful to form a study group with other members of your class and work through these steps together.

REVIEW THE COURSE MATERIAL. Review all of your lecture notes and readings about the topic that you will be tested on. With your study group members, discuss and compare lecture notes and your understanding of the readings.

PART II: SUMMARY WRITING AND ESSAY EXAMS AS WORK IN PROGRESS

ANTICIPATE THE QUESTIONS. Try to anticipate the questions that your instructor will ask. In a sense, you are trying to read the instructor's mind. What did he stress in the lectures? What are the main points that he wants you to know? What would you ask if you were the instructor? Write the questions the way you think your instructor might. If you attended all of the classes and did all of the reading assignments and course work, you should be able to correctly predict at least some of the questions that your instructor might ask. However, be prepared for the fact that you may not always read your instructor's mind correctly.

STUDY AND REHEARSE. Plan answers to your predicted questions. Learn and rehearse key phrases and vocabulary that are relevant to the topic. It is even useful to practice writing out answers to your predicted questions. This rehearsal is important because it will save you time on test day.

PREWRITING ON TEST DAY

The first step for every essay exam is to read all of the questions and directions carefully. Be sure that you understand the test; if you are unsure about any aspects of the test, ask your instructor for clarification if this is permitted. Be sure to ask right away at the beginning of the test so that you do not waste time with doubts or uncertainties.

Once you have read all the questions and the directions, you can focus on preparing good answers. To write successful essay exam answers, you must have successful strategies for completing the task on the day of the test. You must be able to think and write quickly and clearly. The strategies below will give you a "game plan" for test day. Follow these steps for each question that you answer.

READ THE QUESTION CAREFULLY. Underline key words in the question that will help you decide what kind of information to include in your answer. See the chart on page 162 for examples of key words.

BRAINSTORM ON PAPER. Write down notes, words, phrases, facts, dates about the question. Do this on scrap paper. Get down as much information as you can.

REREAD THE QUESTION. Check again to be sure that you know what is being asked. Then go over your notes.

FOCUS YOUR ANSWER. Read through your brainstormed notes and select information for your answer. Cross out irrelevant ideas in your notes; add any ideas that you think are important.

PLAN A GLOBAL STRUCTURE FOR YOUR ANSWER. Decide on the order that you would like to follow when presenting your ideas. Impose an order by preparing a rough outline below your brainstormed notes or by numbering your notes.

WRITE A THESIS STATEMENT. Write one sentence that directly answers the question. Do NOT write a general introduction to your answer; it is not necessary for this type of assignment. Instead, get right to the heart of your answer by writing a thesis statement. If possible, use part of the question to begin that statement:

Example:

Question = *According to Rubin and Thompson, in addition to motivation, there are six psychological traits that relate to language learning. What are these six traits? Explain the significance of each one.*

Introductory sentence for answer =

According to Rubin and Thompson, in addition to motivation, these six psychological traits relate to language learning: attitude, extroversion, inhibition, tolerance of ambiguity, learning style, and eye-ear learning.

TEST DAY: WRITING YOUR ANSWER

WRITE YOUR RESPONSE. Skip lines (unless you are instructed not to).

REREAD YOUR ANSWER. Leave some time at the end of the testing period to reread your answer. Be sure that it is complete. If you want to add something, write it in the space above the sentence where you want to add it and use an arrow.

EDIT YOUR ANSWER. On an essay exam, you will not be able to edit as carefully as you can when writing a drafted paper. Your reader knows this and will most likely tolerate some errors. However, because some mistakes in grammar and even spelling can interfere with communication, it is important that you do some editing.

Take a few minutes at the end of the testing period to edit your answer. If you have an editing acronym (see page 34), use it to help you focus your editing. When you make corrections, cross out neatly and write in the correct form above the error.

PART II: SUMMARY WRITING AND ESSAY EXAMS AS WORK IN PROGRESS

EXAMPLES OF KEY WORDS FREQUENTLY USED IN ESSAY EXAM QUESTIONS*

agree	to show how your opinion is the same as another person's
analyze	to examine an idea by dividing it into and discussing its various parts
choose	to select from a greater number
comment	to give a brief explanation, judgment, or opinion of an idea
compare	to discuss similarities and differences between two ideas
contrast	to discuss the differences between two ideas
criticize	to express a judgment about the good and bad qualities of an idea
define	to explain the meaning of a term or concept
demonstrate	to show by means of specific support
describe	to provide specific information and details about an idea
diagram	to draw a picture or sketch to illustrate
differentiate	to discuss the differences between two ideas
disagree	to show how your opinion is different from another person's
distinguish	to discuss the differences between two ideas
discuss	to write about an idea from several points of view
enumerate	to name ideas one by one
evaluate	to discuss advantages and disadvantages and make a judgment about something
explain	to make an idea clear; to give the causes and effects
give an example	to provide a specific incident or item to make a general idea clearer
identify	to name and briefly describe
illustrate	to provide one or more examples
interpret	to show the possible meaning or implications of an idea
justify	to provide evidence for ideas
list	to name ideas one by one
outline	to give the main ideas or facts, no details
prove	to provide evidence for ideas
relate	to show the connections between ideas
review	to go over the main points
show	to provide specific support or evidence
solve	to figure out and describe an answer to a problem
state	to express the main ideas
summarize	to provide a brief description of the main ideas of a text
support	to provide evidence for ideas
trace	to explain the development or history of something

*Chart adapted from Pauk, Walter. 1984. *How to Study in College*. Boston: Houghton.

CHAPTER 6: WRITING ESSAY EXAMS

TAKING A PRACTICE ESSAY EXAM

Imagine that you are enrolled in an introductory psychology class at this university or college. In your last class period, your instructor announced that in two weeks you are going to have an essay exam on all of the material that you have covered so far this semester.

One of the texts that you have read in the course is entitled *How to Be a More Successful Language Learner*. The essay exam will cover the information about psychological predispositions (pages 277 and 278) and a short chapter on instructional settings (pages 279 and 280).

PREWRITING BEFORE TEST DAY

REVIEW THE COURSE MATERIAL

Exercise 6.1 Reread the section on psychological predispositions. Then read the chapter on instructional settings. Be sure that you understand the material thoroughly. You might find it useful to prepare a study outline of the material. Organizing the information into an outline will help you understand and internalize it.

ANTICIPATE THE QUESTIONS If you were the instructor of an introductory psychology class and you wanted to know how well your students had understood some or all of the ideas from the material *How to Be a More Successful Language Learner*, what questions would you ask?

Exercise 6.2 You already have three possible questions for the content on psychological predispositions (see pages 158 and 159). In study groups, brainstorm together and compose additional possible questions that would elicit a reader's knowledge and understanding of some or all of the course material. Write your questions as you think an instructor might. Compose questions that will elicit paragraph-length, or longer, answers. Compose restatement, analysis, and application questions.

When you have finished composing your questions, discuss them with your classmates. For each question, consider:

① Is it a restatement, analysis, or application question?
② Where in the text can you find the answer to this question?

STUDY AND REHEARSE FOR THE TEST Below, you will find several possible essay exam questions that test a reader's knowledge of the contents of the text, *How to Be a More Successful Language Learner*. These questions are probably very similar to ones that you and your classmates predicted that an instructor would ask.

The next prewriting step involves studying for the test. When you prepare for the test, review all the material that might be covered on a test question. Commit facts, dates, and ideas to memory so that you will be able to write about them easily during the test. It is also a good idea to practice writing some of the key, or important, ideas before test day. This practice gives your brain and your writing hand a chance to "rehearse" some of the work it will do on test day. The rehearsal will make you better prepared for the actual test situation.

Exercise 6.3 With a partner or a small group and the course content, work through some or all of the questions below by doing the following:

① Read each question carefully. Underline the key words in the question.

② With the members of your study group, find the information from the text that relates to and answers the question. Review this information. Then put the text aside.

③ On a piece of scrap paper or in your freewriting notebook, plan and write an answer to the question. This writing is a "dress rehearsal" for test day. Share your rehearsed answers with your study group members. Give each other feedback about your answers.

During this rehearsal, if you find that some of the key words are difficult to remember or spell, practice writing them several times in order to develop "muscle memory" for them.

Remember that you will not be able to use these notes on test day. This is a "dress rehearsal."

Possible Test Questions

1. According to Rubin and Thompson, in addition to motivation, there are six psychological traits that relate to language learning. What are these six traits? Explain the significance of each one.

2. According to Rubin and Thompson, what are the two basic environments in which language can be learned? Describe the characteristics of each setting.

3. Compare and contrast informal and formal instructional settings for language learning. Which setting is most beneficial for you at this point in your language learning? Why?

4. Choose three of the six psychological predispositions described by Rubin and Thompson and show how each one relates to formal and informal instructional settings.

5. According to Rubin and Thompson, in addition to motivation, there are six psychological traits related to language learning. Describe these six traits. Which one of these six do you think is the most important for success? Why? Refer to the course material to help explain your reasons.

6. According to Rubin and Thompson, in addition to motivation, there are six psychological traits that relate to language learning. Describe yourself as a language learner by explaining how each of these six traits does or does not characterize you. Use specific examples from your language learning experience to support your description.

7. A friend of yours who has only studied one semester of beginning Spanish is going to live in Spain for a month. Because she wants to learn as much Spanish as she can during that month, she is trying to decide whether or not it will be worthwhile for her to enroll in a three-week Spanish as a second language course that is offered at the university in the city where she will be living. She asks for your advice. What would you recommend? Justify your recommendation by referring to Rubin and Thompson and to your own experience as a language learner.

Prewriting on Test Day

You have been working on strategies and techniques to use before the day of the essay exam. Now you will practice some techniques to try on test day.

It is difficult to plan under time pressure, especially when you are working in a second language. Below, you will see a list of steps to follow while planning your essay exam answer and a suggested amount of time to spend on each step. You may not use all of these steps for every essay exam that you write. Moreover, the way that you use your time will not always be exactly the same as what is suggested here. These steps and times serve as general guidelines for making good use of your time on test day.

PART II: SUMMARY WRITING AND ESSAY EXAMS AS WORK IN PROGRESS

SUGGESTED TEST-DAY PREWRITING STRATEGIES

1. Read the question and *underline* the key words. (30 seconds)
2. Brainstorm ideas that relate to the topic. (3 minutes)
3. Reread the question and scan your notes. (1 minute)
4. Focus your answer. Select ideas, cross out irrelevant ideas, add ideas. (1 to 2 minutes)
5. Plan a global structure for your answer. (2 minutes)
6. Write a thesis statement. Write that sentence at the top of your answer paper. (1 to 2 minutes)

Exercise 6.4 Use the questions on page 165 to practice these test-day prewriting strategies. Work with a partner or in groups. One person should announce and time each step. The partner or group members should work through each step on scrap paper.

TEST DAY: WRITING YOUR ESSAY EXAM

Exercise 6.5 READ THESE DIRECTIONS CAREFULLY BEFORE YOU BEGIN.

Answer *one* of the questions from page 165. Complete these steps:

① **Read** the questions carefully, and then choose the one you want to answer. **Underline the key words** in your question of choice.

② **Brainstorm** on paper.

③ **Reread** the question to be sure you are on track.

④ **Focus your answer**.

⑤ **Plan a global structure for your answer**.

⑥ **Write a thesis statement** or introductory sentence for your answer.

Go to a clean piece of paper. Write your thesis statement on that paper. Then write the rest of your answer. Skip lines while you are writing.

With ten minutes left in the test, STOP work. Then:

⑦ Finish the sentence you were just working on. STOP writing.

⑧ Reread your answer one time to be sure that the ideas are clear and that you have not omitted anything. If you need to add any words, write them in on your skipped spaces.

⑨ If you have an editing acronym, write it on the top of your page of notes. Reread your answer again, focusing on finding and correcting your three common mistakes. Cross out any mistakes that you find, and write in the correct words above them.

CHAPTER 6: WRITING ESSAY EXAMS

A SECOND CHANCE

When you write an essay exam, you usually only get one chance. Whatever you write during the time limit is what the instructor or the reader evaluates.

Since this is a "practice" situation, you will get a second chance. Now that you have had some time away from your writing, would you do anything differently on that exam if you had a second chance? What?

Exercise 6.6 Reread the questions carefully. Reread your answers carefully. Then reconsider your answers, using the suggestions below to guide you. On your answer sheets, indicate any changes that you feel are appropriate.

SUGGESTIONS FOR REVISING

1. Underline your introductory sentence. Then evaluate it. Does it do the job of a thesis statement? Is it specific enough to focus your answer? Is it too specific? Do you want to make any changes in that thesis statement? If yes, make those changes on your paper.

2. Is your answer complete? Did you include all of the important information and details? If you want to add some information, indicate what it will be and where you will add it.

3. Are all of the ideas in your answer relevant to the question? If no, cross out irrelevant ones with a single line.

4. Is your answer easy to follow? In other words, is it well organized? If you want to change the order of any of the ideas, indicate those changes by using arrows and brackets.

5. Does your answer need more editing? If yes, mark the necessary changes on your paper.

When you have finished planning your revision, work with a partner. Exchange papers, and read each other's answers; then take turns discussing your plans for revision. When you are the writer/talker, explain what you want to do differently in your "second chance" answer and why. When you are the reader/listener, listen to the writer carefully and offer suggestions and feedback that you think will help the writer.

When you have gotten enough feedback from your reader, rewrite your answer.

Freewriting Journal Assignment

Freewrite about the process of writing essay exams.

- What step in the process of writing the exam was the easiest for you? Why?
- What step in the process of writing the exam was the most difficult for you? Why?
- What strategies will you use on the next exam? In other words, what strategies worked well for you? Why?
- What will you try to do differently on your next exam? Why?

PART 3
Sentence Structure and Grammar Exercises as Work in Progress

PART 3: SENTENCE STRUCTURE AND GRAMMAR EXERCISES AS WORK IN PROGRESS

ADJECTIVE CLAUSES — 172
- Restrictive and Nonrestrictive Clauses — 173
- Relative Pronouns as Subjects — 174
- Relative Pronouns as Objects — 175
- Whose + Noun as Subject — 176
- Whose + Noun as Object — 177
- Adjective Clauses of Place — 177
- Adjective Clauses of Time — 178
- Practice Using Adjective Clauses — 178

ADJECTIVE CLAUSES: REDUCED — 181
- Practice Using Reduced Adjective Clauses — 183

ADVERB CLAUSES OF CONCESSION AND CONTRAST — 184
- Practice Using Adverb Clauses of Concession and Contrast — 186

ADVERB CLAUSES OF TIME, CAUSE-EFFECT/ REASON-RESULT, AND PURPOSE — 187
- Practice Using Adverb Clauses of Time, Cause–Effect/Reason–Result, and Purpose and Related Structures — 189

ADVERB CLAUSES: REDUCED — 191
- Reduced Adverb Clauses of Time — 191
- Reduced Adverb Clauses of Cause-Effect — 192
- Practice Using Reduced Adverb Clauses — 193

APPOSITIVES — 193
- Practice Using Appositives — 194

CONDITIONALS — 196
- Patterns with Conditionals — 196
- Factual Conditionals: To State General Truths or Habits — 196
- Using Conditionals to Give Advice or Instructions — 198
- Future Conditionals: To Predict Events — 199
- Counterfactual Conditionals: To Describe Unreal Present Events — 200
- Counterfactual Conditionals: To Describe Unreal Past Events — 203
- Mixed Counterfactual Conditionals: To Describe Present or Future Inferences Drawn from Unreal Past Events — 206
- Additional Information about Conditionals — 207
- Additional Practice Writing Conditionals — 208

COORDINATION — 212
- Simple Coordinating Conjunctions — 212
- Correlative Conjunctions — 213
- Parallelism — 214
- Practice Identifying and Writing Parallel Structures — 215
- Practice Using Simple Coordination — 215
- Practice Using Correlative Conjunctions — 216

DISCOURSE THREADS — 217
- Common Discourse Threads — 218
- Practice Using Discourse Threads — 219

NOUN CLAUSES   223
- THAT-Clauses   223
- WH-Clauses   224
- IF/WHETHER-Clauses   225
- THAT-Clauses of Request or Urgency   226
- Practice Using Noun Clauses   226

PASSIVE CONSTRUCTIONS   228
- Practice Using Passive Constructions   229

REPORTED SPEECH   233
- Reported Statements Using *That*   234
- Sequence of Tenses   234
- Practice Using Reported Speech   236

SENTENCE CONNECTORS   237
- Practice Using Sentence Connectors   239

SOURCES CONSULTED

Celce-Murcia, Marianne, and Diane Larsen-Freeman. 1983. *The Grammar Book: An ESL/EFL Teacher's Course*. Boston: Heinle and Heinle Publishers.

Crowell, Thomas Lee. 1964. *Index to Modern English*. New York: McGraw-Hill, Inc.

Leech, Geoffrey, and Jan Svartvik. 1975. *A Communicative Grammar of English*. London, England: Longman.

PART 3: SENTENCE STRUCTURE AND GRAMMAR EXERCISES AS WORK IN PROGRESS

ADJECTIVE CLAUSES

Adjective clauses, also called relative clauses, are dependent clauses that function like adjectives; that is, they modify noun phrases. A noun phrase can consist of one noun (e.g., *Australia*), one noun and its article (e.g., *a house*), or a noun and its other modifiers (e.g. *the Opera House in Sydney, Australia*).

Remember:	• A clause in English contains at least a **SUBJECT** and a **PREDICATE**. • The predicate consists of a main verb and any auxiliary verbs. • A simple sentence consists of one independent clause. • A complex sentence consists of two or more clauses (e.g., two independent clauses; one independent and one or more dependent clauses).

Many adjective clauses are introduced by a *relative pronoun:* **who, which, that, whom, whose, where,** or **when**. An adjective clause *follows* the noun phrase that it describes, the "head noun." (Think of the "head noun" and its adjective clause as dance partners dancing to a waltz; they should not be split up.)

Study the following examples of sentences with adjective clauses. In each example, the adjective clause is in **bold** type.

1. The Sydney Opera House, **which was designed in 1957,** was completed in 1973.
2. Many people do not know the name of the architect **who designed the Sydney Opera House.**
3. Joern Utzon, **whose design was the most original,** is from Denmark.
4. The architect **whom the contract was given to** is Joern Utzon.
5. The Opera House was built on a peninsula **that extends into the harbor.**
6. This peninsula, **which is in downtown Sydney,** is called Bennelong Point.
7. The site **where the Opera House was built** is right in the heart of the city.
8. The site **on which the Opera House was built** is a perfect setting.
9. In 1973, **when the Opera House was finally completed,** there was a big celebration in Sydney.
10. The Opera House, **which all tourists must see,** is a symbol of Australia.

If you study the example sentences carefully, you can see that some of them have commas, but others do not. You can also see that different relative pronouns were used in different sentences. In short, you can see that there are different adjective clause patterns.

ADJECTIVE CLAUSES

RESTRICTIVE AND NONRESTRICTIVE CLAUSES

How can you know when to use commas with adjective clauses and when not to?

There are two kinds of adjective clauses: restrictive and nonrestrictive. The relationship between a restrictive adjective clause and its head noun is like the relationship between a passport and an international traveler. Just as an international traveler needs his passport for identification, the head noun needs its adjective clause for identification. In other words, a restrictive adjective clause is NECESSARY for your reader; your reader needs the information in that clause in order to identify and understand the head noun and the sentence in which it appears. Because this adjective clause is necessary, you do NOT want to separate it from its head noun; therefore, you do not use commas.

A nonrestrictive adjective clause is like icing on a cake. A cake without its icing is still recognizable as a cake. True, the icing adds flavor to the cake and makes it more interesting. Sometimes the icing is even an important part of the cake. However, the icing is not a necessary ingredient to identify a cake. The same is true for a nonrestrictive adjective clause. This type of clause is not necessary for your reader to be able to identify and understand the head noun and the sentence in which it appears. It is EXTRA information that your reader might find interesting or even important to know. Because it is extra, you want to use commas to separate it from its head noun.

An adjective clause is restrictive:
- if the head noun needs that clause for identification.

An adjective clause is nonrestrictive:
- if the head noun is already identified or definite, such as:
  – when the head noun is a proper noun, that is, the name of a specific person, place, or thing, or
  – when the head noun has been identified for the reader earlier in the text.

The following paragraph provides examples of both restrictive and nonrestrictive adjective clauses. The head nouns and their adjective clauses have been printed in **bold** type so that you can see them clearly.

The University of Colorado, which is located in Boulder, offers a variety of majors. For this reason, many international students decide to attend UC. Before they can be admitted for undergraduate classes, foreign students must submit the required application materials. For example, they must send a complete international application and proof of financial support. **These materials, which must be translated into English,** should reach the admissions office by April 1 for a fall entry. In addition, **international students whose native language is not English** must attain a TOEFL score of at least 500.

The following sentences also show the difference between restrictive and nonrestrictive adjective clauses. One sentence is about a town with one public library facility. The other sentence is about a town with two library buildings. Can you tell which sentence, A or B, is describing the town with one library?

A. The library which is located in the center of town serves many patrons every day.

B. The library, which is located in the center of town, serves many patrons every day.

As you can see from the examples above, the context and the meaning of a sentence usually determine whether an adjective clause is restrictive or nonrestrictive. For this reason, the use of commas with adjective clauses is usually rule-governed.

PART 3: SENTENCE STRUCTURE AND GRAMMAR EXERCISES AS WORK IN PROGRESS

However, sometimes you have a stylistic choice about punctuating adjective clauses. In these situations, you can decide if the clause will be restrictive or nonrestrictive. Consider the following examples:

A. The State University of New York at Buffalo is a large state university, which serves the higher educational needs of the local population.

B. The State University of New York at Buffalo is a large state university which serves the higher educational needs of the local population.

Both of these sentences are correct. The writer of sentence A chose to write the adjective clause as extra information, i.e., as a nonrestrictive clause, because the head noun, "a large state university," is clear for a reader and does not have to be defined or restricted.

Although this head noun does not have to be restricted, it can be. The writer of sentence B chose to limit, or restrict, the head noun. This writer felt that the information about serving the local population is an essential or defining point about this university; therefore, writer B wrote the adjective clause as necessary information.

Remember that more often than not an adjective clause is either obligatorily restrictive or nonrestrictive. You must always consider the meaning and context carefully when trying to determine what kind of adjective clause you have written.

RELATIVE PRONOUNS AS SUBJECTS

With this pattern, the relative pronoun is the subject of the adjective clause. Study the examples below.

Examples of Restrictive Clauses:

1. a. An architectural feat **which amazed the world** was the construction of the Sydney Opera House.
   b. An architectural feat **that amazed the world** was the construction of the Sydney Opera House.

2. a. Most people do not know about the problems **which occurred during the building of the Opera House.**
   b. Most people do not know about the problems **that occurred during the building of the Opera House.**

3. The architect **who designed the Opera House** was from Denmark.

4. The size of the structure always amazes people **who are visiting Sydney for the first time.**

Examples of Nonrestrictive Clauses:

5. The Sydney Opera House, **which was designed in 1957,** was completed in 1973.

6. The Opera House was built on Bennelong Point, **which extends into the harbor.**

7. Joern Utzon, **who designed the Sydney Opera House,** is from Denmark.

8. The Opera House is a treasure for all Australians, **who view it as a symbol of their nation.**

ADJECTIVE CLAUSES

PRONOUN CHART FOR REVIEW

	When the pronoun refers to:	
When the pronoun is:	A PERSON/PEOPLE	A THING/THINGS
SUBJECT in a restrictive clause	*who / that*	*which / that*
SUBJECT in a nonrestrictive clause	*who*	*which*

NOTES:

① The relative pronoun refers to the head noun, and it is the subject of the adjective clause.

② The head noun determines the subject-verb agreement rule inside the adjective clause.

Examples:

The design of the structure amazes people who visit Sydney.

The design of the structure amazes everyone who visits Sydney.

③ In restrictive clauses, use **who** when the head noun names a person. Use **which** when the head noun names a thing. (**Who** and **which** are preferred in written English. Use **that** for a person or a thing in informal spoken English.)

④ In nonrestrictive clauses, use **who** for people and **which** for things.

RELATIVE PRONOUNS AS OBJECTS

With this pattern, the relative pronoun is the direct or indirect object of the adjective clause. Study the examples below.

Examples of Restrictive Clauses:

1. a. Joern Utzon was the architect **to whom the contract was given.** (formal)
   b. Joern Utzon was the architect **whom the contract was given to.**
   c. Joern Utzon was the architect **who the contract was given to.**
   d. Joern Utzon was the architect **that the contract was given to.**
   e. Joern Utzon was the architect **the contract was given to.** (less formal)

2. a. One building **which all visitors to Australia must see** is the Sydney Opera House. (formal)
   b. One building **that all visitors to Australia must see** is the Sydney Opera House.
   c. One building **all visitors to Australia must see** is the Sydney Opera House. (less formal)

PART 3: SENTENCE STRUCTURE AND GRAMMAR EXERCISES AS WORK IN PROGRESS

Examples of Nonrestrictive Clauses:

3. The Opera House, **which all tourists to Australia must see,** is a symbol of the country.
4.
   a. Joern Utzon, **to whom the contract was awarded,** was relatively unknown at the time. (formal)
   b. Joern Utzon, **whom the contract was awarded to,** was relatively unknown at the time.
   c. Joern Utzon, **who the contract was awarded to,** was relatively unknown at the time. (less formal)

PRONOUN CHART FOR REVIEW

	When the pronoun refers to:	
When the pronoun is:	A PERSON/PEOPLE	A THING/THINGS
OBJECT in a restrictive clause	whom / that / Ø / who	which / that / Ø
OBJECT in a nonrestrictive clause	whom who	which

NOTES:

1. The relative pronoun refers to the head noun, and it is the object of the adjective clause.

2. In restrictive clauses, we can use **who, whom, that,** or **Ø** when the head noun names a person; we can use **which, that,** or **Ø** when the head noun names a thing.

3. In nonrestrictive clauses, we use **who** or **whom** for people and **which** for things.

4. **Whom** is considered to be correct and appropriate in formal, written English. **Who** is appropriate in spoken English and in informal written English.

5. You MUST use **whom** when a preposition is used before the relative pronoun. To see examples of this, look back at sentences 1.a. and 4.a. above. Because the preposition **to** comes before the relative pronoun, the writer had to use **whom.**

WHOSE + NOUN AS SUBJECT

Use this pattern to show possession. The relative pronoun is **whose**, and it is always followed by a noun. This pattern shows that the head noun "owns" the noun following **whose**. Study the examples below.

Examples of Restrictive Clauses:

1. The architect **whose design was the most original** won the prize.
2. The Opera House is one structure **whose shape is truly incredible.**

Examples of Nonrestrictive Clauses:

3. Joern Utzon, **whose design was the most original,** won the prize.
4. Everyone is impressed with the Opera House, **whose shape is truly incredible.**

ADJECTIVE CLAUSES

WHOSE + NOUN AS OBJECT

We use this pattern to show possession, too, but **whose + noun** is the *object* of the adjective clause. Study the examples below.

Examples of Restrictive Clauses:

1. The architects **whose designs the committee rejected** were very impressed by Utzon's plan.

2. The Opera House is one structure **whose shape many people considered impossible to build.**

Examples of Nonrestrictive Clauses:

3. The Sydney Opera House, **whose shape and design most people find amazing,** has a prominent location on the Sydney Harbor.

4. Tourists can hear wonderful concerts in the Concert Theater, **whose acoustics most audio technicians only dream of.**

NOTE: We use **whose** for people and for some things. In certain cases, **whose** will sound strange with a thing. Consider this example:

The table whose leg is broken should be thrown away.

In a sentence like this, do not use an adjective clause. Use a different structure:

The table with the broken leg should be thrown away.

ADJECTIVE CLAUSES OF PLACE

You can use an adjective clause to describe a place. With this pattern, use the word **where** to introduce the adjective clause. **Where** carries the meaning of "there" as it refers to a location. It is also possible to use a preposition of place + **which**. Study the following examples.

Examples of Restrictive Clauses:

1. The building **where operas are performed** is the largest of the three.

2. The building **in which operas are performed** is the largest of the three.

Examples of Nonrestrictive Clauses:

3. The Opera House, **where you can hear symphony orchestras and see wonderful ballets**, is the cultural center of Sydney.

4. The Opera House, **in which you can hear symphony orchestras and see wonderful ballets**, is the cultural center of Sydney.

5. The Opera House is located near Sandringham Park, **through which you can stroll after an evening of music.**

PART 3: SENTENCE STRUCTURE AND GRAMMAR EXERCISES AS WORK IN PROGRESS

ADJECTIVE CLAUSES OF TIME

You can use an adjective clause to describe a time event. This type of clause is introduced by the word **when**. Study the following examples.

Examples of Restrictive Clauses:

1. During the first few years **when the Opera House was being built**, no one could have anticipated that it would take so long to complete.

2. I will never forget the moment **when I first caught a glimpse of the Opera House**.

Examples of Nonrestrictive Clauses:

3. My friends were visiting Sydney in 1973, **when the Opera House was finally completed**.

4. Sixteen years earlier, **when the Opera House was first designed**, no one had imagined that the construction would take so long.

PRONOUN CHARTS FOR REVIEW

	When the pronoun refers to:	
When the pronoun is:	A PERSON/PEOPLE	A THING/THINGS
POSSESSIVE in a restrictive or nonrestrictive clause	*whose*	*whose*

	When the pronoun refers to:	
When the pronoun is:	LOCATION	TIME
An ADVERBIAL in a restrictive or a nonrestrictive clause	*where* / preposition + *which*	*when*

PRACTICE USING ADJECTIVE CLAUSES

Exercise 1 Combine the groups of sentences below using adjective clauses. Write adjective clauses in which the relative pronoun is the subject. Make the second sentence the adjective clause and incorporate it into the first sentence. NOTE: The sentences together make up a brief description of Central Library, a library on a university campus. As a result, they form a context. Write them out as separate sentences, but keep in mind that each sentence follows from the one before it. Use commas where necessary. Use your own paper for this and all the other exercises.

1. a. When you walk down University Avenue, you can't miss Central Library.
   b. Central Library is one of the most important buildings on campus.

2. a. On the first floor, you'll find the information desk.
   b. This is a good place to ask questions about the library facilities.

3. a. The main reference area is another good place to ask questions.
   b. It is located behind the stairs on the first floor.

4. a. The people are all trained librarians.
   b. They work behind the reference desk.

5. a. These librarians can help you find reference sources for your research.
   b. They are very kind and friendly.

ADJECTIVE CLAUSES

6. a. The library provides a limited number of rooms.
   b. They can be used for group study sessions.

7. a. These group study rooms are ideal for students.
   b. These students must get together to work on projects outside of class.

Exercise 2 Combine the groups of sentences below using adjective clauses. Wherever possible, write adjective clauses in which the relative pronoun is the object. Make the second (and where there are three, also the third) sentence(s) into an adjective clause. NOTE: The sentences together make up a brief description of Central Library, a library on a university campus. As a result, they form a context. Write them out as separate sentences, but keep in mind that each sentence follows from the one before it. Use commas where necessary.

1. a. When you walk down University Avenue, you can't miss Central Library.
   b. Some people consider Central Library the most important building on campus.

2. a. On the first floor, you'll find the circulation desk.
   b. This is the place to check out books.
   c. You want to take these books home.

3. a. Some of the people are student assistants.
   b. You'll see them working behind the circulation desk.

4. a. To borrow books, you need your student I.D. card.
   b. Your student I.D. card must be valid for the current semester.

5. a. Hand your I.D. and the book to one of the student assistants.
   b. You want to take this book home.
   c. He will enter the relevant information into the library's central computer.

6. a. Through this computer, the library can keep track of all the books.
   b. People borrow these books.

7. a. Books are subject to fines.
   b. People do not return these books by the due date.

8. a. A person will receive a bill.
   b. The computer catches this person with an overdue book.

Exercise 3 Combine the groups of sentences below using adjective clauses. Wherever possible, use **whose, where,** or **when**. Otherwise, use one of the other kinds of adjective clauses that you have studied. Make the second (and third) sentence(s) the adjective clause and incorporate it into the first sentence.

1. a. Many people believe that Akron, Ohio, is an old industrial city.
   b. Everyone lives next to a closed tire factory there.

2. a. These people imagine the city as it was a few years ago.
   b. There was high unemployment in the rubber industry then.

3. a. Akron residents are very impatient with these non-Ohioans.
   b. Akron residents can't understand their image of the city.

4. a. People know it is a city.
   b. They live in Akron.
   c. The city's cultural facilities can compete with those of any other city in the United States.

5. a. The Civic Theater is considered the cultural center of Akron.
   b. Its design makes it a historical landmark.

PART 3: SENTENCE STRUCTURE AND GRAMMAR EXERCISES AS WORK IN PROGRESS

6. a. The Civic was designed in the 1920s.
   b. In the 1920s, Akron was the fastest-growing city in the United States.

7. a. Inside the Civic is a large theater.
   b. You can watch a classic film there.

8. a. The theater is a romantic place.
   b. Its ceiling simulates stars and slowly moving clouds.
   c. You can relax there.

9. a. On a boring Saturday evening, go to the Akron Civic Theater.
   b. You are tired of staying home then.
   c. You can enjoy a wonderful evening there.

Exercise 4 This exercise will give you a chance to review restrictive and nonrestrictive adjective clauses. Below is a letter that a student in an intensive English language program sent to his mother, who reads English. Look at the numbered nouns in each sentence and determine whether or not each noun needs an I.D. card; in other words, ask yourself if the reader of this letter can understand who or what the noun is referring to OR if the reader needs more information.

September 26

Dear Mom,

So far, I'm really enjoying my classes in the E.L.I. Every day, I have two classes: reading/writing and listening/speaking. The class[1] is listening/speaking because, as you know, I haven't had a lot of exposure to spoken English. But, I can tell I'm improving every day.

I have two teachers.[2] The teacher[3] is very nice. However, she gives homework.[4] The reading/writing teacher[5] gives a lot of homework, too. Last week, a really funny thing happened before her class.[6] Because of a scheduling change, we had class in a room.[7] When the teacher[8] came, a group of students[9] were waiting outside the classroom. One student[10] had his back to the teacher.[11] Just as she got to the classroom door,[12] the student[13] threw his arm out and hit her right in the nose. Her nose[14] turned bright red and started to shine like a traffic light! It was really funny! Even the teacher laughed.

But seriously, Mom, I'm learning a lot of English and am studying hard. I know that you will be proud of me at the end of the semester.[15] I am sure that I will pass the TOEFL.[16] Give my love to everyone in the family. And, oh yeah, can you send some money?????

Rewrite the sentences with the nouns numbered 1, 3 to 7, 10, 11, and 13 to 16. When rewriting, add the corresponding sentences below as adjective clauses. Be sure to insert the new information (the clause) into the correct position in each sentence. Use commas where necessary.

1. I'm having the most trouble in this class.

3. I practice listening/speaking with her.

4. The homework is usually pretty difficult.

5. She is also very nice.

6. We have reading/writing class at 4:00.

7. We had never been there before.

10. He is very big.

11. She was walking down the hall.

13. He was talking to his friend and gesturing a lot.

14. Her nose is already a little funny looking.

15. My hard work will pay off then.

16. I have to score 500 on the TOEFL.

SUGGESTIONS • SUGGESTIONS • SUGGESTIONS • SUGGESTIONS

For information about other restrictive and nonrestrictive structures that modify nouns, see:

Adjective Clauses: Reduced .... pages 181 to 183.
Appositives .... pages 193 to 195.

ADJECTIVE CLAUSES: *Reduced*

With an adjective clause whose subject is **who, which,** or **that,** you can sometimes reduce the clause into an adjective phrase. This pattern is a variation on the adjective clause. (See pages 172–181 for information about adjective clauses.)

CLAUSES WITH "TO BE" You can reduce an adjective clause to a phrase:

1. if the *subject* of the adjective clause is **who, which,** or **that**

    and

2. if the verb pattern contains the verb **to be** followed by a present participle (V-<u>ing</u>), a past participle (V-<u>ed</u>), or an adjective.

To reduce the clause, you omit the subject and the verb **to be.**

Example 1:

Here is a sentence with an adjective clause:

The Sydney Opera House, **which was designed in 1957**, was completed in 1973.

Here is the same sentence with an adjective phrase:

The Sydney Opera House, **designed in 1957**, was completed in 1973.

OR

Designed in 1957, the Sydney Opera House was completed in 1973.

Example 2:

Here is a sentence with an adjective clause:

Everyone **who is living in Sydney** considers the Opera House a national treasure.

Here is the same sentence with an adjective phrase:

Everyone **living in Sydney** considers the Opera House a national treasure.

Part 3: Sentence Structure and Grammar Exercises as Work in Progress

Example 3:

Here is a sentence with an adjective clause:

A person **who is capable of designing a structure like the Opera House** must be a genius.

Here is the same sentence with an adjective phrase:

A person **capable of designing a structure like the Opera House** must be a genius.

CLAUSES WITHOUT "TO BE" If there is no form of **to be** in the adjective clause, it is sometimes possible to omit the subject pronoun and change the verb to its *-ing* form.

Example 4:

Here is a sentence with an adjective clause:

The Opera House, **which posed unique challenges for the builders**, took sixteen years to complete.

Here is the same sentence with an adjective phrase:

The Opera House, **posing unique challenges for the builders**, took sixteen years to complete.

OR

Posing unique challenges for the builders, the Opera House took sixteen years to complete.

Example 5:

Here is a sentence with an adjective clause:

Everyone **who visits the Opera House** knows it is an amazing architectural accomplishment.

Here is the same sentence with an adjective phrase:

Everyone **visiting the Opera House** knows it is an amazing architectural accomplishment.

Example 6:

Here is the sentence with an adjective clause:

The Opera House was built on a peninsula **which extends into the harbor.**

Here is the same sentence with an adjective phrase:

The Opera House was built on a peninsula **extending into the harbor.**

NOTES:

① Like adjective clauses, reduced adjective clauses can be restrictive and nonrestrictive. The same comma rules apply to these adjective phrases as to adjective clauses. (See pages 173 and 174 for a discussion of restrictive and nonrestrictive.)

② If the adjective phrase is nonrestrictive and it modifies the subject of the main clause, it can be placed before or after the subject. See examples 1 and 4 above.

ADJECTIVE CLAUSES

PRACTICE USING REDUCED ADJECTIVE CLAUSES

Exercise 1 Combine each pair of sentences below using reduced adjective clauses. Make the second sentence the reduced clause and incorporate it into the first sentence. NOTE: The sentences together form a paragraph about an archaeological discovery made in 1991. Write them out as separate sentences, but keep in mind that each sentence follows from the one before it. Use commas as necessary.

1. a. In September 1991, a tourist spotted something unusual in the snow.
   b. A tourist was hiking in the Italian Alps.

2. a. He found the frozen remains of the Stone Age wanderer.
   b. The wanderer is now called "The Iceman."

3. a. His age is 5,300 years.
   b. His age was determined by radio-carbon dating.

4. a. The discovery has given scientists new insights into our ancestors.
   b. It opened a window on life in the year 3300 B.C.

5. a. Scientists can only speculate about the Iceman's death.
   b. They are studying the body and discovery site.

6. a. It is believed that he might have been a shepherd.
   b. He took care of his sheep high in the Alps.

7. a. For some reason, he separated from his group.
   b. The reason is still unclear to researchers.

8. a. A storm probably forced him off course.
   b. The storm blew up suddenly.

9. a. The Iceman probably fell asleep and froze to death.
   b. He was unable to find his group.

10. a. Soon after his death, a storm dropped a lot of snow.
    b. The snow protected his body and kept him intact.

(NOTE: If you would like more information about the Iceman, consult the following articles: Jaroff, Leon. 1992. "The Iceman." *Time* 26 Oct.: 62–66. Roberts, David. 1993. "The Iceman." *National Geographic* June:36–67.

SUGGESTIONS • SUGGESTIONS • SUGGESTIONS • SUGGESTIONS

For information about other structures that modify nouns, see:

Adjective Clauses . . . . pages 172 to 181.
Appositives . . . . pages 193 to 195.

PART 3: SENTENCE STRUCTURE AND GRAMMAR EXERCISES AS WORK IN PROGRESS

ADVERB CLAUSES OF CONCESSION AND CONTRAST

An adverb clause is a dependent (subordinate) clause. Because of this, it cannot function as a sentence by itself; it must be combined with an independent clause.

Remember:	• A clause in English contains at least a **SUBJECT** and a **PREDICATE**. • The predicate consists of a main verb and any auxiliary verbs. • A simple sentence consists of one independent clause. • A complex sentence consists of two or more clauses (e.g., two independent clauses; one independent and one or more dependent clauses).

An adverb clause begins with a **subordinating conjunction** which indicates the meaning relationship between the idea in the dependent clause and the idea in the independent clause. The first chart below lists some common subordinating conjunctions that are used with adverb clauses to show **concession** and **contrast**.

	SUBORDINATORS
Concession	although, despite the fact that, even though, in spite of the fact that, though
Contrast	whereas, while

Two sentence patterns can be used with adverb clauses of **concession** and **contrast**. The adverb clause can come in initial position before the independent clause or follow the independent clause.

PATTERNS				
Subordinating conjunction	+	clause	, +	clause.
Even though cigarettes pose health risks, many people smoke.				

OR

Clause	+	**subordinating conjunction**	+	clause.
Many people smoke		*even though*		*cigarettes pose health risks.*

ADVERB CLAUSES OF CONCESSION AND CONTRAST

When the adverb clause follows the independent clause and is nonrestrictive (that is, not essential to the meaning of the independent clause), you should set it off with a comma. See pages 173 and 174 for an explanation of restrictive and nonrestrictive.

Contrast clauses introduced by **whereas** or **while** are always nonrestrictive because they combine ideas that are in direct opposition. **Concession** clauses with the other connecting words listed above will be either restrictive or nonrestrictive, depending on the context.

Clause ,	subordinating conjunction	+	clause.
My father smokes three packs a day, whereas my mother has never smoked.			

Additional Examples:

1. In spite of the fact that I hate cold weather, I moved to Minnesota.
2. Although I am undecided about a specific major, I would like to pursue a degree in one of the natural sciences.
3. My father wants me to major in business, whereas I want to study art.

NOTES:

① The subordinating conjunctions **although, despite the fact that, even though, in spite of the fact that,** and **though** signal that the information in the independent clause is unexpected or surprising in light of the information in the adverb clause.

Example:

During the 1992 presidential election, Bill Clinton lost his voice. **Although he was ill,** he made most of his scheduled campaign appearances.

② The subordinating conjunctions **whereas** and **while** introduce an idea that is in direct contrast or opposition to the information in the independent clause.

Example:

In the 1992 presidential election, candidates Clinton and Bush disagreed on many issues. For example, they were in opposite camps on the topic of abortion. **Whereas Bush favored restricting a woman's access to abortion,** Clinton supported a woman's right to choose.

③ The subordinating conjunctions **despite the fact that** and **in spite of the fact that** are followed by a clause. The prepositions **despite** and **in spite of** are followed by a noun phrase.

Examples:

Many people smoke **despite the fact that this habit poses serious health risks.**

Many people smoke **despite the serious health risks.**

In spite of the fact that smoking is dangerous, many young people still take up the habit.

In spite of the dangers of smoking, many young people still take up the habit.

PART 3: SENTENCE STRUCTURE AND GRAMMAR EXERCISES AS WORK IN PROGRESS

PRACTICE USING ADVERB CLAUSES OF CONCESSION AND CONTRAST

Exercise 1 On pages 143 and 144, you will find an article entitled "The Cultures of Medicine." The article reviews a book, *Medicine and Culture*, which contrasts the medical practices of four countries: the United States, Great Britain, France, and Germany. Read that article and complete the exercise below.

Rewrite and complete these sentences with ideas that are logical, based on the article, "The Cultures of Medicine." Restate ideas from the article.

1. Although Americans and the English have the same life expectancy . . .

2. American physicians tend to be aggressive while British doctors . . .

3. Despite the fact that there is no evidence for the effectiveness of the yogurt derivative lactobacillus . . .

4. Whereas Americans visit their doctors on the average of 4.6 times a year, Germans . . .

5. Even though medicine is usually thought of as a science, Lynn Payer . . .

6. Americans are no healthier than their counterparts in western Europe in spite of the fact that . . .

7. Though the subtitle of the article refers to differences in medical practices all over the world . . .

Exercise 2 Think about common ailments (e.g., the cold, the flu, headache, stomach ache) or medical conditions (e.g., pregnancy, labor, delivery, broken bones) and how these illnesses or conditions are typically treated in the United States and in your native country or culture. Make a chart like the one below; complete it with freewritten notes about the differences in the methods of treatment between your country or culture and the United States.

Illness or Condition	Medical Practices in the United States	Medical Practices in Your Country or Culture

After you complete the chart, write ten sentences describing the differences in medical practices between the United States and your native country or culture. Use the structures explained on pages 184 and 185.

ADVERB CLAUSES OF TIME, CAUSE-EFFECT/REASON-RESULT, AND PURPOSE

> **SUGGESTIONS • SUGGESTIONS • SUGGESTIONS • SUGGESTIONS**
>
> For information about other structures that show **concession** and **contrast**, see:
>
> Coordination . . . . pages 212 to 217.
> Sentence Connectors . . . . pages 237 to 240.

ADVERB CLAUSES OF TIME, CAUSE-EFFECT/ REASON-RESULT, AND PURPOSE

An adverb clause is a dependent (subordinate) clause. Because of this, it cannot function as a sentence by itself; it must be combined with an independent clause.

Remember:	• A clause in English contains at least a **SUBJECT** and a **PREDICATE.** • The predicate consists of a main verb and any auxiliary verbs. • A simple sentence consists of one independent clause. • A complex sentence consists of two or more clauses (e.g., two independent clauses; one independent and one or more dependent clauses).

An adverb clause begins with a **subordinating conjunction** which indicates the meaning relationship between the idea in the dependent clause and the idea in the independent clause. The first chart below lists some common subordinating conjunctions that are used with adverb clauses to show **time, cause-effect/reason-result,** and **purpose**. The second illustrates the sentence pattern rules that adverb clauses follow.

SUBORDINATORS

Time	before, after, when, while, until, once, whenever, as soon as, as, since, as long as
Cause-Effect/ Reason-Result	because, since, as, now that
Purpose	so that, in order that

PATTERNS

Clause	+	subordinating conjunction	+	clause.
I came to the United States		*after*		*I finished high school.*

OR

Subordinating conjunction	+	clause	,	+	clause.
After		*I finished high school,*			*I came to the United States.*

PART 3: SENTENCE STRUCTURE AND GRAMMAR EXERCISES AS WORK IN PROGRESS

Additional Examples:

1. I will live in the United States until I finish my degree.
2. After I finish my degree, I will return home.
3. Because I studied for two years at a university in my country, I am applying as a transfer student.
4. I came to this university so that I could study electrical engineering.

NOTES:

① With adverb clauses of time, when the time reference is future, a *present* tense, not a *future* tense, is used after the time word.

Examples:

I **will return** home. I **will find** a job.

After I **return** home, I **will find** a job.

② The subordinating conjunctions **so that** and **in order that** show purpose. They are usually followed by modal auxiliary verbs, either **can, could, will,** or **would. Can** and **could** show the idea of **ability. Will** and **would** show the idea of doing one thing to ensure that something else will happen.

③ Infinitive phrases with **to** and **in order to** also show purpose.

Examples:

I came to the United States **so that I could study English.**
↓
I came to the United States **to study English.**
↓
I came to the United States **in order to study English.**

④ The subordinating conjunction **because** is followed by a clause. The preposition **because of** is followed by a noun phrase.

Examples:

Many people visit Los Angeles **because it has so many wonderful tourist attractions.**

Many people visit Los Angeles **because of its wonderful tourist attractions.**

ADVERB CLAUSES OF TIME, CAUSE-EFFECT/REASON-RESULT, AND PURPOSE

PRACTICE USING ADVERB CLAUSES OF TIME, CAUSE-EFFECT/ REASON-RESULT, AND PURPOSE AND RELATED STRUCTURES

Exercise 1 Combine these sentences using *time clauses*. Try to use as many of the subordinating conjunctions from the chart on page 187 as you can. The information in parentheses will help you decide which time word to use; however, you should not use it in the sentences that you write. (Remember: When the time reference is future, a *present* tense, not a *future* tense, is used after the time word.

Example: I **will return** home. I **will find** a job.

After I **return** home, I **will find** a job.)

1. I graduated from high school. I worked as a salesman.
   (May, three years ago)   (June, three years ago to August, last year)

2. I participated in my school's science fair. I was a junior.
   (May, two years ago)   (September to June, two years ago)

3. I will finish my B.A. Immediately after that, I will return home.
   (in three months)   (in three months and one day)

4. I will live here.   I will finish my studies.
   (for four more years)   (four years from now)

5. I was working at Wang Computer. I was promoted three times.
   (1990–1993)

6. I flew to the United States. I bought life insurance.
   (June 10, last year)   (June 9, last year)

7. I came to the United States. I have eaten food from my country only three times.
   (September last year)   (between September last year and now)

8. I will get used to the food here. I will feel more comfortable.
   (in a few months)   (in a few months)

9. I will never get used to the food here. I will be in this country.
   (for three more years)

10. I see a fast food restaurant. I feel sick.
    (every day)

Exercise 2 Combine these sentences using subordinating conjunctions of *cause-effect/reason-result*. Use words from the chart on page 187.

1. I worked as a computer programmer for three years. I wanted to get experience in that field.

2. I will work for my government. My country needs trained computer programmers.

3. I am studying at this university. I have heard that it is an excellent school.

4. I was a research assistant in the chemistry department. I gained valuable skills in research techniques.

5. I came to study in the United States. My aunt lives here.

6. I am studying at the university. I know I will reach my goals.

PART 3: SENTENCE STRUCTURE AND GRAMMAR EXERCISES AS WORK IN PROGRESS

Exercise 3   Answer each of the following questions truthfully using subordinating conjunctions of *cause-effect/reason-result* in your response. Use words from the chart on page 187.

1. Why did you choose your major field?
2. What kind of job would you like to have in the future? Why?
3. What are some opportunities that you have now but did not have before?
4. What kinds of extracurricular activities were you involved in while you were in secondary school? Why?

Exercise 4   Combine each of the following sentences using **because of.** NOTE: You will have to change the sentence that expresses the *cause* and rewrite it as a noun phrase.

1. This university has an excellent reputation. Therefore, it attracts many international students.
2. Many international students like to study in Florida. The weather there is pleasant all year.
3. Mohammed has had extensive teaching experience. He was offered a teaching assistantship his first semester in graduate school.
4. The famous Olympic skier Pirmin Zurbriggen was not able to win a gold medal in the Alpine Combined in 1988. He had a spectacular fall.
5. Before the 1988 Olympics, U.S. skater, Debi Thomas, did not have much time to relax. She had a very tight schedule.

Exercise 5   Combine these sentences using **so that** or **in order that**. (Remember: **So that** and **in order that** are usually followed by modal auxiliary verbs, so you will have to change the verb forms in the purpose clauses. **Can** and **could** show the idea of ability. **Will** and **would** show the idea of doing something to ensure that something else will happen. Analyze the meaning relationships between the sentences before you combine them.)

1. I decided to study computer science. I wanted to be able to get a good position as a programmer.
2. I am studying English composition. I want to be sure that I am ready for university work next semester.
3. I studied hard in the university. I wanted to be successful in my courses.
4. I plan to be a university professor when I return to my country. I want to be able to share my knowledge and expertise with others.
5. I chose this university. I hoped to do research in the field of polymers.

Exercise 6   Answer these questions truthfully using **so that** or **in order that** in your responses.

1. For what purpose are you studying English composition?
2. For what purpose did you come to this university?
3. For what purpose did you choose your major?
4. What do you hope to do upon graduation from the university? For what purpose will you pursue that goal?

ADVERB CLAUSES OF TIME, CAUSE-EFFECT/REASON-RESULT, AND PURPOSE

Exercise 7 Answer these questions truthfully using **to** or **in order to** in your responses.

1. What is one difficult thing that you have to do this evening? For what purpose do you have to do it?
2. For what purpose do people study English?
3. For what purpose do you write?
4. For what purpose do people watch t.v.?

SUGGESTIONS • SUGGESTIONS • SUGGESTIONS • SUGGESTIONS

For information about other structures that show time, cause-effect/reason-result, and purpose, see:

Adverb Clauses: Reduced .... pages 191 to 193
Coordination .... pages 212 to 217
Factual Conditionals .... pages 196 to 197
Sentence Connectors .... pages 237 to 240

ADVERB CLAUSES: *Reduced*

Some adverb clauses can be reduced to *-ing* phrases. This pattern is a variation on the adverb clause, so it helps a writer with sentence variety. Reduced adverb clauses are dependent structures that must be combined with independent clauses.

REDUCED ADVERB CLAUSES OF TIME

	SUBORDINATORS
Time	before, after, when, while, since

PATTERNS

Subordinating conjunction	**+**	**verb-*ing***	**,**	**clause.**
After graduating from high school			,	*I worked in a store.*

OR

Clause	**+**	**subordinating conjunction**	**+**	**verb-*ing***
I worked in a store		*after*		*graduating from high school.*

PART 3: SENTENCE STRUCTURE AND GRAMMAR EXERCISES AS WORK IN PROGRESS

Additional Examples:

1. Before coming to the United States, I had only seen snow in pictures.
2. While traveling from the airport to the city, I just stared out of the car windows in disbelief.
3. I have survived two blizzards since coming to this country.
4. After having lived in a tropical climate for twenty years, I found the snow overwhelming.

REDUCED ADVERB CLAUSES OF CAUSE-EFFECT

	SUBORDINATORS
Cause-Effect	No subordinating conjunction is necessary. For example, these two sentences have the same meaning: *Because I have a strong background in math, I will study computer science.* *Having a strong background in math, I will study computer science.*

PATTERNS
Verb-*ing* , clause.
Graduating with a high G.P.A., I was able to find a good job in my country.

Additional Examples:

5. Moving from a warm climate to a cold one, I was forced to buy all new clothes.
6. Having grown up in a warm climate, I was not used to the snow.

NOTES:

① Each of the sentences above describes two activities. The subject (or actor) of both activities MUST be the same. In other words, the subject of the verb-*ing* pattern and the subject of the verb in the independent clause must be the same.

② Usually, verb + *ing* is used in the reduced adverb clause. See examples 1 to 3 and 5. However, when the two activities happened in the past and the action described in the phrase was completed BEFORE the action of the main clause, you can use the present perfect participle (**having** + past participle). See examples 4 and 6.

APPOSITIVES

PRACTICE USING REDUCED ADVERB CLAUSES

Exercise 1 Go back to *Exercise 1* and *Exercise 2* on page 189. Which of those sentences can you combine using reduced adverb clauses? Write out each sentence.

Exercise 2 The following sentences are about some athletes who competed in the Winter Olympics in 1988. In the box above the sentences, each athlete's name, country, and sport are listed so that you will know who each one is. Combine each set of sentences using a *reduced adverb clause*.

Name	Country	Event
Katarina Witt	East Germany	figure skating
Debi Thomas	U.S.A.	figure skating
Pirmin Zurbriggen	Switzerland	skiing
Dan Jansen	U.S.A.	speed skating

1. The athletes prepare for the Olympics. They must train for several hours each day.
2. Debi Thomas trained for the Olympics. At the same time, she was a pre-med student at Stanford University.
3. Pirmin Zurbriggen had dreamed of winning the gold medal in the Alpine Combined. He was very disappointed when he fell.
4. Dan Jansen skated in his best event. Jansen learned about his sister's death.
       (in the evening)   (in the afternoon)
5. Katarina Witt has become well known in the United States. She won the gold medal.

SUGGESTIONS • SUGGESTIONS • SUGGESTIONS • SUGGESTIONS

For information about other structures that show time and cause-effect/reason-result, see:

Adverb Clauses . . . . pages 187 to 190
Coordination . . . . pages 212 to 217
Factual Conditionals . . . . pages 196 to 197
Sentence Connectors . . . . pages 237 to 240

APPOSITIVES

Sometimes in your writing you will want to provide your readers with definitions, explanations, or expansions of words or ideas that you present. There are many ways to define or explain words or ideas. For example, you can use adjective clauses (see pages 172 to 181) and reduced adjective clauses (see pages 181 to 183). Another way is to use **appositives.**

An appositive is a word or a group of words that precede or follow a noun phrase (called the head noun) and provide additional information about that noun phrase. Because an appositive describes a head noun, it should always be positioned next to that head noun. (The head noun and its appositive are like dance partners dancing to a slow waltz; they should not be split up.)

PART 3: SENTENCE STRUCTURE AND GRAMMAR EXERCISES AS WORK IN PROGRESS

Appositives can be restrictive or nonrestrictive. (See pages 173 and 174 for an explanation of restrictive and nonrestrictive.) When used to define words, they are usually nonrestrictive. Nonrestrictive appositives are usually set off by commas; you can also use dashes and parentheses.

Examples of Appositives:

1. Joern Utzon, **a Dane,** designed the Sydney Opera House.
2. **A creative and bold architect,** Utzon designed a cluster of three buildings, **all covered with white tiles.**
3. Utzon's plan, **to cover each building with white tiles**, was highly innovative.
4. Construction of the buildings called for special procedures, **fabricating the roof sections as shells and lowering them into place on each building.**
5. His plan, **that each building would look like windblown sails,** proved difficult to implement.
6. As a result, it took years to complete the Sydney Opera House, **an architectural triumph and symbol of Australia.**

NOTES:

① An appositive usually follows the head noun. However, when the head noun is the subject of the sentence, the appositive can precede it. (See sentence 2.)

② An appositive can be a noun (see example 1), a noun phrase (see examples 2 and 6), a noun clause (see example 5), an infinitive (see example 3), or a gerund (see example 4).

PRACTICE USING APPOSITIVES

Exercise 1 Below you will find pairs of sentences about bicycle maintenance and repair. Combine the pairs of sentences using an appositive.

1. With practice, a flat clincher tire is relatively easy to repair.
   A clincher tire is one with a rubber innertube.

2. To remove a clincher tire, you can use tire irons.
   Tire irons are small, flat sticks used to pry the tire off of the wheel.

3. The round end of the tire iron should be inserted under the bead.
   The bead is the inner edge of the clincher tire.

4. After removing the damaged innertube, you must make a decision.
   You must decide whether to patch the hole or replace the innertube.

5. If you don't have a patch kit with you, you have one option.
   That option is to replace the innertube.

6. Once the new innertube is in place, its valve should be straight.
   The valve is the metal device through which air is put into the tube.

7. It is easy to adjust your bicycle's front and rear derailleurs.
   The derailleurs are the changers that move the chain.

8. While the rear derailleur moves the chain across several sprockets, the front one moves it across only two sprockets.
   Sprockets are metal wheels with teeth.

9. Regular maintenance is necessary if you want to keep your bicycle working smoothly.
   Regular bicycle maintenance is a dirty and time-consuming job.

APPOSITIVES

Exercise 2 Below are some sentences about the invention of blue jeans. Expand each sentence by adding at least one appositive. Refer to the article about the history of jeans on pages 146 to 148 to find interesting and relevant details to add. Study the examples before you begin.

1. Levi Strauss invented blue jeans around 1850.

    Levi Strauss, a German immigrant to the United States, invented blue jeans around 1850.

    OR

    A German immigrant to the United States, Levi Strauss invented blue jeans around 1850.

    OR

    Levi Strauss invented blue jeans, the most popular pants in the United States, around 1850.

    OR

    An internationally recognized symbol of America, blue jeans were invented by Levi Strauss, a German immigrant, in 1850.

2. Blue jeans are made from denim.
3. Strauss dyed the cloth indigo.
4. Jacob Davis came up with the idea for Levis' famous trademark.
5. His idea was the result of a miner's complaint about his pockets tearing easily.
6. Blue jeans were first worn by the working people of the west.
7. Today, a large number of blue jeans are sold each year.
8. Levi Strauss International runs a "Western Image Program."

Exercise 3 What are some cultural phenomena or artifacts of your native culture that some of your classmates and teachers may not be familiar with? Think of foods, music, dance, customs, articles of clothing, etc. that are symbolic of your country or culture. Make a list of at least ten words or phrases that refer to such phenomena. Write a sentence defining each word or phrase. Use an appositive for each definition.

Example:

the cultural phenomenon = bluegrass festivals

sentence = Bluegrass festivals, weekend musical events held at campsites all over the United States, are the most popular form of summer entertainment for hard-core fans of bluegrass music.

SUGGESTIONS • SUGGESTIONS • SUGGESTIONS • SUGGESTIONS

For information about other structures that modify nouns, see

Adjective Clauses . . . . pages 172 to 181
Adjective Clauses: Reduced . . . . pages 181 to 183

PART 3: SENTENCE STRUCTURE AND GRAMMAR EXERCISES AS WORK IN PROGRESS

CONDITIONALS

An adverb clause of condition is a dependent (subordinate) clause. Because of this, it cannot function as a sentence by itself; it must be combined with an independent clause.

An adverb clause of condition is combined with an independent clause by a **subordinating conjunction**, usually "if."

Remember:	• A clause in English contains at least a **SUBJECT** and a **PREDICATE**. • The predicate consists of a main verb and any auxiliary verbs. • A simple sentence consists of one independent clause. • A complex sentence consists of two or more clauses (e.g., two independent clauses; one independent and one or more dependent clauses).

PATTERNS WITH CONDITIONALS

Two patterns can be used with IF-clauses. The IF-clause can come in initial position before the independent clause. With this pattern, a comma separates the clauses.

Connecting word	+	clause	,	+	clause.
If a person does not get adequate fluids, he becomes dehydrated.					

The IF-clause can follow the independent clause. With this pattern, a comma is usually not necessary.

Clause	+	connecting word	+	clause.
A person becomes dehydrated if he does not get adequate fluids.				

The choice of pattern depends on the context in which the sentence appears.

FACTUAL CONDITIONALS: TO STATE GENERAL TRUTHS OR HABITS

In factual conditionals, two situations are described. The situation described in the dependent clause (the IF-clause) sets a context for your reader. The independent clause states the results or consequences when that situation occurs.

VERB TENSES AND FORMS In factual conditionals, the verbs in both clauses are simple present. "If" has the same meaning as "when" or "whenever." This conditional, which describes a cause-effect relationship, is often used to describe scientific laws and principles as well as habits.

In the **IF-clause,**	use → simple present
In the **independent clause,**	use → simple present

Examples:

1. Snow begins to melt if the temperature rises above 32°F.
2. If plants are deprived of water, they die.
3. Many second language learners use one strategy for coping with new words when reading: If they meet a new word, they look it up in the dictionary.
4. If a person speaks too quickly, I ask him please to slow down.

Exercise 1 Writing Factual Conditionals: Below are several phrases describing scientific facts or habits. Use these phrases to construct sentences stating general conditions. Follow the examples.

Examples:

a. boil / water . . .
   If you boil water, it evaporates.
b. a friend / ask to borrow money . . .
   If a friend asks to borrow money, I lend it to him.

1. drop / a raw egg . . .
2. cut / your finger with a knife . . .
3. touch / a hot burner
4. heat / butter . . .
5. combine / two hydrogen molecules with one oxygen molecule . . .
6. keep / water at 0°C . . .
7. leave / a piece of steel in the rain . . .
8. my refrigerator / be / empty . . .
9. I / crave chocolate . . .
10. the phone / ring in the middle of the night . . .
11. someone / call during dinner . . .
12. I / forget to water the plants . . .
13. a person / have trouble falling asleep at night . . .
14. my roommate / play the stereo too loudly . . .

PART 3: SENTENCE STRUCTURE AND GRAMMAR EXERCISES AS WORK IN PROGRESS

USING CONDITIONALS TO GIVE ADVICE OR INSTRUCTIONS

Conditionals are often used to give advice or instructions. The IF-clause explains a possible general situation or state; the independent clause describes a recommendation or an action to take when that situation or state exists.

VERB TENSES AND FORMS When you are using conditionals to give advice or instructions, these are the most common patterns of verb tenses and forms:

In the **If-clause,** use	→	simple present		
In the **independent clause,** use	→	should +	main verb	(advice)
		ought to +	main verb	(advice)
		imperative		(instructions and advice)

Examples:

1. If you own a car, you should be prepared for emergency situations.
2. If you travel a lot by car, you ought to join an automobile club like AAA.
3. Call the Emergency Road Service number if your car breaks down.

Exercise 2 Using Conditionals to Give Advice: What is some advice that you would give to students who are living overseas? Rewrite and complete these sentences.

1. If you experience culture shock . . .
2. If you do not make friends easily . . .
3. If your friends speak your native language all of the time . . .
4. . . . go to the library to study.
5. . . . they should complain to their landlord.
6. . . . he ought to find a new roommate for next semester.

Exercise 3 Giving Advice to a Beginning Language Learner: On pages 277 and 278, there is a reading about the psychological traits related to language learning. The article discusses these characteristics: rule-learning, risk-taking, eye-learning, ear-learning, extroversion, inhibition, and tolerance. Read that article and complete the exericse below.

Imagine that a friend of yours at another school is going to take his first foreign language class next semester; he's going to study French 101. Because he knows that you are an experienced language learner, he writes to you for advice. Write a letter back to him giving ten suggestions about how to maximize his learning opportunities. Base your advice on your own experience and on what you learned from reading the article about psychological traits. Complete the letter below. The first piece of advice has been started for you.

Dear _____,

Thanks for your wonderful letter. I'm so glad you are enjoying your first semester at college. And I'm delighted to hear that you are going to study a foreign language next semester; now you'll know what I've been going through trying to learn English!

Yes, I do have some advice for you.

1. *If you are a rule-learner . . .*
2.
3.
4.
5.
6.
7.
8.
9.
10.

Best of luck with your classes. Keep me posted on your progress. Talk to you soon,

FUTURE CONDITIONALS: TO PREDICT EVENTS

Use future conditionals to make predictions. With these conditionals, two events are described; the event in the independent clause is influenced by the events in the IF-clause.

VERB TENSES AND FORMS With future conditionals, these are the most common patterns of verb tenses and forms:

In the **IF-clause** use	→	simple present			
In the **independent clause,** use	→	*will*	+	main verb	(certain)
		should	+	main verb	(probable)
		ought to	+	main verb	(probable)
		may	+	main verb	(possible)
		might	+	main verb	(possible)
		can	+	main verb	(able to)

(Your choice of modal indicates the strength of the prediction.)

Part 3: Sentence Structure and Grammar Exercises as Work in Progress

Examples:

The sentences below make predictions about the consequences of government policy.

1. If the government makes significant reforms in the health care system, medical services will be available to everyone. (certain)
2. If the government cuts defense spending, money should become available for other programs. (probable)
3. Tuition fees may go down if the government reforms educational policies. (possible)
4. If companies have confidence in the economy, they might hire more permanent employees. (possible)

Exercise 4 **Predicting the Future:** Make predictions about what you think will happen to our environment by rewriting and completing the following sentences. Be sure that your ideas are logical.

1. If the world's population continues to grow . . .
2. If the number of cars increases . . .
3. If we do not conserve energy . . .
4. If communities develop good recycling programs . . .
5. If more nuclear power plants are built . . .
6. Landfills will have to be closed . . .
7. Water supplies will become contaminated . . .
8. The quality of air in large cities should improve . . .
9. Future generations might have bigger problems . . .
10. We can have a cleaner world . . .

Exercise 5 **Predicting the Future:** Yen, an international student from Taiwan, is uncertain about his future. Everything depends on whether or not he passes the TOEFL. One day, while thinking about his future, he doodled in his freewriting notebook. He sketched the chart that you see on the following page. Study the chart. Then write at least ten sentences with IF-clauses that make predictions about Yen's future.

Exercise 6 **Predicting the Future:** What about your future? In your own freewriting notebook, doodle some ideas about possibilities for your own future. Think about immediate future and long-term future possibilities. After you sketch out some ideas, write at least ten sentences making predictions about your future.

Counterfactual Conditionals: To Describe Unreal Present Events

Imagine that you want to tell your readers about a situation that does not exist right now, but that you wish did. (For example, you do not have a scholarship for your studies, but you wish that you did.) Or suppose that you want to speculate or guess about the consequences of a situation that does not exist right now. (For example, you want to speculate about what you might do as president of the United States.)

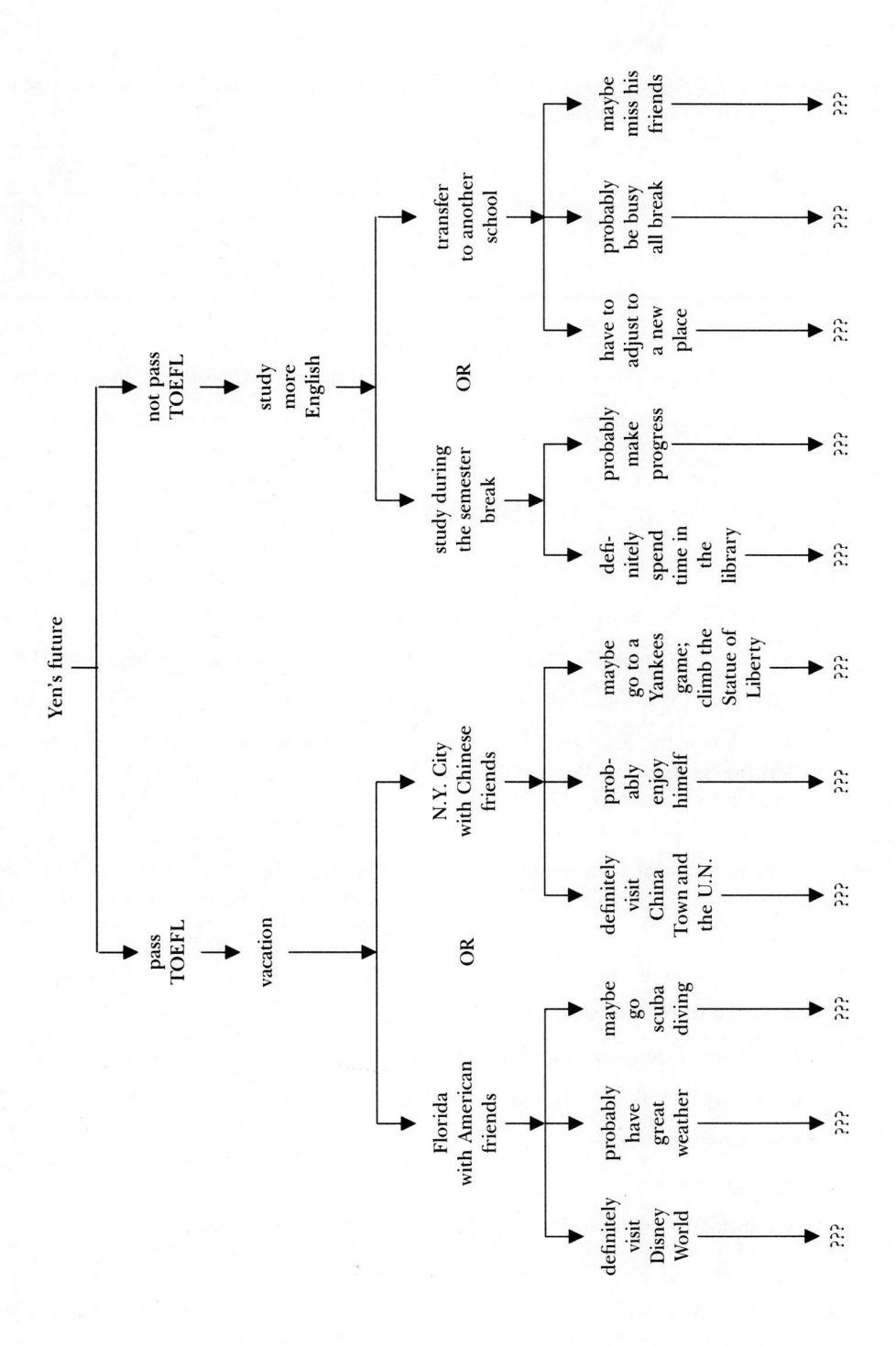

CONDITIONALS

Yen's future

- pass TOEFL → vacation
  - Florida with American friends
    - definitely visit Disney World → ???
    - probably have great weather → ???
    - maybe go scuba diving → ???
  - OR
  - N.Y. City with Chinese friends
    - definitely visit China Town and the U.N. → ???
    - probably enjoy himself → ???
    - maybe go to a Yankees game; climb the Statue of Liberty → ???
- not pass TOEFL → study more English
  - study during the semester break
    - definitely spend time in the library → ???
    - probably make progress → ???
  - OR
  - transfer to another school
    - have to adjust to a new place → ???
    - probably be busy all break → ???
    - maybe miss his friends → ???

201

PART 3: SENTENCE STRUCTURE AND GRAMMAR EXERCISES AS WORK IN PROGRESS

To describe these types of situations, ones which are counterfactual or the opposite of what is currently true, use an IF-clause with a *simple past tense*. The IF-clause describes something that is not real at the present time.

VERB TENSES AND FORMS   With present counterfactual conditionals, these are the most common patterns of verb tenses and forms:

In the **IF-clause,**	use →	simple past			
In the **independent clause,**	use →	*would*	+	main verb	(certain)
		could	+	main verb	(able)
		might	+	main verb	(possible)

Examples:

1. If English did not have such a complicated spelling system, it might be easier to learn.
2. We wouldn't have to memorize the irregular forms if all past tense verbs were regular.

NOTES:

① With this type of conditional, when you use the verb **to be** in the **IF-clause,** always use **were.**

   Examples:

   If I were a millionaire, I would travel around the world.

   If Mohammed were President of the United States, he would abolish the TOEFL.

   If I were you, I would always do my homework.

② Remember that with this type of conditional, even though the verb forms are past, the time reference is present. We use the past forms to show that we are talking about something that is not true right now.

Exercise 7   Writing Present Counterfactual Conditionals: What if you were an English teacher??? Speculate about what you would do by rewriting and completing the following sentences.

1. If I were an English teacher . . .
2. If students came to my class late . . .
3. If a student asked a question I couldn't answer . . .
4. If my students were confused by the English verb system . . .
5. If my students hated to write . . .
6. . . . he might get an A+.
7. . . . she would fail my course.
8. . . . I could retire.
9. I might give pop quizzes . . .
10. I would give more homework . . .

Exercise 8 **Writing Present Counterfactual Conditionals:** Think about your current study habits and living conditions. What if they were different?

Complete the following questionnaire by 1) checking "yes" or "no" for each question; 2) writing a complete sentence to explain your response; 3) writing a "what if" sentence, speculating about how things would be different if your answer were the opposite. Study the example before you begin.

Questions	Yes	No
① Do you ask questions in class?	_____	_____

I don't ask questions in class because I'm afraid to make mistakes. If I asked questions, I could practice speaking English.

OR

I always ask questions in class so that I can be sure that I understand every lesson. If I didn't ask questions, I might get confused.

Questions	Yes	No
② Do you review your lessons every day?	_____	_____
③ Do you always speak English with your friends?	_____	_____
④ Do you ask the teacher for extra help?	_____	_____
⑤ Is your English class too difficult?	_____	_____
⑥ Do your friends ever correct you when you make mistakes?	_____	_____
⑦ Is your apartment or house a good place to study?	_____	_____
⑧ Are your roommates considerate?	_____	_____
⑨ Do you try to create opportunities to use English?	_____	_____
⑩ Are you comfortable living in the United States?	_____	_____

COUNTERFACTUAL CONDITIONALS: TO DESCRIBE UNREAL PAST EVENTS

Imagine that you want to tell your reader about a situation that did not exist or happen in the past, BUT that you wish had happened (e.g., you did not study for a test last week, but you wish that you had!). Or suppose you want to speculate or guess about the consequences of a past event that never happened (e.g., you want to speculate about what your government could have done during a political crisis last year).

VERB TENSES AND FORMS With past counterfactual conditionals, these are the most common patterns of verb tenses and forms:

PART 3: SENTENCE STRUCTURE AND GRAMMAR EXERCISES AS WORK IN PROGRESS

In the **IF-clause**,	use →	past perfect (*had* + past participle)				
In the **independent clause**,	use →	*would*	+	*have*	+ past participle	(certain)
		could	+	*have*	+ past participle	(able)
		might	+	*have*	+ past participle	(possible)

Examples:

1. If Ross Perot had been elected President of the United States in 1992, he would have brought a new kind of politics to Washington.

2. George Bush could have stayed in the White House if he had not lost the election.

3. Bill Clinton might have lost the election if he had not campaigned so aggressively.

Exercise 9 Writing Past Counterfactual Conditionals: Below is John's freewriting entry about his weekend. Read this incredible story and complete the exercise that follows.

Today is Monday, and I am relieved. This past weekend was terrible for me. Friday was the 13th, so as soon as I woke up, I knew it was going to be a bad day. While I was in the bathroom, I broke a mirror. I thought, "Oh, no! Seven years of bad luck!" When I was getting dressed, I ripped my pants. Because I had no other clean pairs, I had to sew the rip. I can't sew well, so it took me a half hour to repair the pants. By the time I got into my car, I only had ten minutes to get to the university in time for my class.

On the way to the university, I had a flat tire. I know nothing about cars. In fact, I don't even know where the spare tire is! At this point, it was too late to get to the university in time for my first class anyway. I decided to read my car owner's manual and to try to change the tire myself. When I looked into the glove compartment, I couldn't find the manual. Then I remembered that I had thrown it out last week when I was cleaning my car. This was not my day!!

While I was sitting in the driver's seat trying to figure out what to do, I glanced into my rear view mirror and saw a police car pulling up behind me. "Great," I thought. "These police officers will help me!" Sure enough, they showed me how to change the tire. However, as standard procedure, they ran my license number through the police computer. The computer reminded me that I had ten unpaid parking tickets totaling $100.00!! One of the officers wrote me a ticket and told me that I had to appear in court the following Tuesday.

By the time the officers left, I had a terrible headache. I was parked in front of a drug store, so I decided to run in for some aspirin. Some painters were touching up the sign on the store, and there were two ladders resting against the building. I walked under both of the ladders. Just as I got to the door of the store, a paint can fell off one of the ladders and splattered paint all over my head and shoulders.

I went home after all of these events, cleaned up, got into bed, and pulled a blanket over my head. I stayed in bed all day Friday and Saturday. Sunday, I ran out to a store and bought a rabbit's foot, a horseshoe, and a four-leaf clover. I am going to carry these good luck charms with me forever.

Rewrite and complete each of the following sentences. The information you add should be based on the story about John. In other words, the meaning of your sentences must be logical and correct based on what you have read about John.

1. If yesterday had not been Friday the 13th . . .
2. If John had been able to sew quickly . . .
3. If John had done his laundry Thursday night . . .
4. If John had not thrown the car manual away . . .
5. If the officers had not run his license through the computer . . .
6. If John had paid his parking tickets . . .

Complete these sentences by adding IF-clauses.

7. John would have been able to change his tire . . .
8. . . . he wouldn't have gone to the drugstore.
9. . . . the painters would not have been there.
10. . . . John would not have thrown the car manual away.
11. . . . John would have been on time for class.

Exercise 10 Writing Past Counterfactual Conditionals: What if Levi Strauss, the inventor of blue jeans, had never been born? What if his life had been different? Would blue jeans have ever been invented? Turn to pages 146 to 148, where you will find a story about the invention of blue jeans. Read that story now. Then complete the exercise that follows.

Below is a list of events about Levi Strauss' life. Using information from the story on pages 146 to 148, speculate about what would have happened if these events had never occurred. Write sentences using past counterfactual conditionals.

FACTS ABOUT THE INVENTION AND POPULARITY OF BLUE JEANS

1. Levi Strauss invented blue jeans.

    If Levi Strauss had not invented blue jeans, he might not have become a wealthy man.

2. Strauss immigrated to N.Y. in 1848.
3. Strauss' brothers did not own land.
4. Strauss was not happy with his life in N.Y.
5. Strauss' sister sent him money.
6. Strauss dyed the canvas blue.
7. Jacob Davis met Alkali Ike.
8. Alkali Ike did not like the pockets on his jeans.
9. Strauss did not live past 1902.
10. The careless construction worker was wearing blue jeans.

PART 3: SENTENCE STRUCTURE AND GRAMMAR EXERCISES AS WORK IN PROGRESS

MIXED COUNTERFACTUAL CONDITIONALS: TO DESCRIBE PRESENT OR FUTURE INFERENCES DRAWN FROM UNREAL PAST EVENTS

Imagine that you want to tell your readers about a situation that did not happen in the past and the consequences of that inaction for the present or future (e.g., last night, you did not study for today's test, so you will probably fail the test today!). Or suppose you want to speculate or guess about how events might be different today or in the future if events in your past had been different (e.g., you didn't learn English as a child. What would be different about your life today if you had learned English then?).

VERB TENSES AND FORMS With mixed conditionals, the IF-clause describes an event or state that was not real at some time in the past. The independent clause describes something that is not real now or in the future.

In the **IF-clause**,	use →	past perfect	(*had* + past participle)
In the **independent clause**,	use →	*would* + main verb (certain) *could* + main verb (able) *might* + main verb (possible)	

Examples:

1. If Levi Strauss had stayed in N.Y., blue jeans might not be popular today.
2. Blue jeans would not have copper rivets today if Alkali Ike had never complained about his pockets always tearing.
3. If Strauss had not dyed the cotton cloth blue, we would probably call blue jeans "brown jeans" today.
4. Tourists to San Francisco could not easily learn about the history of blue jeans if the museum had never opened.

Exercise 11 Writing Mixed Counterfactual Conditionals: Think about the following historical events. Rewrite and complete each sentence with a clause that describes a present or future inference.

What would be different today . . .

1. if doctors had found a cure for AIDS before 1993?

    Tennis great Arthur Ashe would be alive today if doctors had found a cure for AIDS before 1993.

2. if the explorers who settled in North America had come from Spain?
3. if the American people had re-elected George Bush in 1992?
4. if the United States had never started a space exploration program?
5. if Henry Ford had never built a Model T car?
6. if personal computers had never been developed?

Exercise 12 **Writing Mixed Counterfactual Conditionals:** Think about your current living conditions and those of your classmates and friends. Imagine the following situations, all of which are counterfactual. Rewrite and complete each sentence by adding an IF-clause that describes past counterfactual events. Describe events that could have changed the course of your life.

1. I could not afford tuition this semester . . .

   I could not afford tuition this semester if the university had decided to double our fees.

2. My classmates could study my native language . . .
3. I wouldn't speak English every day . . .
4. We could write English fluently . . .
5. I could afford to buy a new house and car . . .
6. We might still be in our home countries . . .
7. My classmates and I would not be in English classes . . .

ADDITIONAL INFORMATION ABOUT CONDITIONALS

If is the most common connecting word to show a condition. The connecting words listed below all show conditions, but they have slightly different emphases in their meaning.

GIVING ADVICE OR INSTRUCTIONS **In case (that)** and **in the event that** are often used when giving advice or instructions. They introduce situations that may arise.

Examples: Carry a spare tire $\begin{bmatrix} \text{in case} \\ \text{in the event that} \end{bmatrix}$ you have a flat.

SPECIFYING NONNEGOTIABLE CONDITIONS **On condition that, provided that, so long as,** and **as long as** specify a condition to which another person must agree. They also carry the added idea of "if and ONLY if."

Examples: I will lend you my car $\begin{bmatrix} \text{on condition that} \\ \text{provided that} \\ \text{so long as} \\ \text{as long as} \end{bmatrix}$ you fill the tank.

USING "UNLESS" **Unless** means "except if."

Examples: Your driver's license is valid for four years unless it is revoked for some reason.

Do not take advanced calculus unless you are willing to work hard.

Part 3: Sentence Structure and Grammar Exercises as Work in Progress

Exercise 13 Read each of the following situations. Combine the sentence describing *the potential situation* and the sentence describing *the resulting action*. Use **in case (that)** or **in the event that.**

1. Imagine that you are taking the vision test for your driver's license.
   Potential situation: You need corrective lenses to pass the vision test.
   Resulting action: Your license will be restricted.

2. Imagine that you are driving down the highway.
   Potential situation: You get a flat tire on the highway.
   Resulting action: Pull the car off the road onto the shoulder.

3. Imagine that you are in an airplane.
   Potential situation: The cabin of the plane loses pressure.
   Resulting action: The overhead compartments will release oxygen masks.

Exercise 14 Read the pairs of sentences below. The first sentence describes a "non-negotiable" condition. The second sentence describes the result if the condition is met. Combine the sentence using **on condition that, provided that, so long as,** or **as long as.**

1. You present the necessary documents.
   The deputy will give you a temporary permit application.

2. The applicants meet all of the entrance requirements.
   The applicants will be accepted to the university.

3. I pass the TOEFL.
   I can begin studies next semester.

4. The benefits package includes comprehensive health insurance.
   I will take the job.

5. You have filed the correct forms.
   You should receive your refund in about a month.

Exercise 15 Rewrite and complete each of the following sentences.

1. My friends and I are going to a movie tonight unless . . .
2. My sister will graduate from the university next semester unless . . .
3. You should not sign up for fifteen credit hours unless . . .
4. A student cannot take advanced geometry unless . . .
5. You will not graduate unless . . .

Additional Practice Writing Conditionals

Exercise 16 Read the following sentences about New York City. After each one, write the time reference of the events described (past, present, future, or mixed) and whether the events are general truths or habits, predictions, advice, or counterfactuals.

Examples:

If you visit New York City, you will see magnificent sky scrapers.
future, prediction

If you were wealthy, you could stay in an expensive hotel.
present, counterfactual

CONDITIONALS

If you visit New York City, you should be cautious.
future, advice

1. If you go to see the New York Ballet, you will be impressed.

2. If I were with you, we could go to see the New York Ballet.

3. If you visit the city before the end of the month, go to the Museum of Modern Art. There is a wonderful exhibition there now.

4. You would not have been able to visit the Statue of Liberty if you had gone to N.Y. during its renovation.

5. If a person visits New York City, he needs a lot of money.

6. If Central Park had not been preserved for recreational purposes, it would probably be all skyscrapers and concrete today.

7. My roommate stays with friends if she goes to N.Y. She can save a lot of money this way.

Exercise 17 Using Conditionals to Describe Habits, Make Predictions, and Give Advice: Below you will find a short essay about the problem of dictionary dependence. Some of the sentences have been omitted from the essay. You will find those sentences decombined and listed in phrases after the essay. Compose complete sentences from the phrases given below, and in each one, use an adverb clause of condition. Use appropriate verb tenses and add modal verbs as necessary. Use the context of the essay and the flow of ideas to help you decide which clause order to use (that is, whether to put the dependent or the independent clause first). Number one has been done for you.

Are you dictionary-dependent? Many people who study a second language are. Their dictionaries are so dogged-eared from overuse that the cover is taped and many pages are worn. While they are reading, they stop and look up every unknown word; they can't continue reading unless they know the meaning of every single word in every single sentence.

1) *If they do not have their dictionaries with them, they cannot read anything*.

And while these language learners often think they are using the only strategy possible, the truth is that this overuse of the dictionary can impede progress in reading.

2) _____.

Read about some of the ways this over-reliance on the dictionary may be harming you.

First, 3) _____
_____. You might lose the thread of the ideas and forget what you just finished reading. 4) _____
_____. This can make your reading process incredibly slow. Also, most words in a language have more than one meaning. 5) _____
_____. However, no dictionary contains all of the possible meanings and usages of all words. Thus, sometimes the dictionary can mislead you. Furthermore, 6) _____
_____. Unfortunately, these small dictionaries are too limited for the needs of an advanced learner.

PART 3: SENTENCE STRUCTURE AND GRAMMAR EXERCISES AS WORK IN PROGRESS

7) _____

_____. This other strategy involves relying on the context to help you understand the meaning of new words. Using the context to figure out the meaning of unknown words is like being a detective; you look for clues to help you discover the mystery word.

8) _____.

---

1. a. they / not have / their dictionaries / with them   (condition)
   b. they / not read / anything   (result)

2. a. you / be / dictionary-dependent   (condition)
   b. read on   (result)

3. a. you / stop / at every new word   (condition)
   b. you / lose / the writer's train of thought   (result)

4. a. this / happen   (condition)
   b. you / have to reread / earlier sections of the text   (result)

5. a. your dictionary / be / fairly comprehensive   (condition)
   b. you / find / thorough explanations of the words   (result)

6. a. you / not want to carry / a 1500-page dictionary / at all times   (condition)
   b. you / sometimes / use / a small pocket dictionary   (result)

7. a. you / use / your dictionary / for every / new word   (condition)
   b. you / not use / another important reading strategy   (result)

8. a. you / come across / an unknown word   (condition)
   b. you / imagine / that you / be / Sherlock Holmes   (result)

Exercise 18 Are you superstitious? Read through the following sentences about Elizabeth, an American student who has developed a fear of Friday the 13th. Then rewrite them in paragraph form, combining each set of sentences into one and rewriting the others. For some of the combinations, use the sentence pattern indicated in parentheses. For the others, choose any pattern that makes sense.

1. a. Some people in the United States get nervous when Friday falls on the 13th of the month.
   b. is is considered an unlucky day.

2. a. They have something important planned.
   b. They postpone it until the 14th. (Use an IF-clause.)

3. a. Elizabeth is one of these people.
   b. They believe in the bad luck of Friday the 13th.

4. a. She developed this fear several years ago.
   b. She had many bad experiences one Friday the 13th.

5. a. She woke up that morning.
   b. She saw a black cat outside her window.

6. a. The cat was there, so the day started out badly. (Rewrite this sentence using a counterfactual IF-clause.)

7. a. Elizabeth stepped out of the shower.
   b. She slipped on a piece of soap.
   c. She fell down.

8. a. The soap was there, so she fell. (Rewrite this sentence using a counterfactual IF-clause.)

9. a. She hurt her shoulder and back.
   b. She felt good enough to go to school.

10. a. She got dressed.
    b. She ate breakfast.
    c. She walked out of her apartment building.
    d. She walked right under a ladder.

11. a. The ladder was resting against the building next to her front door, so she didn't see it in time. (Rewrite this sentence using a counterfactual IF-clause.)

12. a. Elizabeth was crossing the street.
    b. A car almost hit her.

13. a. The driver slowed down, so he didn't hit Elizabeth. (Rewrite this sentence using a counterfactual IF-clause.)

14. a. Elizabeth went to sit down on a park bench for a few minutes.
    b. She wanted to calm down.

15. a. She sat down.
    b. She heard a "crunching" sound under her foot.

16. a. She looked down.
    b. She saw a mirror.
    c. She had broken it with her foot.

17. a. She decided to sit and relax, so she broke the mirror. (Rewrite this sentence using a counterfactual IF-clause.)

18. a. Then she looked to her left.
    b. She saw a "wet paint" sign on the bench.
    c. City workers had painted it early that morning.

19. a. The bench needed new paint, so the city workers had painted it. (Rewrite this sentence using a counterfactual IF-clause.)

20. a. All of these events have made Elizabeth a very superstitious person.
    b. These events happened one Friday the 13th.

21. a. She always thinks the worst will happen.
    b. She carries several good luck charms.

22. a. She carries a rabbit's foot.
    b. She carries a four-leaf clover.
    c. She carries a lucky penny.
    d. She carries a horse shoe.

23. a. She carries these objects forever.
    b. She has good luck. (Use an IF-clause.)

24. a. Many of Elizabeth's friends think she is crazy.
    b. She carries all of these objects.

25. a. Her family knows what happened to Elizabeth on that Friday the 13th.
    b. They understand her fears.

26. a. Her family members know about her experiences, so they tolerate her strange behavior. (Rewrite this sentence using a counterfactual IF-clause.)

PART 3: SENTENCE STRUCTURE AND GRAMMAR EXERCISES AS WORK IN PROGRESS

COORDINATION

Coordination is a way to connect ideas of equal importance within a sentence. Coordinating conjunctions connect words, phrases, and clauses and signal the meaning relationships between the linked ideas.

There are two types of coordinating conjunctions: simple (one-word) coordinators and correlative conjunctions, those with two parts.

SIMPLE COORDINATING CONJUNCTIONS

COORDINATORS	
Cause-Effect	so, for
Addition	and, nor
Concession/Contrast	but, yet
Alternative	or

Examples with Simple Coordinating Conjunctions:

1. My government offered me a scholarship, so I came to study in the U.S.
2. I am always prepared for every class, for I spend five hours every night on my homework.
3. After graduation, I will look for a position with a large company in my country, or I will pursue a master's degree here in the United States.
4. I am undecided about my major, but I have narrowed the possibilities to two. I will study architecture or graphic design.
5. This university does not admit international students with a TOEFL score of less than 500, nor does it offer language courses for students who need more work with English.
6. This university employs world-renowned scholars, and it has excellent research facilities.
7. My favorite subjects in high school were math, biology, and physics.
8. I have a scholarship for my studies, yet I still find it difficult to make ends meet.
9. I took a philosophy course last semester. I found it difficult yet rewarding.
10. My G.P.A. from high school is excellent, but my TOEFL score is low.
11. I enjoy mysteries but hate science fiction.

NOTES:

① All seven simple coordinating conjunctions can combine independent clauses. The conjunctions **and, but, or** and **yet** can coordinate words and phrases as well as clauses. Examples 1, 2, 3, 4, 5, 6, 8, and 10 above show coordination of independent clauses. Examples, 4, 7, 9, and 11 illustrate coordination of words and phrases.

② When coordinating conjunctions combine independent clauses, a comma follows the first clause. When coordinating clauses combine two words or phrases, no comma is used. When **and** combines three or more words or phrases in a series, use a comma between the items and before **and.**

3. The coordinating conjunction **nor** connects two negative clauses. **Nor** carries the negative for the verb in the second clause, and, because it starts the second clause, the negative inversion rule applies. This means that the verb in the second clauses uses question word order. See example #5 above.

4. The coordinating conjunction **so** introduces the *effect-clause* in a cause-effect relationship.

   Example:

   I finally passed the TOEFL, so I can start my academic courses next semester.
         (cause)   (effect)

   The coordinating conjunction **for** introduces the *cause-clause* in a cause-effect relationship.

   Example:

   I can start my academic courses next semester, for I finally passed the TOEFL.
        (effect)   (cause)

5. The coordinating conjunction **but** is used to show contrast and concession; **yet** is most often used to show concession.

   Example:

   Maria has only completed one semester of English, yet she hopes to begin her academic courses next semester.

   Maria applied to the university three months ago, but she has not received a reply.

CORRELATIVE CONJUNCTIONS

COORDINATORS	
Addition	both . . . and, not only . . . but also neither . . . nor
Alternative	either . . . or

Examples with Correlative Conjunctions:

1. A person can learn a language in either a formal, classroom setting or an informal, natural environment.

2. Both formal and informal environments can help second language learners improve quickly.

3. Studying a language in a classroom setting provides a secure environment for not only making mistakes but also learning from them.

4. I know that neither a teacher nor a test can accurately determine my progress in English.

5. Not only are successful language learners tolerant of ambiguities, but they also seek out opportunities to use their second language.

PART 3: SENTENCE STRUCTURE AND GRAMMAR EXERCISES AS WORK IN PROGRESS

NOTES:

① **Both . . . and** and **neither . . . nor** connect words and phrases. **Not only . . . but also** and **either . . . or** connect words, phrases, and clauses.

② When **not only . . . but also** connects two clauses, the first clause is introduced by "not only" and the negative inversion rule applies. This means that the verb in the first clause uses question word order. See example #5 below.

PARALLELISM

When a writer presents coordinated ideas (two or more ideas in a series) within a sentence, those ideas should be presented in similar grammatical structures. This principle is known as parallelism. By using the same structures, the writer keeps the readers on track and helps them clearly understand the relationship between the ideas.

The simple and correlative conjunctions in the charts above are often used to present two or more ideas in a series. Therefore, when you use these words, you should be sure that your ideas are parallel.

Note the use of parallelism in the sentences below. Parallel words and phrases are underlined.

1. <u>Both doctors and nutritionists</u> agree that <u>vegetables and fruits</u> are essential to a healthy diet.
2. <u>Neither doctors nor researchers</u> are completely sure of the benefits of vitamin supplements.
3. Some people believe that vitamins <u>not only supplement their diets but also fight off heart disease and cancer</u>.
4. Vitamins come from two sources: They are <u>either produced within the body or ingested</u>.
5. <u>Not only children but also senior citizens</u> can benefit from vitamin supplements.
6. <u>Not only can vitamins supplement deficiencies in our diets, but they can also reduce the risk of some diseases</u>.
7. If people <u>can't eat a balanced diet or don't eat much</u>, they might consider taking vitamin supplements.
8. People who are <u>healthy but fatigued</u> might benefit from vitamin pills.
9. Many people wonder <u>how many vitamins are needed and what is the best way to get them</u>.
10. Should people get vitamins <u>in food or in pills</u>?

NOTES:

① Parallelism can apply at the phrase and clause level of structure. Sentences 1, 2, and 5 above show parallel noun phrases; sentences 3, 4, and 7 show parallel verb phrases; sentence 8 shows parallel adjective phrases; sentence 10 shows parallel prepositional phrases. Sentences 6 and 9 show parallel clauses.

② Remember that when **not only . . . but also** is used with two clauses, the first clause is introduced by **not only**. The negative inversion rule applies, so the main verb in the first clause should use question word order. See the example below and example #6 above.

Not only do vitamins supply important nutrients, but they also fight off certain diseases.

COORDINATION

③ When you use **either . . . or, neither . . . nor,** and **not only . . . but also** with subjects, the proximity principle applies. The proximity principle determines subject-verb agreement; the noun closest to the verb governs the verb.

1. a. Neither doctors nor the foremost researcher in the field of nutrition is sure about the benefits of vitamin supplements.
   b. Neither the foremost researcher in the field of nutrition nor doctors are sure about the benefits of vitamin supplements.
2. a. Either vitamin pills or a balanced diet is necessary for good health.
   b. Either a balanced diet or vitamin pills are necessary for good health.

PRACTICE IDENTIFYING AND WRITING PARALLEL STRUCTURES

Exercise 1 Analyze the example sentences on pages 212 and 213. Underline the parallel structures and circle the coordinating conjunctions in each example.

Exercise 2 Rewrite and complete the sentences below by adding information that will logically complete the meaning. Make the information that you add parallel to the underlined structure.

1. Many students in the United States wonder how they will cover the rising cost of <u>tuition</u> and . . .
2. Many students in the United States wonder <u>how they will survive their academic programs</u> and . . .
3. <u>Not only is the tuition rising every year</u>, but . . .
4. Students are faced <u>not only with higher tuition costs</u> but also . . .
5. Some students will have to <u>either work part time</u> or . . .
6. <u>The high cost of tuition</u>, . . ., and . . . are making it more and more difficult for some students to get a higher education.
7. Confronted with the decision <u>to delay college</u>, . . ., or . . ., some students try to come up with creative solutions to the problem.
8. For many students, neither <u>student loans</u> nor . . . will be enough to ease the burden of the cost of higher education.

PRACTICE USING SIMPLE COORDINATION

Exercise 3 Combine the following sets of sentences using a simple coordinating conjunction from the list on page 212. Be sure that the coordinated structures are parallel.

1. I came to this university. The chemical engineering program is world-renowned.
2. I like living here. I will stay here for a few years.
3. I like living here. I will probably move back to my hometown after I graduate.
4. Because this university does not offer computer engineering, I will transfer after next semester. I will change my major.

PART 3: SENTENCE STRUCTURE AND GRAMMAR EXERCISES AS WORK IN PROGRESS

5. My advisor recommended that I take nine credit hours my first semester. Twelve would be too many to manage.

6. For some people, living in a new country is exciting. It helps them learn more about themselves and their native culture.

7. For other people, living in a new country is not exciting. It is not rewarding.

8. When universities experience financial difficulties, they raise tuition. They cut services.

PRACTICE USING CORRELATIVE CONJUNCTIONS

Exercise 4 The sentences below are about an important archaeological discovery made in 1991. Two hikers in the Alps discovered the remains of a 5,300-year-old man on the border between Austria and Italy. Named the Iceman, the body is the oldest intact human ever found. See page 183 for some introductory sentences about the Iceman. Then, read and combine the following sets of sentences using a correlative conjunction from the list on page 213. Be sure that the coordinated structures are parallel.

1. The hikers did not realize the significance of the discovery.
   The initial rescuers did not realize the significance of the discovery.

2. Austria claimed the Iceman as its own.
   Italy claimed the Iceman as its own.

3. The rescuers found the Iceman's body.
   They also retrieved pieces of clothing and equipment.

4. The Iceman left his group to find material for tools.
   He left his group to hunt for food.

Exercise 5 Imagine that you are trying to find a new roommate for next semester. You have been interviewing possible roommates all week and have narrowed your choices to the two people described below. Now you are trying to decide which person to live with. To help you clarify your thoughts, freewrite some sentences about your choices. Use a correlative conjunction in each sentence.

CHRIS	TERRY
will be my roommate??	will be my roommate??
has not lived with a foreign student before	has not lived with a foreign student before
is extroverted	is shy and quiet
seems friendly	seems friendly
studies hard	studies hard
stays up late	goes to bed early
sleeps late	gets up early
likes to party	likes to read
listens to loud music	listens to classical music
does not clean	seems tidy
does not cook	is an excellent cook
is interested in international affairs	is interested in international affairs
does not like pets	loves dogs and cats
will major in math??	is a music major
will major in physics??	will work in McDonald's??
will live with me??	will get a job on campus??
will move back home??	

Examples:

1. Either Chris or Terry will be my roommate next semester.
2. Both Terry and I like to read.

DISCOURSE THREADS

A well written American English text is coherent; that is, the ideas of each sentence build on the preceding ideas and add to them. A coherent text flows smoothly, so the reader can follow the ideas easily.

When you organize your ideas and consider the global structure of a paper, you are paying attention to coherence. You should also think about coherence when you are analyzing and revising your sentences. One way to achieve coherence in your writing is through the use of **discourse threads,** grammatical and vocabulary patterns that help maintain the flow of ideas.

Discourse threads are like street signs. To understand this comparison, think about street signs for a minute. What do they do? They guide people around the streets of a city and keep them going in the right direction. When you know where you are going, for example, when you are in a familiar neighborhood, you do not pay conscious attention to the street signs; you do not have to because you understand where you are going and your trip is easy and smooth. However, when you travel to new neighborhoods, the street signs become very importnat. You stop and look at each one to check your progress and make sure that you are going in the right direction.

Like street signs, discourse threads in a written text guide the reading process. When you are writing for others, you will use threads to help your readers get through your texts and understand your ideas easily. The threads will keep your readers on the right track.

Part 3: Sentence Structure and Grammar Exercises as Work in Progress

Some threads in English refer to previously mentioned ideas and serve as a tie between "given" information and "new" information. "Given" information is information that you have already told your readers earlier in the text. New information is built on—or added to—what you have already mentioned. An example of this type of thread is a *pronoun;* a pronoun usually refers back to a noun that was previously mentioned.

Other threads establish the meaning relationship between two ideas to serve as bridges, links, or transitions between them. An example of this kind of thread is a *sentence connector*.

Below is a list of some of the common discourse threads used in English. The examples come from, or have been adapted from, the article "The Jeaning of America—and the World"; see pages 146 to 148.

Common Discourse Threads

PRONOUNS (PRO) Use personal pronouns (e.g., *she, her, he, him, it, they*) and demonstrative pronouns (e.g., *this, that, these, those*) to refer back to previously mentioned nouns or ideas. This makes your writing economical by avoiding unnecessary repetitions.

Example:

When **Strauss** ran out of canvas, **he** wrote **his** two brothers to send more.

Example:

When Strauss arrived in N.Y., he found **that his brothers were not wealthy landowners but peddlers. This** surprised him.

REPETITION (REP) Repeat the same word across two sentences or use a word from the same word family. When you repeat a noun, use *the, this, that, these, those* + a noun phrase.

Example:

This is the story of a sturdy American **symbol** which has now spread throughout most of the world. **The symbol** is not the dollar. It is a simple pair of pants called blue jeans, and what the pants **symbolize** is what Alexis de Tocqueville called "a manly and legitimate passion for equality. . . ."

SYNONYMS (SYN) Use a word which has the same meaning as a previously mentioned word. You might use synonyms that are different parts of speech. When the synonym is a noun, use *the, this, that, these, those* + a noun phrase.

Example:

Once again, **the idea** worked so well that the word got around; in 1873 Strauss appropriated and patented **the gimmick**.

CLASSIFIERS (CLASS) Use a noun phrase to classify or generalize a word or idea stated earlier in the text. The noun phrase can substitute for a word, phrase, or entire clause. You will often use *the, this, that, these, those* + a noun phrase. You can also use *such* + a noun phrase.

Example:

> When a married sister in San Francisco offered to pay his way West in 1850, he jumped at the opportuntiy, taking with him bolts of canvas he hoped to sell for **tenting.** It was the wrong kind of canvas for **that purpose,** but . . . .

Example:

> As a kind of joke, Davis took the pants to a blacksmith and **had the pockets riveted;** once again, **the idea** worked so well that the word got around . . . .

Example:

> Instead, he found them pushing **needles, thread, pots, pans, ribbons, yarn, scissors and buttons** to housewives. For two years he was a lowly peddler, hauling some 180 pounds of **sundries** door-to-door. . . .

Example:

> It was Jacob W. Davis, a tailor from Virginia City, Nevada, who first **added the copper rivets to the pockets of a pair of Levis.** How did he come up with **such an idea**?

CONNECTING WORDS (CON WORD) You can use sentence connectors, coordinating conjunctions, and subordinating conjunctions to signal meaning relationships across the clauses. (For information about sentence connectors, see pages 237 to 240; about coordinating conjunctions, see pages 212 to 217; about subordinating conjunctions, see pages 184 to 191 and pages 196 to 211.)

Example:

> They were landowners, they had told him; **instead,** he found them pushing needles, thread, pots . . .

PRACTICE USING DISCOURSE THREADS

Exercise 1 Read through the text, "The Jeaning of America—and the World," looking for examples of the discourse threads described above. Underline and label several examples of each type of thread. You will find this text on pages 146 to 148.

Exercise 2 Read through another text of your choice. Look for and underline examples of the discourse threads described above. Share your findings with another writer or a small group of writers in your class.

Exercise 3 Read through the first part of one student writer's draft in which she shared her expertise about sailing. Fill in each blank with an appropriate discourse thread. Note that in some instances, more than one correct answer is possible.

PART 3: SENTENCE STRUCTURE AND GRAMMAR EXERCISES AS WORK IN PROGRESS

Imagine the huge ocean, the blue sky, and the warm sun. You are sailing, crossing the crystalline water. You can feel the force of the wind against your face. The view is marvelous. Don't you think you should try it?

Mainly a summer sport, sailing is a fantastic way to exercise and have great experiences. As a beginner, you must have some theoretical ideas about the sailboat; (1) _____ will help you understand why the boat moves the way that it does.

There are many different kinds of sailboats. If you start sailing young, like at the age of eight until eleven years old, there are small (2) _____ (about 1.5 meters long and less than a meter wide) called "Optimis." (3) _____ don't sail fast because the stern, the front part, and the aft, the back part, are cut; they don't have a sharp shape. Other sailboats, like the 4-20 and the 4-70, are bigger, about 2.5 meters long. Different from the Optimis, which is used by only one person, the 4-20 and 4-70 are used by two people. One navigator is responsible for the helm, which is made of wood or metallic material and is used to control the direction of the boat. (4) _____ takes care of the sails and the balance of the boat. Two other sailboats are the Puma and the Furia, distinguished by small differences in their shapes. (5) _____ have to be sailed by at least three (6) _____.

Now that you know a little about different types of sailboats, let's focus on just the 4-20. See Figure A, which shows the main parts of (7) _____.

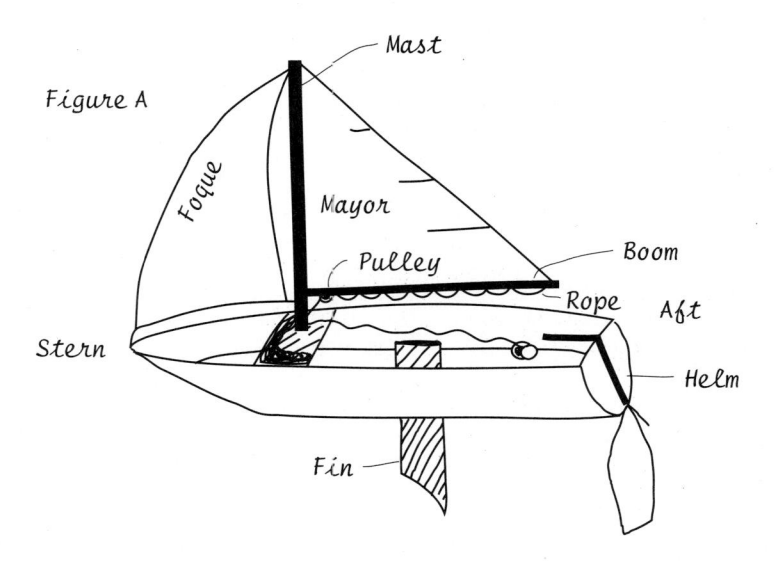

Figure A

Labels: Mast, Foque, Mayor, Pulley, Boom, Rope, Aft, Helm, Stern, Fin

When sailing a 4-20, one of the (8) _____ must sit at the back of the boat and never lose the helm. The fin under the sailboat helps to control the balance. The 4-20 has different sails, but the principal ones are "la mayor" and "el foque." Depending on the direction of the wind, you set (9) _____ in one position or another. If (10) _____ blows from the aft, you have to loosen some or most of the rope from the mayor sail so that the boom becomes perpendicular to the sailboat. With (11) _____ you catch more wind and can move faster. See Figure B. If the wind comes from the stern, you have to grab the rope and keep the boom near the sailboat; see Figure C.

Figure B

Figure C

Exercise 4 Read through the first part of one student writer's draft in which he shared his experience about learning how to swim. Fill in each blank with an appropriate discourse thread. Note that in some instances, more than one correct answer is possible.

Many people are afraid to swim. Some have had a bad experience in the water, others don't know the proper technique, and still others are hydrophobic. (1) _____ prevent these people from enjoying the wonderful sport of swimming. If you are afraid to swim, ask yourself "why?" before you read this article.

At the age of eight, I went swimming for the first time with my cousin. When I saw the swimming pool, I leaped into the water even though I knew nothing about how to swim. Although I was in the shallow part of (2) _____ and the water was only to my chest, I didn't know (3) _____. I thought I was in over my head. I tried to catch something to hang onto, but there was nothing. I struggled, drank in a lot of water, became scared and screamed. Hopeless, helpless, and hapless, I thought I was going to drown. Fortunately, I ultimately caught a rope from a lifeguard who hauled me up from the pool. It was like a nightmare; (4) _____ caused me to be afraid of swimming.

I didn't go swimming again for several years until I saw a movie about a man who feared to swim, just like me. Because of (5) _____ of the water, he lost a dear friend who drowned in the ocean while they were on vacation. He just stood on the beach and watched his friend disappear. Everyone was trying to save her, but he was afraid to even touch the water. (6) _____ made me think about my inability to swim. I didn't want to be like (7) _____. Besides, some of my friends always teased me. I decided to learn to swim.

PART 3: SENTENCE STRUCTURE AND GRAMMAR EXERCISES AS WORK IN PROGRESS

Even though knowing the proper swimming technique was important, conquering my mind was more (8) _____. I told myself that I could do what others could do. Did I want to be teased all the time? Did I want to be like the man in the movie? Was it reasonable to fear swimming when I had only tried one time? It was my mistake that I had leaped into the water without knowing how to swim. (9) _____ didn't mean that I had no potential for swimming. Why did I fear swimming without really trying? How did I know it was hard? Whenever I felt fear about learning how to swim, (10) _____ came into my head and pushed me to try.

The first time back in the water, I was scared. With encouragement from my family, friends, the instructor and particularly my own firm aspiration, I gradually walked into a swimming pool. Learning started by kicking my legs on the surface of the water; (11) _____ took me two days to master. When I was used to kicking, I started learning breath control, a vital (12) _____ in swimming. Although I felt fear every time I got in the water, I encouraged myself by posing the questions listed above. Day by day, (13) _____ disappeared.

After my fear disappeared and I had become used to the water, it was time to try real swimming. First was the crawl. I turned over, made my body parallel to the surface of the water, and swung my arms. After around two weeks, I tried the backstroke; (14) _____ was similar to the crawl, just moving on my back. I kept practicing (15) _____ until I was comfortable with both of them. Then, I went on to the advanced strokes: the breast stroke, in which the swimmer acts like a frog, and the butterfly. Both of (16) _____ needed lots of skill. I've been practicing (17) _____ for about ten years now, so today, I can swim very well. In fact, swimming is my favorite sport.

If you are afraid of swimming, ask yourself "why?" again. Do you want to learn to swim? I hope that my experience can encourage and help you reach your goal. I don't want you to be like the man in the movie. Some day, you will be proud of yourself and see that you are lucky because you can swim. It's never too late. Be brave and start now.

NOUN CLAUSES

Noun clauses function as nouns in a sentence; that is, they can be subjects, objects, or complements. Because they are dependent clauses, they must be included in an independent clause.

Remember:	• A clause in English contains at least a **SUBJECT** and a **PREDICATE**. • The predicate consists of a main verb and any auxiliary verbs. • A simple sentence consists of one independent clause. • A complex sentence consists of two or more clauses (e.g., two independent clauses; one independent and one or more dependent clauses).

THAT-CLAUSES

Noun clauses formed from statements are introduced by the word **that.**

Examples:

1. Many people believe **that avalanches do not pose serious risks for skiers.**
    (object of the verb "believe")

2. This belief, **that avalanches are not serious,** can result in tragedy.
    (nonrestrictive appositive, explaining the word "belief")

3. **That avalanche deaths occur each winter** should alert people to the risks.
    (subject of the verb "alert")

4. The fact **that people have survived avalanches** is a miracle.
    (restrictive appositive, explaining the word "fact")

5. One problem is **that some skiers are unprepared for changes in the weather.**
    (complement after the verb "is")

6. Some people are surprised **that the weather can change so quickly.**
    (complement after the adjective "surprised")

With some nouns and adjectives, two THAT-clause patterns are possible. When writing, you should use the pattern that maintains the flow and balance of ideas within the context that you have set. Usually, Pattern B is preferred when the THAT-clause is long and complex.

PATTERN A:	THAT-clause + *to be* + [noun / adjective].
PATTERN B:	It + *to be* + [noun / adjective] + THAT-clause.

7. **That the skiers survived** was a miracle.

8. It was a miracle **that the skiers survived.**

9. **That people die in avalanches every year** is unfortunate.

10. It is unfortunate **that people die in avalanches every year.**

PART 3: SENTENCE STRUCTURE AND GRAMMAR EXERCISES AS WORK IN PROGRESS

NOTES:

① When the THAT-clause is a direct object or a complement, you can omit the connecting word "that."

Examples:

Many people believe **avalanches do not pose serious risks for skiers.**

One problem is **some skiers are unprepared for changes in the weather.**

Some people are surprised **the weather can change so quickly.**

② When the THAT-clause comes in subject position, it often follows a head noun such as "fact," "idea," "belief," or "news." In this case, the THAT-clause is an appositive. See examples 2 and 4 above. (For more information about appositives, see pages 193 to 195.)

WH-CLAUSES

Noun clauses formed from WH-questions are introduced by the WH-question words: *who, whom, what, why, when, where, how, which,* and *whose.*

Examples:

1. **Where people can ski safely** is not always easy to judge.
   (subject of the verb "is")

2. I do not understand **why anyone would ski avalanche terrain without a beacon.**
   (object of the verb "understand")

3. **Why anyone would ski avalanche terrain without a beacon** is a mystery.
   (subject of the verb "is")

4. One concern for avalanche victims is **how they can prevent frostbite.**
   (complement after the verb "is")

5. All skiers must know **what they should do in an avalanche.**
   (object of the verb "know")

6. Some skiers can't judge **when it is wiser to stay home and not ski.**
   (object of the verb "judge")

7. The judgment, **when it is safe to ski,** is not always an easy one.
   (an appositive explaining the word "judgment")

8. **Who survives an avalanche** is sometimes a matter of luck.
   (Subject of the verb "is")

NOTES:

① In noun clauses, the WH words DO NOT signal questions. For this reason, use statement word order inside the WH-clause, not question word order.

Examples:

Some people asked this question: "Why did the skiers go out in bad conditions?"

Some people asked **why the skiers went out in bad conditions.**

② WH-clauses (except those introduced by "why") can sometimes be reduced to infinitive phrases if the subject of the infinitive phrase is clear to the reader.

Examples:

Where to ski safely is not always easy to judge.

One concern for avalanche victims is **how to prevent frostbite.**

All skiers must know **what to do in an avalanche.**

③ For more information about appositives (see example 7 above), see pages 193 to 195.

IF/WHETHER-CLAUSES

Noun clauses formed from *yes/no* questions are introduced by **if** or **whether.**

Examples:

1. **Whether a person survives an avalanche** depends on skill and luck.
    (subject of the verb "depends on")
2. The skiers wondered **if they would survive.**
    (object of the verb "wondered")
3. **Whether conditions are safe enough** is a question that every skier must ask.
    (subject of the verb "is")
4. The question, **whether conditions are safe,** is not always easy to answer.
    (appositive explaining the word "question")

NOTES:

① You can add "or not" to clauses with **if** or **whether.** Study the examples below to see the patterns with "or not."

Examples:

The skiers wondered **whether they would survive or not.**

The skiers wondered **whether or not they would survive.**

The skiers wondered **if they would survive or not.**

② When the noun clause is in subject position, use **whether.** See examples 1 and 3 above.

PART 3: SENTENCE STRUCTURE AND GRAMMAR EXERCISES AS WORK IN PROGRESS

THAT-CLAUSES OF REQUEST OR URGENCY

The verbs and adjectives listed below express the idea of a request, an order, advice, or urgency. They are followed by THAT-clauses which contain a subjunctive verb. The subjunctive verb form is always the base form.

VERBS

advise	direct	prefer	suggest
ask	forbid	propose	urge
beg	insist	recommend	
command	move	request	
demand	order	require	

ADJECTIVES

advisable	desirable	important	right
best	essential	mandatory	urgent
better	fitting	necessary	vital
crucial	imperative	proper	wise

Examples:

1. Ski patrol members **recommend** that a back country skier **wear** an avalanche beacon.
2. It is **advisable** that any person skiing in a remote area **carry** a shovel and supplies.
3. That a skier **dress** properly is **imperative**.

NOTES:

① The adjectives listed above are often used after "It is . . ." and before a THAT-clause. When the THAT-clause is long and complex, the pattern with "it is" is preferred.

② The use of the subjunctive verb is appropriate for formal written English. You can use **should** + base form in informal situations.

Examples:

My friend suggested that we **should** rent avalanche beacons at the local ski shop.

PRACTICE USING NOUN CLAUSES

For Exercises 1 to 3:

In February 1993, five cross-country skiers in Colorado survived five days in a blizzard. The sentences below are about their experience and about avalanche survival in general. Combine each pair of sentences using a noun clause.

Noun Clauses

Exercise 1 Combine these sentences using THAT-clauses.

1. Rescuers feared *this*. The five cross-country skiers were lost in an avalanche.
2. *This* was amazing. The skiers came out alive.
3. *It* seemed foolhardy. Some of the skiers didn't bring waterproof gear.
4. *The fact* helped the skiers survive. They were all expert mountain climbers.
5. Many skiers do not realize *this*. Avalanches are often unpredictable.
6. Ski patrol squads urge *this*. A skier stays within ski area boundaries.

Exercise 2 Combine these sentences using WH-clauses.

1. Many people asked *this*. Why did the skiers go out in such dangerous conditions?
2. *This* posed a major problem for the skiers. How would they shelter themselves at night?
3. The first night out, the skiers decided *this*. Where should they dig a snow cave?
4. The rescuers wondered *this*. When would the weather break?
5. Because of the weather conditions, the ski patrol was unsure about *this*. What could they do to save the skiers?

Exercise 3 Combine these sentences using IF/WHETHER-clauses.

1. The resucers wondered *this*. Would the skiers make it?
2. Will a buried skier survive an avalanche? *This* depends on how quickly he is found.
3. In the backwoods, it is difficult to determine *this*. Are the conditions safe?
4. At the trailhead, a local resident asked *this*. Had the skiers heard the weather forecast?
5. Did the skiers act carelessly? *This* was a matter of opinion.

Exercise 4 Imagine that your friend's brother is planning to travel overseas for the first time. Before the trip, you write a letter to your friend, including some advice and some orders for your friend's brother and his family.

Complete these sentences with your advice and orders:

1. I suggest that your brother . . .
2. Your parents should insist . . .
3. Your parents should request . . .
4. It is important . . .
5. It is vital . . .
6. It is best that you . . .

SUGGESTIONS • SUGGESTIONS • SUGGESTIONS • SUGGESTIONS

For more information and practice with noun clauses, see:

Reported Speech . . . . pages 233 to 237

PART 3: SENTENCE STRUCTURE AND GRAMMAR EXERCISES AS WORK IN PROGRESS

PASSIVE CONSTRUCTIONS

Passive constructions are frequently used in scientific and official writing, where an impersonal style is appropriate. A passive construction focuses the readers' attention on the action of the verb and on the receiver of that action, not on the performer. In a passive construction:

(1) The person or thing which **receives** the action is mentioned first. In other words, in the subject position of the sentence, the writer places the name of the person or thing on which the action is performed.

(2) The verb describes the **action.**

(3) The **performer,** that is, the person or thing that carries out or does the action, is mentioned after the verb, if necessary, or not at all.

EXAMPLES OF PASSIVE CONSTRUCTIONS Study the following examples of sentences with passive constructions. Answer the questions that follow each example. Note: All of the sentences describe the process of applying to a university.

1. *The application form is filled out.*
   a. What is the action? _____
   b. Who or what receives the action? _____
   c. Who or what performs the action? _____

2. *This form is submitted to the admissions office.*
   a. What is the action? _____
   b. Who or what receives the action? _____
   c. Who or what performs the action? _____

3. *The application form must be signed by the applicant.*
   a. What is the action? _____
   b. Who or what receives the action? _____
   c. Who or what performs the action? _____

4. *Official transcripts are required and should be sent directly to the admissions office.*
   a. What are the actions? _____
   b. Who or what receives the actions? _____
   c. Who or what performs the first action? _____
      the second action? _____

5. *A financial statement has to be furnished with the application.*
   a. What is the action? _____
   b. Who or what receives the action? _____
   c. Who or what performs the action? _____

6. *All decisions regarding the applicant's status will be made as soon as the relevant documents are received.*

   a. What are the actions? _____

   b. Who or what receives the first action? _____
      the second action? _____

   c. Who or what performs the first action? _____
      the second action? _____

7. *The applicant is notified by mail, usually within four weeks.*

   a. What is the action? _____

   b. Who or what receives the action? _____

   c. Who or what performs the action? _____

FORMING THE PASSIVE To form a passive construction:

① The receiver of the action is placed in subject position.

② The verb consists of the verb **to be** + **the past participle of the main verb.** The verb **to be** carries the tense of the sentence. In other words, the verb **to be** expresses the time reference for the sentence.

③ The verb is followed by the preposition **by** + **the performer of the action,** if necessary. The **BY-phrase** is omitted when:
   a. The performer is unknown.
   b. It is not necessary or important for the reader to know who or what the performer is.
   c. The reader already knows who or what the performer is through the context.

PRACTICE USING PASSIVE CONSTRUCTIONS

Exercise 1 To see how a writer can use passive constructions effectively in his writing, read through the essay below. It describes how to get a driver's license in Ohio. Underline all the passive constructions that you can find. For each construction, identify the performer, the action, and the receiver of the action.

Part 3: Sentence Structure and Grammar Exercises as Work in Progress

Although every state in the U.S. has its own requirements for obtaining a driver's license, the requirements in Ohio are typical of many states. The first step is to visit the nearest deputy registrar office where driver's licenses are issued and apply for the license. You must bring documentary proof of your age, identity and Social Security number. A birth certificate and Social Security card are normally required, but other documents identifying the Social Security number are acceptable: military records, state photo identification, or official correspondence from the IRS, banking institutions or insurance companies. After checking your birth certificate, the deputy will complete your application and give you a temporary permit application packet. Do not fold, tear off or write on any of the forms in your application packet. These forms must be retained and taken with you through each step of the licensing process. At this time, certain fees must also be paid.

After you receive your application packet, you should go to an Ohio Highway Patrol driver's license station to take the written and vision exams. No appointment is required. The written exam is divided into two sections: one section on laws (20 questions) and the other on signs (20 questions). The questions are multiple choice and are based on the material in the "Digest of Ohio Motor Vehicle Laws." At this station, your vision will also be tested to determine if it meets minimum standards established by law. If you need corrective lenses to meet these standards, your license may be restricted to driving only when you are wearing such lenses.

The next step in getting your Ohio license is the road test. An appointment must be made for this test. The road test has two parts—driving and a maneuverability test. During the driving test, the examiner will ask you to perform a number of driving tasks. These may include stopping and starting; turning around; backing up; making proper left and right turns; and giving hand signals or using mechanical turn signals. You will not be asked to do anything against the law, and the examiner will not try to "trick" you. The maneuverability test is conducted in two steps. Each step is to be completed in one continuous motion. The only instructions that you will be given by the examiner will be to steer to the right or left of a point marker.

When you have successfully completed your road test, the examiner will give you an "examination passed" form which must be taken to a deputy registrar. The deputy will collect another fee. Then, your photo license will be issued on the spot. The license will be valid until your fourth birthday after the date of issuance.*

Exercise 2 Practicing the Passive with Different Time References: Below is a list of sentences in which the only difference is the verb tense. Change each sentence to the passive. Be sure that the verb **to be** expresses the time reference of the sentence.

1. The applicant's sponsor signs the financial statement.
2. The applicant's sponsor is signing the financial statement.
3. The applicant's sponsor signed the financial statement.
4. The applicant's sponsor was signing the financial statement.
5. The applicant's sponsor will sign the financial statement.
6. The applicant's sponsor is going to sign the financial statement.
7. The applicant's sponsor has signed the financial statement.

*Adapted from "Digest of Ohio Motor Vehicle Laws," Ohio Department of Highway Safety, 1988, 2-4.

8. The applicant's sponsor used to sign the financial statement.
9. The applicant's sponsor had signed the financial statement.
10. The applicant's sponsor could have signed the financial statement.
11. The applicant's sponsor should sign the financial statement.
12. The applicant's sponsor has to sign the financial statement.
13. The applicant's sponsor must sign the financial statement.

Exercise 3 Practicing the Passive with Different Time References: Use the words below to construct sentences using the passive construction. Only use the **BY-phrase** when necessary. Use the time clues to help you choose an appropriate verb tense for each sentence. (Write the time information in your sentence *unless* it is in parentheses.) Study the example before you begin.

Performer	Action	Receiver	Time Clue
embassy	process	my visa application	(now)

My visa application is being processed.

	Performer	Action	Receiver	Time Clue
1.	I	mail	my visa application	yesterday
2.	embassy	process	my application	not yet (It will do this next week.)
3.	the consul	must approve	a visa application	(in general)
4.	the consul	approve	the visa application	tomorrow
5.	the English Program	will issue	an I-20	immediately
6.	the English Program	issue	sixty I-20s	last semester
7.	the university	admit	Ali	before he applied to the English Program
8.	the high school	should send	official records	(in general)
9.	the sponsor	sign	the financial statement	(in general)
10.	the applicant	can sign	the financial statement	if he is independently wealthy

Exercise 4 In this next exercise, you must decide when to use passive or active verb forms. The story below is a freewriting journal entry about one writer's "strange" Christmas. You must fill in the blanks. Following the story, you see the information to use for each blank. Before you fill in the blank, decide:

① Whether you should use active or passive. Sometimes either will be correct; sometimes one or the other will be more appropriate for the context. When you choose passive, decide whether or not you need a BY-phrase.

② What the time reference and verb form should be.

PART 3: SENTENCE STRUCTURE AND GRAMMAR EXERCISES AS WORK IN PROGRESS

In the United States, (1) _____ in many different ways. While some people begin to celebrate several days before December 25th, many begin the holiday on December 24th, Christmas Eve. On that day, (2) _____ _____ in the evening. Usually, (3) _____. After dinner, (4) _____. (5) _____ on the tree.

Like so many other families, (6) _____ _____ this way. However, last year, (7) _____ _____ in a strange way. (8) _____ in an airplane. (9) _____ for December 23. However, (10) _____ _____ because of a heavy snow storm. (11) _____ to stay in the airport for 24 hours. On the 24th, (12) _____ _____. (13) _____ _____ to leave at 1:00 p.m. (14) _____ at 12:30. However, (15) _____ _____. (16) _____ _____ for 12 more hours. When I finally arrived home on the 25th, (17) _____ _____.

① action = celebrate
performer = people
receiver = Christmas

② action = prepare
performer = people
receiver = a big meal

③ action = serve
performer = people
receiver = turkey

④ action = decorate
performer = people
receiver = the Christmas tree

⑤ action = put
performer = people
receiver = ornaments and lights

⑥ action = celebrate
performer = my family
receiver = Christmas

⑦ action = celebrate
performer = I
receiver = Christmas Eve

⑧ action = spend
performer = I
receiver = December 24th

⑨ action = schedule
performer = I
receiver = my flight home

⑩ action = cancel
performer = airlines
receiver = my flight

⑪ action = force
performer = the cancellation
receiver = I

⑫ action = announce
performer = the airlines
receiver = a new flight

⑬ action = schedule
performer = the airlines
receiver = the flight

⑭ action = board
performer = the airlines
receiver = we

⑮ action = discover
performer = the pilot
receiver = a mechanical problem

⑯ action = have to delay
performer = the airlines
receiver = the plane

⑰ action = save
performer = my family
receiver = one small piece of turkey for me

REPORTED SPEECH

To paraphrase or restate someone else's ideas and then present them in your own writing, you can use a reporting verb and a noun clause. The main clause of the sentence includes the name of the source from whom you borrow the idea and the reporting verb. The noun clause restates the borrowed idea. Because it is a complete clause, it contains a subject and a predicate. (For more information about noun clauses, see pages 223 to 227.)

Example:

Roger Tougas contends that foreign students do not contribute to the United States (qtd. in Baker 1987, 73).

(source) (reporting verb)   (noun clause with borrowed idea)

PART 3: SENTENCE STRUCTURE AND GRAMMAR EXERCISES AS WORK IN PROGRESS

REPORTED STATEMENTS USING THAT

Reported statements are introduced by the word **that**. Below is a list of common *reporting verbs* that are followed by a **THAT-clause**.

REPORTING VERBS		
acknowledge	emphasize	point out
add	exclaim	remark
admit	explain	repeat
allege	hint	reply
announce	imply	report
answer	indicate	reveal
assert	inform	say
claim	mention	state
contend	promise	tell
declare		

NOTES:

① Most of these verbs are followed directly by the THAT-clause.

② However, **tell** and **inform** must be followed by an indirect object before the THAT-clause. Also, the verb **promise** can be followed by an indirect object.

Examples:

Michael Schuh, an American Ph.D. engineering student, tells <u>us</u> that pursuing his advanced degree will not give him any financial advantage in the job market (qtd. in Baker 1987, 73).

Goodwin and Nacht inform <u>us</u> that about 327,000 foreign students were in the United States in 1981-82 (1983, 26).

SEQUENCE OF TENSES

When you use reported speech to borrow and report someone else's ideas, you must be careful about the verb tenses in the main clause and in the noun clause. The rule that governs which tenses to use is called the sequence of tenses rule.

PRESENT TENSE IN THE REPORTING VERB If the verb in the main clause, that is, the reporting verb, is in the present tense, then the verb in the noun clause should be in whatever tense is appropriate to express the correct meaning. Study the examples below.

Examples:

1. Goodwin and Nacht mention that in 1981-82, eighty percent of the foreign students in the United States were supported by personal, family, or home government resources (1983, 26).

   (present tense)   (past tense)

2. Baker makes the point that welcoming foreign students to the United States is good for promoting international relationships (1987, 73).

    (present tense)   (present tense)

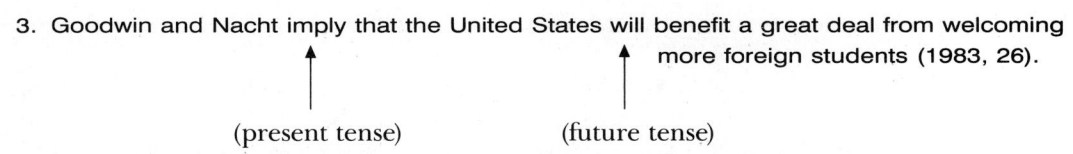

3. Goodwin and Nacht imply that the United States will benefit a great deal from welcoming more foreign students (1983, 26).

    (present tense)   (future tense)

NOTE: When you are reporting borrowed material in a paper and the original source is a fairly recent publication, it is acceptable to use the simple present tense in the reporting verb.

Examples:

    Mark Rentz points out that . . .

    James Baker maintains that . . .

PAST TENSE IN THE REPORTING VERB If the reporting verb is in the past, the verb in the noun clause must be in one of the past tense forms. NOTE: This is the rule for formal written English. We do not always follow this rule in spoken English or in informal written English.

Examples:

1. Goodwin and Nacht mentioned that in 1981–82, eighty percent of the foreign students in the United States had been supported by personal, family, or home government resources (1983, 26).

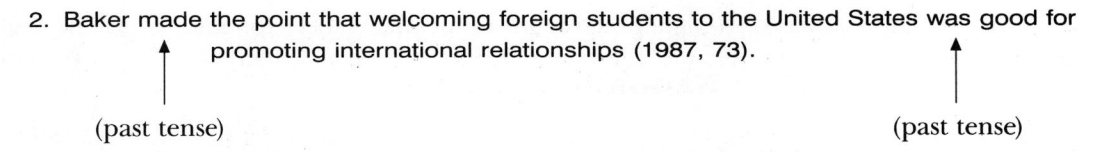

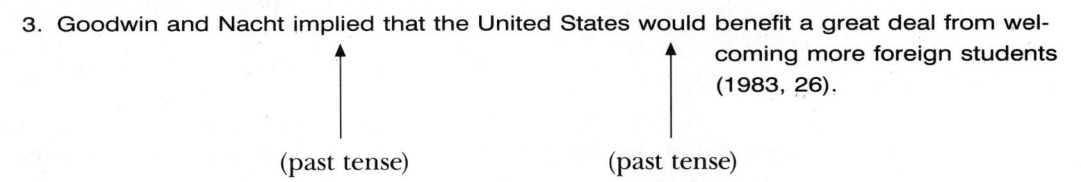

    (past tense)   (past perfect tense)

2. Baker made the point that welcoming foreign students to the United States was good for promoting international relationships (1987, 73).

    (past tense)   (past tense)

3. Goodwin and Nacht implied that the United States would benefit a great deal from welcoming more foreign students (1983, 26).

    (past tense)   (past tense)

PART 3: SENTENCE STRUCTURE AND GRAMMAR EXERCISES AS WORK IN PROGRESS

WHICH PAST TENSE FORM TO USE? The past tense form that you choose for the noun clause depends on what the verb tense of the original idea was. Study the list below.

<u>Original Idea</u> → <u>Borrowed and Reported</u>

1. Many foreign students <u>study</u> math. → John said that many foreign students <u>studied</u> math.
2. Many foreign students <u>studied</u> math. → John said that many foreign students <u>had studied</u> math.
3. Many foreign students <u>are studying</u> math. → John said that many foreign students <u>were studying</u> math.
4. Many <u>have studied</u> math. → John said that many <u>had studied</u> math.
5. Many <u>have been studying</u> math. → John said that many <u>had been studying</u> math.
6. Many <u>were studying</u> math. → John said that many <u>had been studying</u> math.
7. Many <u>are going to study</u> math. → John said that many <u>were going to study</u> math.
8. Many <u>can study</u> math. → John said that many <u>could study</u> math.
9. Many <u>will study</u> math. → John said that many <u>would study</u> math.
10. Many <u>may study</u> math. → John said that many <u>might study</u> math.
11. Many <u>have to study</u> math. → John said that many <u>had to study</u> math.
12. Many <u>must study</u> math. → John said that many <u>had to study</u> math.

PRACTICE USING REPORTED SPEECH

Exercise 1 The sentences below come from some of the articles in Appendix D. Restate each sentence using reported speech. Paraphrase the ideas of the original speaker and present them in your own words.

From "Foreign Students Under Fire," pages 265 to 267.

(1) "We're shooting ourselves in the foot if we send foreigners home. It's because of them we're not further behind." (Robert Weatherall, job-placement director at MIT)

(2) "In Chinese Society, a higher degree means people respect you and your family will be proud." (Ching Bin Liaw, a Taiwanese student in mechanical engineering at the University of California, Berkeley)

(3) "Foreign students are not productive citizens. If they are going to reap the benefits, I just want them to pay for it." (Roger Tougas, a Massachusetts state representative in 1987)

From "Foreign Students Still Flock to the U.S.," pages 269 to 270.

(4) "At the national level, the State Department or a newly created Department of Trade should be charged to facilitate the flow of foreign students to our shores." (Craufurd Goodwin and Michael Nacht)

(5) Foreign students "help to educate American students at a time when sophisticated understanding of the world is crucial." (Craufurd Goodwin and Michael Nacht)

From "Diplomats in Our Backyard," pages 273 to 274.

(6) "One-third to one-half of the world's top positions in politics, business, education and the military will be filled in the next 25 years by foreign students attending colleges and universities in the United States." (Lawson Lau, author of "The World at Your Doorstep")

Exercise 2 The sentences below come from articles in Chapter 5. Restate each sentence using reported speech. Paraphrase the ideas of the original speaker and present them in your own words.

From "Speaking Through an Interpreter," page 140.

① "At whom does one look when oral translation of a foreign language is involved?"

② "When the interpreter is translating what the student says, nod at the interpreter to show that you understand, but direct your looks of reaction at the student with whom you are, however cumbersomely, conversing."

From "The Cultures of Medicine," pages 143 and 144.

③ "The practice of medicine, finally, is an art. And like painting and sculpture, it reflects the culture from which it comes." (Matt Clark)

④ "American medicine owes a lot to the aggressive, 'can do' spirit of the frontier." (Matt Clark)

⑤ The French "put more stock in the theory that underlies a treatment than any experimental evidence that it actually works." (Matt Clark)

Exercise 3 To complete Exercise 4.4, page 96, you discussed the issue of a tuition increase for international students with at least two people and took notes during the discussions. Read through your notes now. Write sentences reporting the ideas of your interviewees.

SENTENCE CONNECTORS

Sentence connectors do not combine clauses. They keep two sentences separate, but make the meaning relationship between them explicit and clear. The first chart below lists some of the common sentence connectors in English. The second chart shows the sentence pattern rules that you should follow when using these connectors.

	CONNECTORS
Time	then, next, first, second, third, last, finally, meanwhile, at the same time, simultaneously, at this point, at this time
Cause-Effect/ Reason-Result	therefore, as a result, hence, consequently, thus, for this reason, accordingly
Purpose	for this purpose, to do this, to this end
Concession and Contrast	however, nevertheless, nonetheless, on the other hand, on the contrary, in contrast, to be sure, admittedly
Addition	moreover, furthermore, in addition, also
Exemplification	for example, for instance
Condition	otherwise
Restatement	in other words, that is

Part 3: Sentence Structure and Grammar Exercises as Work in Progress

Patterns

Clause	.	Sentence connector	,	Clause.
I am interested in math.		*For this reason,*		*I will major in computer science.*

OR

Clause	;	sentence connector	,	clause.
I am interested in math;		*for this reason,*		*I will major in computer science.*

Additional Examples of Sentence Connectors:

1. This university's chemical engineering program is excellent. For this reason, I am pleased to be able to study here.

2. I want to pursue a degree in polymer science; to do this, I came to the United States.

3. I hope to graduate in three and a half years. Then, I will return to Korea and look for a job with a corporation or large company.

4. I hope to be accepted to the graduate program in biology. Otherwise, I will return to my country.

NOTES:

① When you use these sentence connectors, use a period (.) or a semicolon (;) after the first sentence. Place a comma after the sentence connector if there is a noticeable break in the continuity of thought. If no such break occurs, do not separate the connector by a comma.

② The most common position for a sentence connector is between the two sentences (like in the examples above). However, a sentence connector can also be placed between the subject and the predicate of the second sentence or at the end of the second sentence if it is short.

Examples:

a. Many international students adjust quickly to life in a new country. **However,** some experience severe culture shock.

b. Many international students adjust quickly to life in a new country. Some, **however,** experience severe culture shock.

c. Many international students adjust quickly to life in a new country. Some experience severe culture shock, **however.**

SENTENCE CONNECTORS

PRACTICE USING SENTENCE CONNECTORS

Exercise 1 Most visitors to another country experience culture shock. Culture shock often progresses through four stages: the honeymoon period, rejection, adjustment, and acceptance. The chart below lists common characteristics and symptoms of each stage.

Stages	Characteristics	Symptoms
honeymoon	excitement desire to acculturate desire to learn about the new country	seek opportunities to use the second language try food participate in local customs
rejection	anger disdain for the new country frustration	spend time with people from native country speak native language criticize new culture feel tired and bored stay at home
adjustment	tolerance for the new experiences	establish a routine begin to feel comfortable participate in activities in the local community
acceptance	acculturation	feel like a member of the community

Rewrite the following sentences about culture shock. After each one, add a sentence of your own to further develop the ideas in the original sentence. Use the clue in parentheses to decide how to develop each sentence. Use a sentence connector from the list on page 237 to relate your sentence explicitly to the original. Study the example before you begin.

1. During the honeymoon stage, visitors are excited about life in the new country. (What is a result of this excitement?)

   During the honeymoon stage, visitors are excited about life in the new country. Consequently, they try to participate in local events and to use their new language.

2. They seek out opportunities to meet residents. (Think of some examples.)

3. They make every effort to speak the new language. (What else do they do to experience the culture?)

4. The honeymoon stage can last several weeks. (What stage comes next?)

5. During the rejection stage, the visitors feel anger and disdain for the new country. (What is the result of these feelings?)

6. The visitors often stay home. (What else do they do?)

7. They close themselves off from the new culture. (Give some examples.)

8. They know they should practice speaking the language of their new country. (What do they do instead?)

9. During the rejection stage, visitors face a conflict. On the one hand, they want to avoid the new language. (What conflicts with this desire?)

239

Part 3: Sentence Structure and Grammar Exercises as Work in Progress

10. They want to distance themselves from the new culture. (How do they achieve this purpose?)

11. In order to enjoy life in the new country, visitors must get through the rejection stage. (What happens if they do not?)

12. Fortunately, most visitors survive the rejection stage. (What stage comes next?)

13. During the adjustment and acceptance stages, the visitors begin to establish a routine. (What is the result of this?)

14. In the acceptance stage, visitors acculturate. (Restate this in simple terms.)

15. They do not lose their native culture. (What happens instead?)

APPENDICES

APPENDIX A

Editing Checklist

APPENDIX B

Editing Correction Symbols

APPENDIX C

Word Processing

APPENDIX D

Readings and Worksheets

APPENDICES

APPENDIX A: *Editing Checklist*

An editing checklist provides you with a systematic way to proofread a final draft. The checklist below explains the rules for some areas of English that commonly cause problems for second language writers. It also gives you steps to follow when editing your writing.

You can use every page of the checklist every time that you edit a paper, or you can use select pages, those that cover aspects of English that cause you difficulty.

EDITING FOR AGREEMENT — **243**
- Subject/Verb Agreement — 243

EDITING FOR ARTICLE USAGE — **245**
- Understanding Article Usage — 245
- Using the Article Editing Chart — 248

EDITING FOR MECHANICS — **249**
- Paragraph Indentations — 249
- Spelling — 249
- Capitalization — 250

EDITING FOR PREPOSITIONS — **250**
- Prepositions of Time — 251
- Prepositions of Space — 252
- Other Prepositions — 253

EDITING FOR PUNCTUATION — **254**
- Period — 254
- Comma — 255
- Semicolon — 256
- Colon — 256
- Question Mark — 256

EDITING FOR VERB TENSES AND FORMS — **257**
- Past — 258
- Present — 259
- Future — 259

SOURCES CONSULTED:

Celce-Murcia, Marianne, and Diane Larsen-Freeman. 1983. *The Grammar Book: An ESL/EFL Teacher's Course*. Boston: Heinle and Heinle Publishers.

The Chicago Manual of Style. 13th ed. 1982. Chicago: The University of Chicago Press.

Crowell, Thomas Lee. 1964. *Index to Modern English*. New York: McGraw-Hill, Inc.

Leech, Geoffrey, and Jan Svartvik. 1975. *A Communicative Grammar of English*. London, England: Longman.

Editing for Agreement

SUBJECT/VERB AGREEMENT In English, the subject and verb in a clause must agree in number. You only have to worry about this rule with the verb TO BE (am, is are, was, were) and with the 3rd person singular verb in the simple present (She *studies* math).

Study the chart below to learn some of the rules of subject/verb agreement.

Agreement Editing Chart

Subject		+ Verb	Examples
another, anybody, anyone, anything, each one, either, everybody, everyone, everything, neither, nobody, none, no one, nothing, one, somebody, someone, something		+ SINGULAR VERB	Anything goes. Everyone is early. I don't recommend those books. Neither has an interesting plot. Because of the ice storm nobody was here on time. Somebody wants to speak with you on the phone.
another, each, every, either, kind of, neither, one, some of, sort of, type of	+ SINGULAR COUNT NOUN	+ SINGULAR VERB	Every book on the list is interesting. Neither book is very expensive. Some of the page was illegible. That type of novel holds my interest.
a lot of, all (of), little (of), most (of), much (of), some (of)	+ MASS NOUN	+ SINGULAR VERB	A lot of the equipment is new. All the money was stolen. Much of the water is polluted.
each of, every one of, one of, neither of, none of, the number of	+ PLURAL NOUN	+ SINGULAR VERB	Every one of the books on the required reading list is interesting. One of the books has an especially intricate plot. The number of books on the required reading list seems just right for a semester.
a few (of), a lot of, all (of), both (of), few (of), many (of), most (of), a number of, numerous, other, several, some (of), various	+ PLURAL NOUN	+ PLURAL VERB	All the books that you recommended are interesting. Some people prefer non-fiction to fiction. Other readers love poetry. A number of my friends like to read comic books.
COORDINATED SUBJECT (connected by **and**)		+ PLURAL VERB	Stephen King and Dick Francis are my favorite authors at the moment.
GERUND (e.g., swimming, studying)		+ SINGULAR VERB	Swimming is an excellent aerobic sport.
NOUN CLAUSE (e.g., what I want to know, that you did so well on the last exam)			What I want to know is how the legislators arrived at their decision.

APPENDICES

Subject	+ Verb	Examples
UNIT WORDS (e.g., units of distance, time, or money)	+ SINGULAR VERB	Fifteen thousand miles <u>is</u> too far to drive by myself. Three thousand dollars <u>was</u> not a bad price for such a low-mileage car. Ten minutes <u>passes</u> quickly when you are freewriting.
COLLECTIVE NOUN (e.g., committee, family, staff, team) With collective nouns, the subject/verb agreement rule depends on whether the writer views the noun as a single unit (i.e., singular) or as a collection of separate individuals (i.e., plural).	+ SINGULAR OR PLURAL VERB	The committee <u>has</u> made <u>its</u> recommendation. The committee <u>have</u> made <u>their</u> recommendation.
FRACTIONS (e.g., one-third of, one-half of) PERCENTAGES (e.g., fifteen percent of, forty-seven percent of)	+ MASS NOUN	+ SINGULAR VERB	One-third of the equipment <u>is</u> broken. Fifty percent of the water used in my city <u>comes</u> from another state.
FRACTIONS (e.g., one-third of, one-half of) PERCENTAGES (e.g., fifteen percent of, forty-seven percent of)	+ PLURAL NOUN	+ PLURAL VERB	One-third of the machines <u>are</u> broken. Fifty percent of the people <u>are</u> against the new law.

Exercise 1 Read the following text. Find and correct errors with agreement. Refer to the Agreement Editing Chart above as necessary.

A fire broke out on the ground floor of the library over the weekend. None of the employees were there during the fire because everyone were already gone for the day. Fortunately, no one were injured. Because of quick action by the fire department, damage to the building itself was minimal. The most significant loss was the destruction of several pieces of equipment. Because the library had recently upgraded its on-line catalog, a lot of the equipment were brand new. In fact, a lot of the computer terminals were only two months old. Fifty percent of the equipment are functioning, so the library plans to open on Monday. The staff have been requested to work its regular hours.

EDIT NOW

Reread your draft. As you read, look for places where you have used some of the words listed in the chart above. Check to be sure the verb agrees with the subject.

Editing for Article Usage

UNDERSTANDING ARTICLE USAGE To use articles (*a, an, the, some* or Ø) correctly in written English, you need to understand:

- how nouns work in English, and
- that article choice depends not only on the type of noun being used but also on the bigger context, including the words and sentences before and after the noun and the relationship and amount of shared knowledge between the writer and the readers.

Below you will find some information about nouns and some of the usage rules for articles. This information will help you make decisions while you are editing your writing.

NOTE: The charts and rules below explain the *basic* rules for article usage, *but not all*. The article system in English is very complicated and there are many exceptions and variations to the rules. After using the charts, if you still have some questions about your article usage in the paper that you are editing today, ask a native English speaker for advice.

Types of Nouns	Explanation	Examples
COMMON NOUNS	name a person, place, or thing.	city, man, building, book, bread, water, peace, furniture, money
Count Nouns	name a person, place, or thing that can be counted; these nouns are singular when referring to only one item but plural when referring to two or more.	one city/five cities, one man/three men, one building/eight buildings, one book/two books
Mass Nouns	name something that cannot be counted; mass nouns are grammatically singular.	bread, water, peace, furniture, money, health, beauty, sleep
PROPER NOUNS	name a specific person, place, or thing.	New York, President Bill Clinton, Radio City Music Hall, *Work in Progress*, Brownberry Whole Wheat Bread

APPENDICES

Uses of Nouns	Explanation	Examples
DEFINITE	refers to a person, place, or thing that has a definite reference for both you, the writer, and your readers. The noun will be definite because: • it is unique, or • it is identified for the reader through the written context or because of shared knowledge.	1. The earth revolves around the sun. 2. I finished a book about U.S. politics last night. In the book, the author described how the two-party system works in this country. The book that I read before this one was also about U.S. politics. 3. In 1992, Governor Bill Clinton won the U.S. presidential election.
INDEFINITE	refers to a common noun that: • has a definite reference for you, the writer, but not yet for the readers. You are introducing this noun for the first time in this piece of writing, or • is not definite for you or your readers.	1. I finished an interesting detective novel last night. 2. I want to begin a new novel tonight, but I can't decide which one to read. I'd like to read a mystery. Can you recommend one?
GENERIC	refers to a whole class or category.	1. A student must study hard to succeed. 2. Students must study hard to succeed.

NOTES:

① When you are not sure whether a noun is count or mass, consult a grammar book or a dictionary for ESL learners. Nouns that are count in your language may be mass in English, and vice versa.

② Some nouns can be both mass and count, depending on the context and the meaning. When a mass noun is used as a count noun, it refers to "an instance of," "a kind of," or "a unit of" the mass noun.

Examples:

I love coffee. (mass)
I'd like two coffees, please. (count)

Freedom is a right, not a privilege. (mass)
The freedoms guaranteed by the United States Constitution are upheld by the judicial system. (count)

APPENDIX A

③ Although many English nouns are made plural by adding -S or -ES, some are irregular. Consult a grammar book or a dictionary for ESL learners if you are not sure of the irregular plural form of a noun.

Examples of Irregular Noun Plurals:

singular	plural	singular	plural
man	men	child	children
woman	women	tooth	teeth
person	people	foot	feet
datum	data	fish	fish
analysis	analyses	species	species

④ Although most proper nouns do not use an article in the singular, there are some exceptions.

a. Use "the" with names of countries containing the word "Union," "United," or "Kingdom."

Examples:

The United States
The United Kingdom

b. Use "the" with lakes, mountains, or islands that comprise a group.

Examples:

the Great Lakes
the Finger Lakes of New York
the Rockies
the Alps
the Catskills
the Canary Islands

APPENDICES

USING THE ARTICLE EDITING CHART If you understand the basic rules for article usage, use the Article Editing Chart on this page to guide you while editing your writing. Ask yourself these questions:

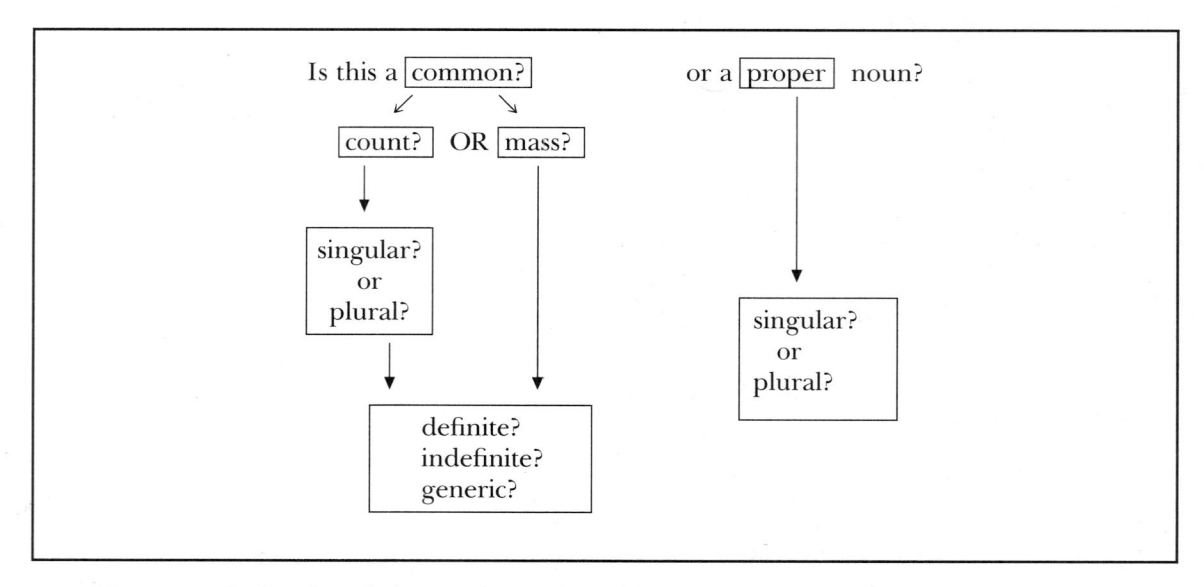

```
              Is this a  common?         or a  proper  noun?
                        ↙     ↘
                    count?  OR  mass?
                      ↓                          ↓
                  singular?                  singular?
                     or                          or
                  plural?                    plural?
                    ↓        ↓
                   definite?
                   indefinite?
                   generic?
```

Now, consult the chart below to determine which, if any, article to use.

ARTICLE EDITING CHART

PROPER NOUNS			COMMON NOUNS		
			count		mass
singular	plural		singular	plural	
Ø	the	**DEFINITE**	the	the	the
		INDEFINITE	a/an	some/Ø	some/Ø
		GENERIC	a/an	Ø	Ø

Exercise 2 Read the following text and fill in the blanks with the correct articles (**a, an, the** or **some**). If no article is necessary, put an X in the blank. Refer to the Article Editing Chart above to guide your editing.

(1) _____ tea is (2) _____ international beverage, consumed all over (3) _____ world. There are many varieties of (4) _____ tea. (5) _____ tea preferred in (6) _____ Taiwan is different from that favored by most Americans.

(7) _____ people in (8) _____ Taiwan drink (9) _____ oolong tea, (10) _____ kind of green tea with (11) _____ slight smell and (12) _____ strong taste.

APPENDIX A

To make green tea in (13) _____ Taiwan, you need (14) _____ special equipment; you need (15) _____ tea kettle, (16) _____ teapot, (17) _____ tea pan, and (18) _____ cups. (19) _____ tea kettle is (20) _____ container in which (21) _____ tea is brewed. (22) _____ tea leaves are placed in (23) _____ kettle and (24) _____ water is poured over them. To get (25) _____ best flavor, (26) _____ water should be boiling. Once (27) _____ tea is ready, it is poured into (28) _____ teapot, which sits in (29) _____ hot water inside (30) _____ tea pan. (31) _____ teapot keeps (32) _____ tea fresh before it is poured into (33) _____ cups.

EDIT NOW

Now edit your own paper. Read it carefully, considering each noun. Use the Article Editing Chart above to determine: 1) what type of noun it is, and 2) how it is being used in the sentence. Then check to see what article you should use, if any.

EDITING FOR MECHANICS

Read the editing steps below one by one. Follow the directions given with each step. When you finish a step, move on to the next one.

PARAGRAPH INDENTATIONS How many paragraphs does your draft have? _____.

Each paragraph should begin with a space (called an indentation) about one inch in from the *left* margin of your paper. If you have written your paper on a computer or a typewriter, the indentation should be five spaces.

EDIT NOW

Scan your paper and look to be sure that each paragraph begins with an indentation. Make corrections as necessary.

SPELLING Read your draft again carefully. As you read, underline any words that you think may be spelled incorrectly.

EDIT NOW

Go through the paper underlined word by underlined word, checking each one in the dictionary. Make corrections as necessary.

If you are using a computer, run your file through the spell checking program.

APPENDICES

CAPITALIZATION Here are the basic rules of capitalization in English:

① Capitalize the first word of every sentence.

② Capitalize the pronoun "I" wherever it appears.

③ Capitalize all proper nouns and names (e.g., *Chicago, Joe*).

④ Capitalize geographical names and words that are formed from them.

Examples:

America	American food
Paris, France	French cuisine

⑤ Capitalize dates, months, days of the week, and holidays.

Examples:

Monday   September   Christmas

EDIT NOW

Reread your draft. As you read, be sure that each sentence begins with a capital letter and that you have applied the other rules for capitalization that are explained above. Also, be sure that you do not use capital letters when they are not needed.

EDITING FOR PREPOSITIONS

Prepositional phrases consist of a preposition and a noun phrase. Prepositions signal meaning relationships of time, space, degree, and manner, as well as those among people and/or objects. English prepositions may pose a problem for you because the rules for their usage may be very different from the rules in your native language.

If prepositions cause you difficulty when writing, study the charts below. These charts explain some of the uses of prepositions in English, *but not all.*

NOTE: Some prepositions combine with verbs and adjectives to form a vocabulary item. Be sure to learn these verbs and adjectives with their prepositions. If you are not sure of the combination when editing, consult a dictionary for ESL learners. Look up the verb or adjective, and the dictionary will list the preposition that co-occurs with it.

Examples of Verb + Preposition Combinations

result from	The budget deficit has <u>resulted from</u> poor economic planning.
speak on (+ a topic)	The president will <u>speak on</u> the economy.
speak to (+ a person)	He will <u>speak to</u> the Congress.
succeed in	I hope he <u>succeeds in</u> his plan to reduce the deficit.

Examples of Adjective + Preposition Combinations

capable of	You are <u>capable of</u> great things.
interested in	I am <u>interested in</u> a career in criminal justice.
similar to	Your background is <u>similar to</u> mine.
upset about	The president is <u>upset about</u> his low approval rating.

APPENDIX A

PREPOSITIONS THAT SIGNAL TIME RELATIONSHIPS

To Write About	Use	Examples
a specific hour and with these time words: noon, night, midnight, dawn, dusk, sunrise, sunset, daybreak	at	I'll be home at 9:30. Meet me at noon. I always jog at sunrise. Let's meet at dusk. I want to get home before dark.
a specific month, year, or season and with these time phrases: the past, the present, the future, the morning, the afternoon, the evening	in	The semester break comes in December. I was born in 1975. Flowers bloom in spring. Many people hate to get up early in the morning. I prefer to study in the evening. In the near future, doctors hope to find a cure for AIDS.
an approximate time	about around	The explosion occurred about 4:00 a.m. Come over to my house around 8:30.
an earlier time	before	Before my trip, I had many things to do. Come before 11:00. I want to talk to you before the start of class.
a later time	after	I will return to my country after graduation.
a deadline	by	Mail your application by Thursday. I must finish my assignment by tomorrow.
an intermediate time	between	I'll be in my office between 2:00 and 3:00.
a length of time	during + an event for + a period of time	During the 1992 presidential campaign, Bill Clinton pledged to change the U.S. health care system. During the campaign, Clinton lost his voice for several days.
a length of time up to the present	for + time period since + a point in time	I have lived in the United States for three years. My friend has worked for that company since 1990.
a starting and finishing time	from . . . to from . . . until	Classes are scheduled from 9:00 a.m. to 3:00 p.m. Classes are scheduled from 9:00 a.m. until 3:00 p.m.
an end point of time	until	We lived in N.Y. until last year. I will study until 3:00.
a future end point after a period of time	in + period of time	The movie starts in ten minutes. We're moving to a new city in a month.
a day or a date	on	I was born on August 10, 1975. Our appointment is on Tuesday.

APPENDICES

PREPOSITIONS THAT SIGNAL SPATIAL RELATIONSHIPS

To Write About	Use	Examples
a point as:		
a position •X	at	The accident happened at the corner.
a target ○	at	The president waved at the crowd.
a general area	at	Meet me at the mall.
a → direction →X	to	Let's go to Florida for vacation.
a ← direction X→	from	My sister moved from California to Florida last year.
a surface or line as:		
a position	on	Niagara Falls is on the U.S.-Canadian border.
a → direction	on (to)	Put your homework on the desk.
a ← direction	off	Keep your feet off the table.
a passage	across	When the player runs across the goal line, he scores.
an area or volume as:		
a position	in	We keep our dog in the yard.
a → direction	in (to)	I hate to drive into the city.
a ← direction	out of	Traffic is bad coming out of the city.
passage	through	The boy ran through the park and jumped through the window.
a position higher than another	above over	The police ordered the man to raise his hands above his head. The window over the kitchen sink is broken.
contact between two objects	against	I put the hot plate against the plastic bowl and it melted.
a position lower than another	below under	Hang this picture below that one. Your book is under that pile of papers.
an intermediate position	between	Philadelphia is between N.Y. and Washington, D.C.
a position that is close	by next to near beside	Your glasses are by the t.v. We live next to a fire station. Our house is near the university. The grocery store is beside the bank.
a distance	for	We drove for 500 miles today.
a ↑ direction X↑	up	We should not drive up the mountain in the dark.
a ↓ direction X↓	down	The children love to ride their bikes down the hill.

APPENDIX A

PREPOSITIONS THAT SIGNAL OTHER MEANING RELATIONSHIPS

To Indicate	Use	Examples
the performer of an action (with a passive construction)	by	If the applicant is under the age of 18, the application must be signed <u>by a parent or guardian</u>.
the means to accomplish something	by	The police entered the house <u>by kicking in the door</u>. Many people travel to work <u>by subway</u>.
a source	from	I had to borrow money <u>from the bank</u>.
an instrument	with	Heat the test tube <u>with a Bunsen burner</u>.
manner (the way in which something is done)	with like	The candidate spoke <u>with confidence</u>. I'm starting to sound <u>like my mother</u>.
cause	because of on account of	<u>Because of the ice</u>, the car skidded off the road. <u>On account of the economic crisis</u>, the government decided to raise taxes.
contrast	despite in spite of	The university decided to raise tuition <u>despite its promise not to</u>.
a temperature	at	We keep the thermostat <u>at 68°</u>.
an approximation	about around	Add <u>about a tablespoon of salt</u>.
a degree higher than another	above	I'm not sure how cold it is, but I think it is <u>above freezing</u>. Your test scores are always <u>above average</u>.
a degree lower than another	below	It is so cold that it must be <u>below freezing</u>. This machine performed <u>below the norm</u>; we should replace it.
an intermediate degree	between	Buy <u>between two and three pounds of beef</u>.
a degree of success or failure	by	In the 1993 Super Bowl, the Dallas Cowboys beat the Buffalo Bills <u>by 35 points</u>.

NOTE: The concept of "degree" refers to how much something happens or the extent to which something happens. Prepositional phrases of degree usually answer the question, "How much?" They often refer to an amount or quantity.

Exercise 3 Read the following sentences and correct any errors. Refer to the Preposition Editing Charts above to guide your editing.

1. I was born in June 22, 1975.

2. I lived at a small city since 10 years.

3. When I was 11, I moved into the biggest city in my country.

4. From 1986 to 1992, I attended a public school at the city.

5. I studied hard, so my grades were always more than average.

6. I was in school at 7:30 a.m. to 2:30 p.m., so I got home near 3:00.

7. I worked hard the same like my parents and my brothers and sisters.

8. The reason of our hard work, we had a wonderful life together.

APPENDICES

EDIT NOW

Read your draft carefully; underline any prepositions that you are uncertain about. For each one that you underline, ask yourself:

What kind of meaning relationship does the prepositional phrase express? Time? Space? Degree? Other?

Look at the appropriate chart above. Then,

① Locate the meaning in the left column of the chart.

② Find the correct preposition in the middle column.

③ Verify your choice by comparing your sentence to the example sentences in the right column. Check to see if the meaning that you want to express in your sentence is similar to the meaning expressed in the example sentences.

④ Make corrections on your draft as necessary.

EDITING FOR PUNCTUATION

Punctuation marks in writing are like traffic signals. They help direct the readers through your text so that your meaning is clearly communicated.

PERIOD The period (.) shows your readers that one complete thought or idea has ended.

① Use a period to signal the **end** of a grammatically complete sentence that expresses a statement. A sentence in English can have one, two, three, or even four clauses.

When a statement sentence is one clause, it will begin with a capital letter and end with a period.

Example:

> My plane trip was exciting.

When a statement sentence contains two or more clauses, it will begin with a capital letter, end with a period, and have connecting words (and sometimes commas) between the clauses.

Examples:

> After the plane took off, we developed some engine trouble, so we had to return to the airport immediately.

Remember: In English, when you have two or more clauses and *no* connecting words between them, you *must* use a period. Study the following example:

> The plane took off at 3:40, we developed some engine trouble about ten minutes later, we had to return to the airport, everyone was very frightened.

How many clauses are there in this text? How many connecting words? What is the correct way to punctuate this text?

② Use periods with most abbreviations.

Example:

> The plane was headed to N.Y. and then L.A. We departed on Tues., Nov. 3 at 3:40 p.m.

COMMA Unlike the period, the comma (,) does not mark the end of a complete thought or idea; instead, it marks a slight pause after a phrase or a clause. Below you will find some of the rules for comma usage.

① Use a comma after dependent clauses, introductory phrases, or sentence connectors that come at the beginning of a sentence if there is a noticeable break in the continuity of thought.

Examples:

When the plane landed safely, we were all happy.

After the safe landing, we were all happy.

The plane landed safely. At that time, we were all happy.

② Use commas to set off sentence connectors that appear in mid-sentence position.

Example:

The pilots and flight attendants remained calm throughout the crisis. Most of the passengers, however, became very anxious.

③ Use a comma between coordinated clauses connected by these words: *and, but, so, or, nor, for, yet*.

Example:

I hate to fly, so I usually take a train.

④ Use commas with some adjective clauses, reduced adjective clauses, and appositives. If these structures are necessary to identify the head noun (the noun they are describing), do not use commas; the reader needs the structure to understand the head noun. If these structures are extra, not essential, information, use commas. NOTE: When these structures come at the end of a sentence, use one comma and a period.

Examples:

The books written by Dick Francis are very interesting.
(no commas because the reader needs the adjective clause to understand which books the writer is describing.)

Longshot, written by Dick Francis, is very interesting.
(commas because the writer has identified the book by its proper name.)

I really enjoyed reading *Longshot*, a novel written by Dick Francis.

⑤ Use commas to separate three or more items in a series. These items can be phrases or clauses.

Example:

I enjoyed reading *Longshot, Banker, Twice Shy,* and *Blood Sport*.

APPENDICES

SEMICOLON The semicolon (;) works like a period in some contexts and like a comma in others.

   ① Use the semicolon between clauses that are very closely related in meaning. This use of the semicolon tells your reader that the two clauses could be joined by a coordinating word: *and, but, so, or,* or *nor.*

   Example:

      During the vacation, I might go to Florida; I might go to Washington, D.C.

   ② Use the semicolon between three or more items in a series when those items themselves contain commas.

   Example:

      During the vacation, I might go to Orlando, Florida, to visit friends; to Washington, D.C., to sightsee in the Capitol; or to Los Angeles to spend some time on the beach.

COLON The colon (:) functions like an equal sign; it signals that the information after it explains or expands on the idea before it.

   ① You can use a colon before a list or before a phrase that illustrates or extends the preceding idea.

   Example:

      When you travel to the eastern states, there are several places that you must see: Niagara Falls, New York City, Boston, and Washington, D.C.

   ② You can use a colon between independent clauses when the second clause illustrates or extends the ideas of the first.

   Example:

      Be sure to visit Niagara Falls: It is one of the natural wonders of the world.

QUESTION MARK Use a question mark (?) with sentences that ask a question.

Examples:

   Have you ever been to Niagara Falls?

   Do you plan to visit N.Y.?

   When will you go?

APPENDIX A

Exercise 4 Read the following text. Edit for errors with punctuation.

Although most people think of bees as a nuisance these insects are indispensable to the agriculture industry. Farmers need bees in order to grow a variety of fruits and vegetables, apples, cherries; avocados; carrots, celery and sunflowers. By buzzing from blossom to blossom bees pollinate plants and create the reaction necessary for the plants to reproduce.

Have you ever wondered how farmers manage to pollinate acres and acres of crops, how do they get the bees to their farms just when they need them. They rely on migratory beekeepers special farmers who move their bee hives from farm to farm. These beekeepers who follow the growing season from the south to the north arrive with truckloads of hives which they rent to farmers, when the bees' work is done the beekeepers pack up their hives, they move on to the next farm.

EDIT NOW

Reread your draft. As you read, check the clause and phrase structure of each sentence. Be sure that you have used periods, commas, other punctuation marks, and connecting words appropriately. Make corrections as necessary.

EDITING FOR VERB TENSES AND FORMS

Verb tenses tell your readers the time reference for the activities and events that you describe in your writing. To ensure that your readers understand your ideas, you must choose the correct tenses. You must also write these verb tenses in the correct forms.

If verb tenses and forms are a problem for you in English, study the Verb Tense Editing Chart on the following pages.

(To read more about bees and migratory beekeepers, see Mairson, Alan. 1993. "America's Beekeepers: Hives for Hire" *National Geographic* May: 73–93.)

APPENDICES

Verb Tense Editing Chart

IF PAST, was the action or event

Condition		Tense

completed at a specific past time?
`├──── to N.Y. ────┤`
`1986          now`
	→	***SIMPLE PAST**
		(verb + ED or irregular)
		I moved to N.Y. in 1986.

OR		

habitual at a specific past time?
`├─ x-x-x-x-x ─┤`
`last year       now`
	→	***SIMPLE PAST**
		(verb + ED or irregular)
		I studied in the library every day last year.

OR		
a state, a sensory/mental perception, or emotion? e.g. be, seem, appear, hear, see, know, love, have, own	→	***SIMPLE PAST** (verb + ED or irregular) *The president heard the protesters.* *My children loved going to the beach.* *John had a sports car.*
OR		

in progress at a specific past time?
`     8:00-10:00`
`├────┤────┤`
`last night    now`
	→	**PAST PROGRESSIVE**
		(*was/were* + verb + ING)
		I was watching t.v. from 8:00 to 10:00 last night.

OR		

completed at an unspecified past time?
`├─── ? ───┤`
`            now`
	→	**PRESENT PERFECT**
		(*has/have* + verb – P.P.)
		I have studied math.

repeated at unspecified past times?
`├─ ?-?-?-?-? ─┤`
`            now`
	→	**PRESENT PERFECT**
		(*has/have* + verb – P.P.)
		I have visited that museum many times.

OR		

started in the past and continues to the present?
`├────────→`
`3 years ago   now`
	→	**PRESENT PERFECT**
		(*has/have* + verb – P.P.)
		I have lived in the United States for three years.

OR		

started in the past and in progress in the present?
`├────────→`
`started     now`
`homework`
	→	**PRESENT PERFECT PROGRESSIVE**
		(*has/have* + BEEN + verb + ING)
		I have been doing my homework for three hours.

OR		

completed before another past time?
`├────┤────┤`
`in Tokyo  to U.S.  now`
	→	**PAST PERFECT**
		(*had* + verb – P.P.)
		I had lived in Tokyo before I came to the United States.

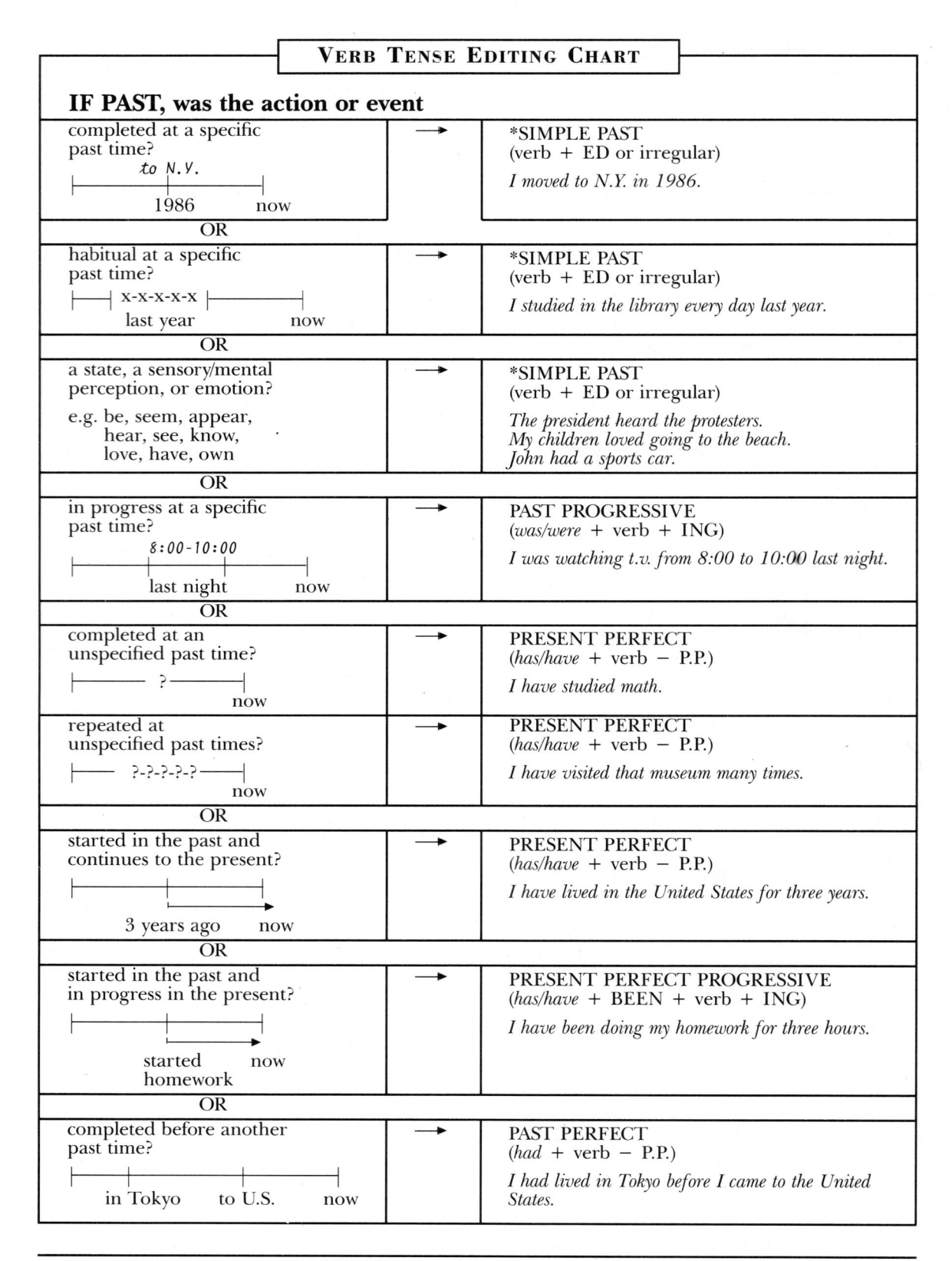

*Note: With simple past, use *did* for questions and *did not* for negatives. Use *was* or *were* for the verb "to be."

APPENDIX A

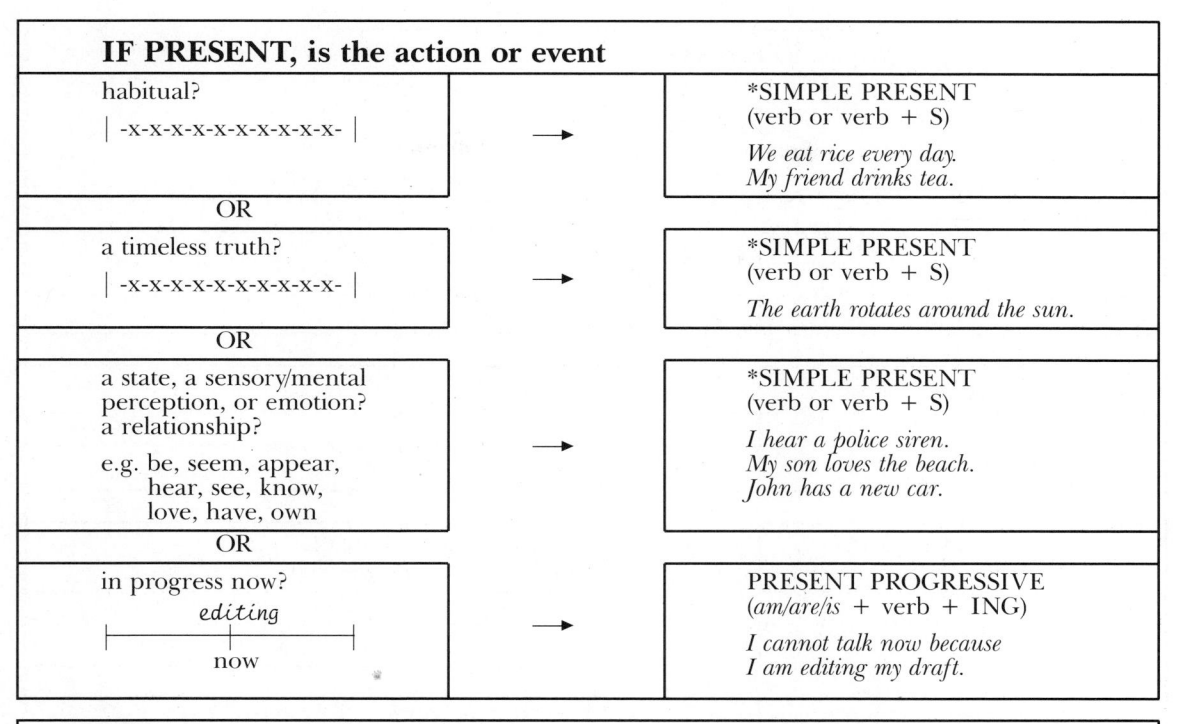

IF PRESENT, is the action or event

habitual? |-x-x-x-x-x-x-x-x-x-|	→	*SIMPLE PRESENT (verb or verb + S) *We eat rice every day.* *My friend drinks tea.*
OR		
a timeless truth? |-x-x-x-x-x-x-x-x-x-|	→	*SIMPLE PRESENT (verb or verb + S) *The earth rotates around the sun.*
OR		
a state, a sensory/mental perception, or emotion? a relationship? e.g. be, seem, appear, hear, see, know, love, have, own	→	*SIMPLE PRESENT (verb or verb + S) *I hear a police siren.* *My son loves the beach.* *John has a new car.*
OR		
in progress now? *editing* now	→	PRESENT PROGRESSIVE (*am/are/is* + verb + ING) *I cannot talk now because I am editing my draft.*

IF FUTURE, is the action or event

at some definite time? *graduate* now 3 years	→	WILL + verb *I will graduate in three years.*
OR		
a prediction? *rain* now tomorrow	→	WILL + verb BE GOING TO + verb *It will rain tomorrow.* *It is going to rain tomorrow.*
OR		
the result of a present intention? now visit N.Y.	→	BE GOING TO + verb *I am going to visit my friend in N.Y. during the break.*
OR		
the result of a present cause? now rain	→	BE GOING TO + verb *Look at the storm clouds rolling in. It is going to rain.*
OR		
the result of a present plan or arrangement? now next semester	→	PRESENT PROGRESSIVE (*am/are/is* + verb + ING) + future time adverbial *I am taking 15 credits next semester.*

*Note: With simple present, use *do* or *does* for questions and *do not* or *does not* for negatives. Use *am, is,* or *are* for the verb "to be."

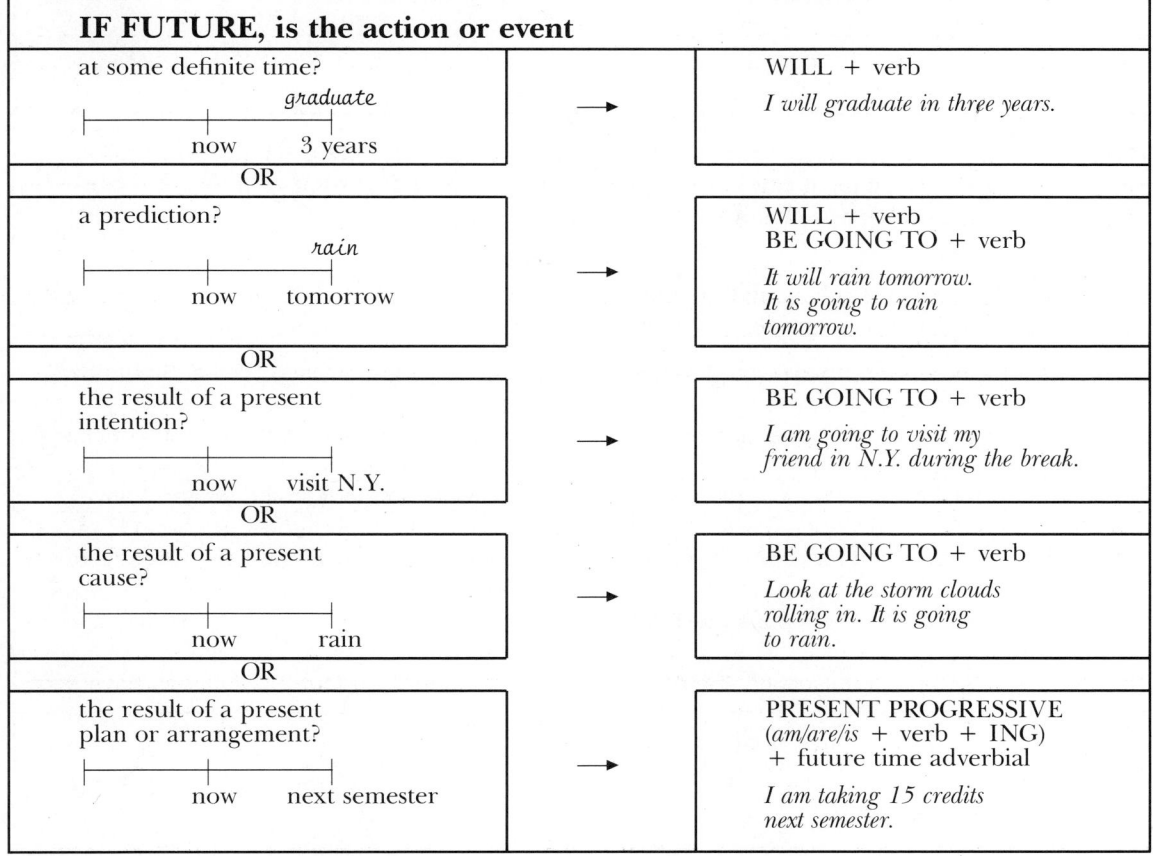

APPENDICES

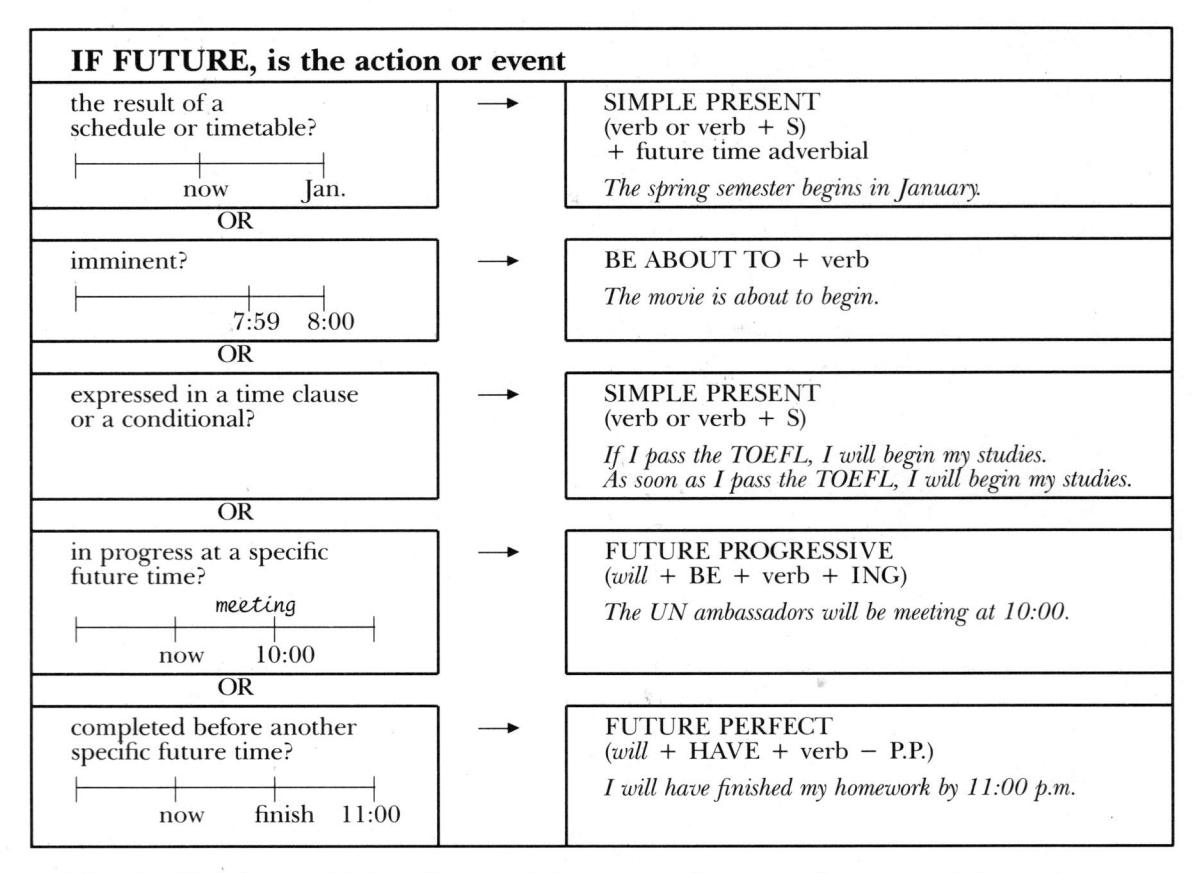

IF FUTURE, is the action or event		
the result of a schedule or timetable? ⊢——┼——┼——⊣ now　　Jan.	→	**SIMPLE PRESENT** (verb or verb + S) + future time adverbial *The spring semester begins in January.*
OR		
imminent? ⊢——┼——┼——⊣ 　　7:59　8:00	→	**BE ABOUT TO + verb** *The movie is about to begin.*
OR		
expressed in a time clause or a conditional?	→	**SIMPLE PRESENT** (verb or verb + S) *If I pass the TOEFL, I will begin my studies.* *As soon as I pass the TOEFL, I will begin my studies.*
OR		
in progress at a specific future time? 　　　　*meeting* ⊢——┼——┼——⊣ 　now　10:00	→	**FUTURE PROGRESSIVE** (*will* + BE + verb + ING) *The UN ambassadors will be meeting at 10:00.*
OR		
completed before another specific future time? ⊢——┼——┼——⊣ 　now　finish　11:00	→	**FUTURE PERFECT** (*will* + HAVE + verb − P.P.) *I will have finished my homework by 11:00 p.m.*

NOTE: The Verb Tense Editing Chart explains commonly used verb tenses and forms, *but not all*. After using the chart, if you are still unsure of the accuracy of some of the verb forms in your draft, ask another writer in the class for help.

Exercise 5 Read the following text and correct any errors with verb tenses or forms. Use the Verb Tense Editing Chart to guide your editing.

I have lived in Bangkok until 1993, when I was moving to the United States. Right now, I study English in an intensive language program. Every day, I am taking three hours of classes. I am also having one hour of independent study each week in the learning center. I have study in this program for only two months, but I am feeling that my English has already improve a great deal. If I will pass the TOEFL at the end of the semester, I will be studying computer science at the university. The next semester is beginning in four months, so I have a lot of English to learn by then.

APPENDIX A

EDIT NOW

Reread your draft. Follow these steps.

① With a pencil, underline the main verb inside each clause. (The main verb is the verb that is marked, or inflected, for tense. An infinitive, gerund, or participial phrase is not a main verb.)

② Go through your draft focusing on each main verb one by one. For each verb, ask yourself these questions:

   a. What is the time reference for this clause? Past? Present? Future?

   b. How do I know the time reference? (In other words, what are the meaning clues that indicate the time reference?)

③ After you have identified the time reference, use the Verb Tense Editing Chart on the previous pages to help ensure that you write the correct verb forms.

APPENDIX B: *Editing Correction Symbols*

art	= article. I wanted to study in ∨̂ⁿ university with ∨̂ⁿ good reputation.
CAP	= capitalization. I want to study ~~english~~ *English*.
CLS	= clause structure. I went to California after ∨̂ᴵ graduated from high school.
CON	= connection. I am interested in the field of medicine, ∨̂ˢᵒ I want to be a nurse.
P	= punctuation I loved math in high ~~school, because~~ *school. Because* of that, I hope to be a math teacher some day.
prep	= preposition. I am interested ~~with~~ *in* studying engineering.
pro-agr	= pronoun agreement. One of my hobbies is listening to music. ~~They~~ *It* can always help me relax.
S-PL	= singular or plural?? My oldest ~~sisters~~ *sister* studied in the United States last year. One of my ~~friend~~ *friends* recommended this university.
sp	= spelling. I hope to ~~graduete~~ *graduate* in two years.
VB-agr	= verb agreement. Music ~~help~~ *helps* me relax.
VF	= verb form Last year, I took a course in English while I was ~~work~~ *working*.
VT	= verb tense Last year, I ~~study~~ *studied* English while I was working.
WO	= word order. The admissions officer was very kind (who I interviewed with).
WF	= word form. My country is a ~~development~~ *developing* nation and needs trained engineers.
WW	= word choice. The ~~judgment~~ *evaluation* system in my country is different from the one in the United States.
¶	= Begin a new paragraph.
???	= I don't understand what you mean here. Please talk to me about it.

APPENDIX C: *Word Processing*

The computer is a wonderful tool for you as a writer. It makes the drafting, revising, and editing steps easier because with a few keystrokes or movements of a mouse, you can make major and minor changes in your writing. You can then assess the effects of those changes, decide whether to keep them or reject them, and go on to make other changes as necessary.

Below are some suggestions for how to take advantage of the computer at each step in the writing process.

WRITING A FIRST DRAFT ON THE COMPUTER

1. Type your first draft at the terminal.
2. Before you begin, set the line spacing to 2.
3. Type your ideas as they flow. Do not be overly concerned with organization, grammar, spelling, or typing errors (typos) at this point.
4. When you are finished inputting the sentences, print out a "hard" copy of your draft.

WRITING A SECOND DRAFT ON THE COMPUTER

1. Reread the writing assignment carefully to be sure that you are staying on task. Be sure that you have a clear idea of your purpose and your audience.
2. Reread the computer printout of your first draft carefully.
3. Think about the feedback and suggestions that you received from your readers. Try to look at your writing with a fresh and constructively critical eye. Should you omit any information? Should you add any information? Should you reorganize any of the ideas? (You want your second draft to be fairly well organized and complete, so spend some time on this step.)
4. On the computer printout of your first draft, mark down any changes that you plan to make in your second draft.
   a. If you plan to reorganize any ideas, try using brackets and arrows to show the new order.
   b. If you plan to omit any ideas, cross them out with one line.
   c. If you plan to add any information, write it in the margin or in blank spaces, and somehow indicate to yourself where it will be inserted.
5. Open the file containing your first draft and make your changes.
6. When you have finished revising the draft, read through it on the screen carefully. Make additional changes that you feel are necessary.
7. If your word processing program has the capability, use a spell check program at this time.
8. Print out a copy of your second draft.

APPENDICES

⑨ Read through this "hard" copy. If you see any more changes you would like to make, open the file and make them. Print a new hard copy.

WRITING A THIRD DRAFT ON THE COMPUTER

① Reread your second draft carefully.

② Read your readers' comments carefully; ask for clarification or additional information if necessary.

③ On the computer printout of your second draft, mark down any changes that you plan to make in your third draft.

   a. If you plan to reorganize any ideas, try using brackets and arrows to show the new order.
   b. If you plan to omit any ideas, cross them out with one line.
   c. If you plan to add any information, write it in the margin or in blank spaces, and somehow indicate to yourself where it will be inserted.
   d. If you plan to change any sentence patterns, mark those changes in the margins or blank spaces of your second draft.
   e. If you see any corrections that you should make in your grammar, spelling, or punctuation, make them on your second draft.

④ Open the file containing your second draft and make your changes.

⑤ When you have finished revising the draft, read through it carefully. Make any additional changes.

⑥ If your word processing program has the capability, use a spell check program at this time.

⑦ Print out a copy of your third draft.

⑧ Read through this "hard" copy. If you see any more changes you would like to make, open the file and make them. Print a new hard copy.

APPENDIX D: *Readings and Worksheets*

"FOREIGN STUDENTS UNDER FIRE," BY JAMES N. BAKER

"FOREIGN STUDENTS STILL FLOCK TO THE U.S.," BY CRAUFURD GOODWIN AND MICHAEL NACHT

"FOREIGN STUDENTS ARE A BURDEN TO AMERICA," BY GEORGIE ANNE GEYER

"DIPLOMATS IN OUR BACKYARD," BY MARK RENTZ

WORKSHEET FOR SOURCES RELATED TO THE TOPIC OF INTERNATIONAL STUDENTS IN THE UNITED STATES

"PSYCHOLOGICAL PREDISPOSITIONS," BY JOAN RUBIN AND IRENE THOMPSON

"INSTRUCTIONAL SETTINGS," BY JOAN RUBIN AND IRENE THOMPSON

Foreign Students Under Fire

Resentment rises as more come to the U.S.

Massachusetts likes to call its capital city the "cradle of liberty" and compare it to ancient Athens. But these images of enlightenment have come under challenge in Boston's gold-domed Statehouse. The number of foreign students coming into Massachusetts, state Rep. Roger Tougas said, has "gotten out of hand." He argued that the students have been "poshly subsidized by tax dollars," even if they were from countries associated with terrorism. To discourage foreign students, Tougas introduced legislation to raise their tuition at public colleges. His bill passed easily, and Gov. Michael Dukakis signed it into law last June. Starting in 1988, foreign undergraduates have to pay as much as 38 percent more than American youngsters from out of state. "Foreign students are not productive citizens," said Tougas. "If they are going to reap the benefits, I just want them to pay for it."

Scattered episodes—large and small—indicate that resentment of foreign students is also rising around the country. Louisiana increased tuitions this year, and Tougas says he's gotten inquiries from legislators in other states. An embarrassing incident took place at the University of Rochester in upstate New York. Because the university's graduate business school had accepted a Japanese employee of Fuji Photo Film Inc., the Eastman Kodak Co.—fearful of corporate spying at its Rochester headquarters—threatened to withdraw the 230 students it provides yearly to various programs at the school. The school caved in and rescinded the young man's acceptance, but last month, after a public outcry, invited him back. (He had already enrolled at the Massachusetts Institute of Technology.)

Source: Baker, James N. 1987. *Newsweek.* Oct. 19:73–74.

Five years ago, when the number of foreign students hit 300,000, concerned college administrators predicted a backlash of quotas, prohibitive tuition hikes and growing xenophobia. The resentment has been building gradually, though foreigners account for less than 3 percent of the total college population. Fears that foreign graduates will snatch away good jobs from Americans—particularly engineers whose profession draws the most foreigners—persist despite evidence to the contrary. The Immigration and Naturalization Service says the majority of foreign students return home, and the Department of Labor reports that non-Americans constitute only 4 percent of the country's engineering work force.

Statistics also show that the 343,777 foreign students now in the United States—two-thirds of whom pay their own way—are a good national investment. Not only do they pump $2 billion to $3 billion into the economy every year, they bring distinction to second-rate colleges, keep graduate programs afloat and contribute to U.S. technology. Making foreign students welcome has always been a source of goodwill. Under the best of circumstances, the policy makes lifelong, sometimes influential, friends for the United States—for example, both Corazon Aquino and Zachary Onyonka, Kenya's foreign minister, graduated from U.S. colleges. Proponents of an open-door policy expect the same not only from the Malaysians and Taiwanese who are here in large numbers now but also from the students from oil-rich Iran and Nigeria who flocked here in the early 1980s.

Why then do foreign students encounter resentment from Americans? Perhaps it's because they're highly visible in certain disciplines. They earn from 27 to 41 percent of the doctorate degrees awarded in engineering, life sciences, architecture, computer science and mathematics. Some schools have consciously set out to lure talent from overseas to enhance the reputation of their graduate programs. The University of Southwestern Louisiana in Lafayette, for example, built an $8 million computer system for studying factory automation—the only one of its kind on an American college campus—knowing it would attract the best minds in the world to study computer science there.

Bachelor's degree: Still, foreign students are not supplanting Americans in graduate schools; they're filling empty spaces. Americans simply aren't going to graduate schools in force anymore. At Syracuse University, where foreigners account for 70 percent of the graduate engineering enrollment, dean Theodore Bickart admits, "Quite frankly, they are sustaining our higher education." Eager to make money, Americans tend to rush into the marketplace armed with only a bachelor's degree. "Financially, it was foolish of me to carry on," says Texan Michael Schuh, a Ph.D. candidate in mechanical engineering at the University of California, Berkeley. "Someone who's been working for as long as I've been in grad school will be making the same money." More patient foreigners tend to be motivated by other goals. Schuh's classmate Ching Bin Liaw of Taiwan says, "In Chinese society, a higher degree means people respect you and your family will be proud."

As the debate about foreign students heats up, educators, professionals and legislators offer controversial—and often contradictory—images of the 1990s. Some imagine university faculties clogged with foreigners; others envision important scientific research left undone because all the Ph.D.'s went home after all. The problem boils down to the absence of qualified Americans, a situation that can be remedied only over time by recruiting bright students for careers in scientific fields. "We're shooting ourselves in the foot if we send foreigners home," says Robert Weatherall, job-placement director at MIT. "It's because of them we're not further behind." His point is hard to dispute. Imagine what might have happened if we'd booted out Chinese-born Paul Chu

> in 1968, right after he received his Ph.D. in physics from the University of California, San Diego. Earlier this year Chu stunned the world when he used yttrium to make a high-temperature superconductor. The news may have reached the Massachusetts Statehouse: last week a legislative committee recommended repealing last summer's tuition hike.

WORKSHEET "Foreign Students Under Fire," *Newsweek*, October 19, 1987, pages 73 and 74.

  I. Pre-Reading:

  A *Easing into the Text and Tapping Prior Knowledge*

  1. Number the paragraphs 1 to 7.

  2. Read the title and the subtitle. Then freewrite answers to the following questions and discuss them with your classmates.

   a. What might cause resentment towards foreign students?
   b. Who might feel resentful? Why?
   c. Why do you think that the number of foreign students in the United States is increasing?
   d. At this point, do you expect this article to discuss the disadvantages of allowing foreign students to come to this country, the advantages, or both? Why?
   e. What do you already know about this topic? Freewrite some notes.

  B *Getting in Deeper and Forming Hypotheses about the Text*

  Read the first paragraph and the first sentence of paragraphs 2 to 7. At this point, what do you think the writer's topic is? What do you think the writer's purpose and main idea are? What do you think the global structure of the entire text is?

  Discuss with your classmates what you expect to learn from the article.

  II. Reading: Read the article through one time quickly, just to get the "big picture." Then read it a second time, paying attention to the details. While you are reading the second time, highlight or underline main ideas.

  III. Post-Reading: Make a graphic representation of the text

  OR

  Prepare a study outline.

  IV. Critical Analysis: You have read the article carefully and understand the contents. Now, critically analyze and evaluate some of the ideas within the article. The questions below will help you draw inferences, judge the validity of some of the arguments, and interpret and apply some of the ideas to your own life, context, and paper. Freewrite answers to these questions and then discuss them with your classmates.

  1. Reread sentence one of paragraph 1. What does "cradle of liberty" mean? Is it a good thing to say about Boston or a bad thing?

   Now, reread sentence two. What seems to be the writer's opinion about the Massachusetts state law regarding tuition for foreign students? What does he imply about the legislators, and even the governor at the time, Governor Michael Dukakis?

APPENDICES

2. In paragraph 1, Tougas asserts, "Foreign students are not productive citizens."

   a. What are some inferences that you can draw from Tougas' statement. In other words, what is Tougas implying about foreign students?

   b. Do you agree with Tougas' idea that foreign students are not productive? If yes, why? If no, provide some counterevidence to his assertion.

3. Paragraph 1 informs us that the tuition increase in Massachusetts would mean an increase of "as much as 38 percent more than American youngsters from out of state [pay]."

   a. If your state follows the example of Massachusetts in 1987, what would a 38% increase mean for foreign students? How much would foreign undergraduate tuition be for one semester?

   b. What would that kind of increase mean for you and/or your friends? Would it affect you? How?

4. Paragraph 2 gives two examples to prove that resentment of foreign students is rising.

   a. What other examples can you think of that support this idea?

   b. What counterevidence can you think of to disprove it?

5. Paragraph 4 states that foreign students bring in $2 billion to $3 billion a year.

   a. What do foreign students spend their money on?

   b. What areas of the economy are they pumping money into?

6. Paragraph 4 gives examples of influential friends of the United States who are former foreign students.

   a. In what ways does it benefit the United States to make these friends?

   b. Can you think of other examples?

7. In paragraph 6, the article states that foreign students are "filling empty spaces" in graduate schools.

   What are some inferences that you can draw from that statement?

8. In several places in the article, the writer mentions foreign students' contributions to research and technology.

   What examples do you know of? Do you know of any examples of this happening at your university or college?

9. In paragraph 7, Robert Weatherall of MIT says, "We're shooting ourselves in the foot if we send foreigners home. It's because of them we're not further behind."

   a. Does Weatherall agree with Tougas' legislation or disagree?

   b. What is Weatherall's job? What is Tougas' job? Who do you think is probably more knowledgeable about the impact of foreign students on this country? Why?

10. Read the last sentence of the article.

    a. What does this imply about the Massachusetts legislature?

b. Do you think Tougas is a member of the committee that is recommending repeal of the law?

11. What does the writer of this article think about the issue? How do you know?

Foreign Students Still Flock to the U.S.

The U.S. has one major export industry that is depression-proof: higher education. The number of foreign students here climbed from about 135,000 in 1969–70 to at least 327,000 in 1981–82. Four of every five of these had their primary source of funds in personal resources, family support or home governments. They were paying customers. Their contribution to the U.S. balance of payments runs in the billions. Moreover, the trend seems steadily upward. Students come from virtually all countries. They come for professional education in engineering, business administration and computer science, but also for the liberal arts. It is time we recognize, understand and encourage this trend.

The conventional wisdom after World War II was that as higher education in older countries was reformed and reconstructed, and as the systems of new nations took shape, students would no longer flock to our shores. That is not what happened. While the international competitiveness of our auto and steel plants declined, that of our colleges and universities improved. Some observers speculate that foreign students in this country may reach one million by the turn of the century.

Why they keep coming isn't entirely clear. Several reasons suggest themselves. First, for some the free and open spirit of American education together with its close relationship to pioneering research afford an experience that cannot be duplicated in other places. For others the practical orientation of American post-secondary education, in subjects from hospitality management to fire science, responds to their wants. Overall the reputation and prestige of an American degree remains great and is a source of upward professional mobility. For a few, of course, an American education can be a first step to permanent U.S. residence or citizenship.

Foreign students yield various side benefits. They contribute significantly in the seminars and research laboratories of professors in fields vital to the national interest, such as engineering and science, where fashion, market conditions or national policy have kept American students away. They also, by their mere presence, help to educate American students at a time when sophisticated understanding of the world is crucial. Moreover, foreign students have filled the classrooms and dormitories of many institutions, public and private, faced with reduced domestic demand.

For colleges and universities the results of educating foreigners are not all rosy. Costly advisory services must be provided and the foreign student may create a host of challenges for an institution, from admissions and housing to record-keeping and community relations. In the classroom the impact is complex: on the one hand foreigners contribute a breadth of perspective and richness of experience; on the other, their linguistic problems and cultural differences sometimes constitute an educational "drag" because of their

Source: Goodwin, Crauford D., and Michael Nacht. 1983. *The Wall Street Journal* July 21:26.

APPENDICES

constrained participation in seminars and classes, and their service as occasionally incomprehensible graduate-student instructors. Numbers are the key. Up to a point, which is difficult to identify, benefits outweigh costs; after this point, the lines cross.

Two powerful arguments are raised against foreign students: national security and economic competitiveness. Why, some ask, should American universities train citizens of potential adversaries in skills that can be used to develop military capabilities that could threaten the U.S.? Others argue that it is the height of economic folly to provide expertise in solid-state electronics, managerial effectiveness or agricultural productivity to citizens of our trading rivals who will use this knowledge to undermine the competitiveness of American industry. These serious concerns deserve careful scrutiny; thus far, however, little evidence can be marshaled in their defense.

What is most surprising about the foreign student scene is that so few people are paying serious attention to it. And those who are manifest a negative attitude inconsistent with the facts. State legislators demand quotas or differential pricing which bear little relationship to the costs and benefits. Congress has recently considered changing immigration regulations governing students to constrain opportunity for in-service training after formal education.

The education of foreign students, like banking and insurance, is the sale abroad of a valuable service. Like agriculture, the market is highly competitive and warrants the support and encouragement of public authorities at all levels. Moreover, the public and the business community should appreciate their good fortune in having a promising export growth industry unnoticed right under their noses. Individual colleges and universities should decide for themselves how many and by what means foreign students should be welcomed. State governments must reconsider their recent negative attitude. At the national level, the State Department or a newly created Department of Trade should be charged to facilitate the flow of foreign students to our shores. America has too few export success stories of this magnitude to permit the foreign student to continue to oscillate between nationalism and neglect.

Mr. Goodwin, dean of the Graduate School at Duke University, and Mr. Nacht, associate professor of public policy at Harvard's Kennedy School of Government, recently completed a study on foreign students in America.

WORKSHEET "Foreign Students Still Flock to the U.S." Wall Street Journal, July 21, 1983, page 26.

I. Pre-Reading

   A *Easing into the Text and Tapping Prior Knowledge*

   1. Number the paragraphs 1 to 8.

   2. Read the title. Note the source. Read the information about the authors at the end of the article.

   3. Freewrite answers to the following questions and discuss them with your classmates.

a. Who wrote the article?
b. What are their credentials?
c. What kind of source is the *Wall Street Journal*? Why would an article on this topic appear in this periodical?

B *Getting in Deeper and Forming Hypotheses about the Text*

1. Read the first paragraph and the first sentence of each paragraph 2 to 8.

2. Read the last paragraph completely.

3. Freewrite answers to these questions and discuss them with your classmates.

   a. Would these authors agree or disagree with Representative Roger Tougas?
   b. Would they agree or disagree with Robert Weatherall?

II. Reading: Read the article through one time quickly, just to get the "big picture." Then read it a second time, paying attention to the details. While you are reading the second time, highlight or underline main ideas.

III. Post-Reading: Make a graphic representation of the text.

OR

Prepare a study outline.

IV. Critical Analysis: You have read the article carefully and understand the contents. Now, critically analyze and evaluate some of the ideas within the article. The questions below will help you draw inferences, judge the validity of some of the arguments, and interpret and apply some of the ideas to your own life, context, and paper. Freewrite answers to these questions and then discuss them with your classmates.

1. Now that you have read the entire article, what seems to be these writers' attitude towards foreign students in the United States? On what do you base your answer?

2. In paragraph 3, how many possible reasons are given to explain why foreign students come to the United States? What are those reasons?

   Based on your experience and background knowledge, do you agree that these are likely reasons why foreign students come to the United States? Do you know of any others? What are they?

3. In paragraph 4, how many benefits of foreign students are listed? What are they?

   Can you think of specific examples at your own college or university to illustrate each benefit? What are they?

   What are other benefits that you can think of?

4. In paragraph 5, how many drawbacks of foreign students are listed? What are they?

   Can you think of specific examples at your own college or university to illustrate each drawback? What are they?

   What are other drawbacks that you can think of?

5. In paragraph 6, the writers dismiss two worries that some people raise against foreign students; they claim that there is not enough evidence to support these worries.

   Based on your background knowledge and experience, do you think that these worries are valid? Explain your answer.

Foreign Students Are a Burden to America

The world's tired and hungry and those "yearning to be free" still are struggling to the United States. Among them is a new group whose presence is creating myriad new problems for the country.

It consists of the 300,000 foreign students now in the United States, a number that soon will soar to half a million. In Southern California community colleges, 15% to 30% of the students now are foreigners.

Though there is a prevalent idea in the Third World that America owes these students an education and should take them tuition-free, the contradictory facts are these: The massive influx of foreign students brings in about $2 billion a year, but students pay only about 60% of their costs. Taxpayers are subsidizing almost all these students, particularly at state schools.

It is time, then, that we forge some national policy on foreign students. And a group of leading educators is trying to do just that.

"We have to ask, what is our national policy?" says Richard Berendzen, the dynamic young president of American University. "I personally think we have to develop a global concern.

"The immigration situation and the foreign student situation are intimately linked. I don't know if the American people really understand the momentum of what is happening here. We are becoming a global village."

Berendzen heads the National Commission on Foreign Students and Institutional Policy, an adjunct of the American Council on Education. The commission is trying to hammer out policy directives for the future. But what should they be?

In formulating these directives we should keep in mind these risks:

The first danger is that we let the influx of foreign students add a further disintegrative note to an American society already divided by other immigration difficulties. Any responsible nation must know who is actually here, and where and why, or it will soon cease being a nation.

The second danger lies in accepting students as if we were a kind of technology drugstore and nothing more. Every foreign student should be required to know or study English (something many, ironically, now complain about) and to take an appropriate amount of American Studies courses. It is crucial that this country not be perceived as a country without pride in its institutions and ideas; it is crucial that foreign students know what we stand for.

Third, we must clean up the misleading "come-ons" of colleges needing students, not to speak of such outright corrupt practices as issuing false documents to bring foreign students here.

Given these long-overdue clarifications, we should welcome foreign students even more generously than before—and learn from them while they are here.

Berendzen's "global village" is indeed upon us. More than ever we need to be clear about the law and principles that allow us to live sanely and with civility within that global village.

Source: Geyer, Georgie Anne. 1981. *The Plain Dealer* July 8:21A.

Diplomats in Our Backyard

How we treat foreign students on our campuses can have lasting consequences for our country

Last year, after we invited my foreign students to dinner, my wife and I were astonished to learn that we were in all likelihood breaking bread with future world leaders. One of my students, Khaled, in replying to another student's question, mentioned that his father had been president for five years.

"Of what company?" I asked.

"Of my country," he replied.

His wife nodded, adding "President Abdullah al-Sallal, Khaled's father, is commonly referred to as having given birth to North Yemen."

From around the table came other foreshadowings of greatness: architects from Thailand and Mexico pursuing postgraduate degrees; the fifth- and 57th-ranked undergraduate students in all of Tunisia; a Japanese educator; a brilliant and highly awarded Korean opera singer; the daughter of an Egyptian national assemblyman. That night I realized the possibilities of international diplomacy and envisioned a blockbuster sequel to Dale Carnegie's best seller—"How to Win Friends and Influence Nations."

According to Lawson Lau, author of "The World at Your Doorstep," one-third to one-half of the world's top positions in politics, business, education and the military will be filled in the next 25 years by foreign students attending colleges and universities in the United States. Some of the puzzled and bewildered and sometimes unimpressive-looking sojourners in our dorms, cafeterias and classrooms may one day assume national responsibilities in their countries. How we treat them now could have lasting global consequences.

The next time you see a friendless foreign student, just remember that the presidents, prime ministers and princes of the following countries studied in our own backyard: El Salvador (José Napoleón Duarte at Notre Dame); Philippines (Corazon Aquino at College of Mount St. Vincent, New York); Mexico (Miguel de la Madrid at Harvard); Zimbabwe (the Rev. Canaan Sodindo Banana at Wesley Theological Seminary, Washington, D.C.); Malawi (Dr. Hastings Kamuzu Banda at University of Chicago and Meharry Medical College in Tennessee); Sweden (Ingvar Carlsson at Northwestern); Greece (Andreas G. Papandreou at Harvard); Jamaica (Edward Philip George Seaga at Harvard); Belize (Manuel Esquivel at Loyola); Iceland (Steingrimur Hermannsson at Illinois and California Institutes of Technology); and King Birendra Bir Bikram Shad Dev of Nepal (Harvard).

Although most foreign students are satisfied with their academic experience in the United States, many also have said that they hate America because they feel that Americans don't know or even care if they exist. For example, in a study published in 1976, 40 percent of the 247 foreign students surveyed at 38 Southern universities felt "unwelcome, lonely, and isolated," and the situation is not much different in the North. One of my foreign students, representing the view of many, made this damning observation: "Americans are very friendly, but they don't make good friends."

Since a number of foreign students had asked me for advice on how to make friends with Americans, I helped develop a program in the English language and

Source: Rentz, Mark D. 1987. *Newsweek* Feb. 16: 10.

culture division which seeks to pair foreign and American students for an hour or so a week of friendly conversation. The first time we tried to run "Conversation Partners," we were inundated with requests from foreign students who were willing and wanting—but mostly had to wait because we couldn't attract enough American students. We finally contacted church groups and community-service organizations so our students could meet face to face and on a regular basis with average Americans.

Peace Corps: Making a foreign friend is really one of the easiest things in the world to do. They don't necessarily need us to do things *for* them, they just need us to do things *with* them. They are, by and large, courteous, ambitious, bright and sociable. According to the Institute of International Education, they are unmarried (80 percent), male (70.7 percent) and supported by personal or family funds (67.1 percent). Almost one out of five is working toward a master's degree; one in 10 is enrolled in a doctoral program. They come from 187 different countries and all 343,777 of them are spread across the United States. Alaska has 234 international students.

Making a foreign friend is easy, but turning a foreigner into an enemy is apparently easier still. Stereotypes abound, but not every Arab is a terrorist from Libya or Lebanon and not every Asian is responsible for our country's trade imbalance. What a great irony it is that we alienate on our own soil the citizens of nations we journey great lengths to influence. The U.S. government annually allocates $15 billion, divided almost equally into military and economic aid, to foreign countries. To add a personal touch, we have sent, since 1961, more than 120,000 Peace Corps volunteers to 92 nations. Yet when we entertain strangers in our midst, instead of saying, "Welcome to our home," the words many foreigners seem to hear, expressly or not, are "Go home."

Apparently we did not endear ourselves to Lt. Col. Mengistu Haile Mariam, who trained at the Aberdeen Proving Grounds, a U.S. Army ordnance base in Maryland. After he seized power in Ethiopia, Mengistu expelled more than 341 American military men and civilians and signed cooperative accords with the U.S.S.R.

The strategic possibilities of forging friendships with foreign students are so beneficial that Richard Berendzen, president of American University in Washington, D.C., has advocated increased government support for international education. The "future leaders of the developing world," he has said, not only will get a diploma in the United States but also will gain "some understanding of our culture ranging from our form of government to our sports, from our TV to our food, from our business life to our spiritual life." The political benefits are obvious. The next wave of world leaders is here. Influence the world; go out and make a foreign friend.

Rentz teaches English in the department of international studies at Arizona State University.

WORKSHEET FOR SOURCES RELATED TO THE TOPIC OF INTERNATIONAL STUDENTS IN THE UNITED STATES Use the chart below to help you organize the information that you have learned through your sources on the issue of foreign students in the United States. In the spaces at the left, write in the name of each source of information. In note form under each category, write the ideas expressed by that source. Follow the examples that have been completed for you.

APPENDIX D

IMPACT OF FOREIGN STUDENTS

economic	educational, technological	cultural/ social	global	other
$2-3 billion/ year (p. 73) Source: James Baker "F.S. Under Fire" Newsweek	research —e.g., Paul Chu (p. 74)			
Source:				
Source:				
Source:				
Source:				
Source:				

APPENDICES

IMPACT OF FOREIGN STUDENTS

economic	educational, technological	cultural/ social	global	other
Source:				
Source:				
Source:				
Source:				
Source:				
Source:				

Psychological Predispositions

A number of psychological traits appear to be related to successful language learning. One of them, motivation, is so important that it is discussed separately in Chapter 2. In this chapter we examine several other traits that have a significant effect on language mastery.

Attitude—*Emotions are important.*

If aptitude is an intellectual trait, attitude is an emotional one. On the one hand, it may have to do with the way learners feel about the foreign culture and its people. They may admire them and want to learn more about them by becoming fluent in their language. Or, they may like the people who speak the foreign language and wish to be accepted by them. Research has shown a definite relationship between attitudes and success when foreign-language learners have an opportunity to know people who speak the language they are studying. Such positive attitudes usually help learners to maintain their interest long enough to achieve language mastery. Thus, if you find France and the French people attractive, if you wish to learn more about them or wish to become more like them, you are likely to succeed at learning to speak French well.

Some people are remarkably successful in mastering a language without feeling powerfully drawn to the country or the people who speak it. They may need the language for academic or career purposes, so their attitude is purely pragmatic. These two attitudes are not mutually exclusive: it is entirely possible that a person may want to learn Spanish because he or she wants to understand the Spanish people better *and* wants to study in Spain. More important than specific attitude is that the language learner experience a real need to communicate and make meanings clear.

Extroversion—*Practice is important.*

It should not be surprising that personality influences the way a person goes about learning a foreign language. Although we cannot, at present, sketch the ideal language-learning personality, several traits appear to be related to success. Of these, extroversion is repeatedly mentioned as a positive trait. When everything else is equal, a sociable person who uses every opportunity to talk with other people may be more successful because by initiating and maintaining more contacts he or she has more occasion to hear and use the new language.

Inhibition—*Make yourself comfortable.*

People who are painfully aware of their limitations and worry about their ability to use the language are usually less willing to engage in either classroom practice or in real-world communication. Shyness and inhibition can stand in the way of progress in speaking (perhaps less in the way of reading) a foreign language. They can also prevent a person from taking risks or seizing opportunities to practice and learn. Fear of making a mistake or being misunderstood can keep a learner from adopting an open-minded, active, and creative approach to language learning. Everything else being equal, a person who has an open, receptive attitude towards the foreign language, who is not afraid to use it, and who feels at ease in foreign-language situations is more likely to learn from his or her language experiences.

Thus, if you have an open, inquisitive, worry-free approach to learning a foreign language, if you find the whole experience enjoyable and rewarding, you will probably learn better. You may want to review your life situation in general and ask yourself the following questions: Is my self-esteem low in language class? If so, what can I do to raise it? (If your teacher is highly intolerant of errors, you may find it helpful, when you can, to change teachers.) Is there anything wrong with my study habits? Do I expect too much of myself? Do I really have the time to devote to language learning, or do I have too many other pressing matters on my mind?

Tolerance of Ambiguity—*Everything is not black and white.*

Tolerance of ambiguity allows a person to reconcile and accommodate ideas that may be contradictory or information that may be inconsistent. A person who is tolerant of ambiguity does not see everything in terms of black and white and does not put information in air-tight compartments. Such a person is willing to accept the fact that there are many shades of grey and that uncertainty and inconsistency must be accommodated. Tolerance of ambiguity has been noted as an asset in learning a foreign language because there are so many inconsistencies in language rules that even native speakers cannot always agree on correct usage or explain certain language phenomena. Also, whether a turn of speech is right or wrong may depend on the situation rather than on an ironclad rule. A person who can accept an evasive answer, such as, "Well, I suppose you could say it that way under certain circumstances," is more likely to have an open, flexible system for accommodating new information as knowledge of the language increases.

Learning Style—*Rules or risks?*

Learning a foreign language is just one form of learning in general; therefore, each individual will employ the approach that he or she usually applies to other learning situations. When it comes to foreign languages, one kind of learner prefers a highly structured approach with much explanation in the mother tongue, graded exercises, constant correction, and careful formulation of rules. This type of learner is very analytical, reflective, and reluctant to say anything in the foreign language that is not grammatically perfect. This person is a rule learner. A second type of learner relies more on intuition, the gathering of examples, and imitation. He or she is willing to take risks. There is no evidence that one type of learner is more successful than the other. What is more important perhaps is that the learner's style be appropriate to the particular task. If the task is to communicate, then risk taking is in order. If the task is to say or write something correctly, then rules should be consulted.

It is important that each learner's preferences be accommodated in the classroom. You may thus wish to examine your own preferences, and communicate them to your teachers. For instance, if you feel that you need rules, you may be quite uncomfortable in a classroom dedicated to imitation and repetition of dialogues and should ask the teacher for more explanations. If, on the other hand, you feel that you learn more from being exposed to the language and from making your own inferences, you may feel ill-at-ease in a classroom where the teacher painstakingly explains the new grammar in English and should ask the teacher for more practice in speaking.

Eye–Ear Learning

When learning a foreign language, some students depend on their eyes; others depend on their ears. Some learners feel that they learn better if they can see the language written out, while others prefer to listen to tapes and records. It is not clear to what extent "eye-mindedness" and "ear-mindedness" are related to foreign-language mastery. You may want to experiment to find out whether a single method or a combination of the two works best for you.

Instructional Settings

There are two basic environments in which a language can be learned: formal and informal. When a language is learned mainly in a classroom or through audio-visual means, we often call this foreign language learning, whereas when it is learned in an informal setting, it is commonly referred to as second language learning.

Informal Settings—*The biggest classroom is the community.*

In an informal environment, that is, outside of the classroom or the language laboratory, communication is not generally organized around the learner's needs. It is not simplified, graded, or repetitive. An informal environment does, however, offer a great deal of information about the nature of interaction and about appropriate ways of speaking. It usually also offers clues to the meaning of a conversation, since the setting, the relationship between participants, and the topic are generally clear. Further, and more important, it offers one of the strongest reasons for learning—the need to communicate. Most people learn a language in order to talk to other people. In informal environments in which the listeners speak only the foreign language, the need to make oneself understood is crucial. Hence, informal environments offer unlimited opportunities for practice as well as instant reward—being understood. Punishment is just as instant and obvious—one fails to communicate.

In informal settings, learners are neither particularly aware that they are learning nor able to describe what they have learned. Since the primary use of language in informal settings is communication, persons learning another language in such settings usually go through a number of stages before attaining mastery. In the early stages they make lots of mistakes and rely heavily on their first language. With additional practice, they begin to make fewer mistakes and rely less on their native tongue. Eventually, they may reach a stage at which their speech approximates that of native speakers. Often learners in informal settings go through a silent period; they just listen to the new language and do not speak until they feel ready.

Formal Settings—*The classroom is safe.*

In formal environments, learning materials are generally graded, simplified, and arranged around specific linguistic structures and vocabulary lists. This situation provides an opportunity to learn in progression, although the progression may have little to do with the learner's real-life language needs. The teacher usually provides feedback by correcting mistakes and emphasizing rules. Often the mother tongue is used for explanation and communication between teacher and students about everything not contained in the lesson.

Formal classroom environments do not, as a rule, offer strong motivation to communicate or the opportunity to observe the way language is used in real life. The emphasis is on knowing *about* the language, on being able to produce correct sentences on cue, and knowing why they are correct or incorrect. In the classroom, when a student speaks, he or she usually concentrates on producing correct grammar, with the content of the message often quite irrelevant. After all, when one is practicing the plural forms of nouns, it is relatively unimportant whether one pluralizes vegetables or pieces of furniture as long as one does so correctly. The focus is not on *what* is expressed but on *how* it is expressed. In real-world settings, however, confusing the endings on nouns is much less serious than confusing *vegetables* with *furniture*, or asking for *chairs* instead of *cherries*.

In formal settings, people usually first learn a structure and then try to practice it in different contexts. Once the "structure of the day" is mastered, the teacher proceeds to the next, until the students have completed a list of structures considered essential. There is no guarantee, however, that they will be able to use these structures when they need to convey a message and are concentrating on its meaning.

Combining Formal and Informal Settings—*Combine the best of the two worlds.*

Foreign-language educators argue about which is more beneficial for adult learners: studying a foreign language in the classroom or using it in real-life situations. The answer to this question is that both are needed.

When beginning foreign-language learners study in the classroom without a chance for real-life interaction with native speakers, their only sources of input are the teacher, the textbook, and language tapes. They benefit from error correction, explanation of rules, and graded practice, which reduce information overload and provide a certain amount of security. The instructor often makes a conscious attempt to use simplified and familiar language, and this makes the students feel good. As the knowledge of the language increases, however, such study becomes less valuable than the use of the language outside the classroom.

An intermediate or advanced student usually profits more from a stay in the country where the language is spoken than from continuing classroom study. At the advanced level, it is more profitable to use the language as a tool to study other subjects: literature, politics, history, culture, and the like.

Both settings may also be helpful at the same time. Since most adults are more comfortable in structured situations yet also need the motivation to communicate that comes from informal settings, they should try to take advantage of both environments.

From: Rubin, Joan and Irene Thompson. 1982. *How To Be a More Successful Language Learner.* Boston, MA: Heinle and Heinle.

Answer Key

TO THE STUDENT: Below are answers to most of the exercises in Part 3. Use this key to check your sentences after you have completed the exercises. Ask your teacher or tutor if you have any questions.

Please note that some of the exercise items focus on grammatical form and have only one right answer or a limited number of formal variations given the grammatical and the meaning contexts. For these exercises, the key provides the correct answers and, if there are any, some acceptable variations. Other variations may be possible, so be sure to ask your teacher if you have questions.

Other exercise items focus on form while allowing you to supply your own content. These exercises will elicit a certain sentence structure but are open-ended in that the ideas expressed will depend on your own experiences and interpretations. For the open-ended exercises, the key supplies representative answers that illustrate the structure being practiced. Ask your teacher if you have any questions about your answers.

PRACTICE USING ADJECTIVE CLAUSES

Exercise 1 Page 178

1. When you walk down University Avenue, you can't miss Central Library, which is one of the most important buildings on campus.
2. On the first floor, you'll find the information desk, which is a good place to ask questions about the library facilities.
3. The main reference area, which is located behind the stairs on the first floor, is another good place to ask questions.
4. The people who work behind the reference desk are all trained librarians.
5. These librarians, who are very kind and friendly, can help you find reference sources for your research.
6. The library provides a limited number of rooms which can be used for group study sessions.
7. These group study rooms are ideal for students who must get together to work on projects outside of class.

Exercise 2 Page 179

1. When you walk down University Avenue, you can't miss Central Library, which some people consider the most important building on campus.
2. On the first floor, you'll find the circulation desk, which is the place to check out books that (or which or Ø) you want to take home.
3. Some of the people whom (or who or Ø) you'll see working behind the circulation desk are student assistants.
4. To borrow books, you need your student I.D. card, which must be valid for the current semester.
5. Hand your I.D. and the book that (or which or Ø) you want to take home to one of the student assistants, who will enter the relevant information into the library's central computer.
6. Through this computer, the library can keep track of all the books that (or which or Ø) people borrow.
7. Books that (or which or Ø) people do not return by the due date are subject to fines.
8. A person whom (or who or Ø) the computer catches with an overdue book will receive a bill.

Exercise 3 Page 179

1. Many people believe that Akron, Ohio, is an old industrial city where everyone lives next to a closed tire factory.
2. These people imagine the city as it was a few years ago when there was high unemployment in the rubber industry. (If you wish, you can use a comma after "a few years ago." See page 174 for an explanation.)

ANSWER KEY

(3) Akron residents are very impatient with these non-Ohioans, whose image of the city they can't understand.
or
Akron residents, who can't understand this image of the city, are very impatient with these non-Ohioans.

(4) People who live in Akron know it is a city whose cultural facilities can compete with those of any other city in the United States.

(5) The Civic Theater, whose design makes it a historical landmark, is considered the cultural center of Akron.

(6) The Civic was designed in the 1920s, when Akron was the fastest-growing city in the United States.

(7) Inside the Civic is a large theater where you can watch a classic film. (If you wish, you can use a comma after "theater." See page 174 for an explanation.)

(8) The theater, whose ceiling simulates stars and slowly moving clouds, is a romantic place where you can relax. (If you wish, you can use a comma after "place." See page 174 for an explanation.)

(9) On a boring Saturday evening when you are tired of staying home, go to the Akron Civic Theater, where you can enjoy a wonderful evening. (If you wish, you can use a comma after "a boring Saturday evening." See page 174 for an explanation.)

Exercise 4 Page 180

(1) The class that (or which or Ø) I'm having the most trouble in is listening/speaking because, as you know, I haven't had a lot of exposure to spoken English.
or
The class in which I'm having the most trouble is listening/speaking . . . .

(3) The teacher whom (or who or Ø) I practice listening/speaking with is very nice.
or
The teacher with whom I practice listening/speaking is very nice.

(4) However, she gives homework which is usually pretty difficult.

(5) The reading/writing teacher, who is also very nice, gives a lot of homework, too.

(6) Last week, a really funny thing happened before her class, which we have at 4:00.

(7) Because of a scheduling change, we had class in a room where we had never been before.

(10) and (11) One student, who is very big, had his back to the teacher, who was walking down the hall.

(13) Just as she got to the classroom door, the student, who was talking to his friend and gesturing a lot, threw his arm out and hit her right in the nose.

(14) Her nose, which is already a little funny looking, turned bright red and started to shine like a traffic light!

(15) I know that you will be proud of me at the end of the semester when my hard work will pay off. (If you wish, you can use a comma after "the end of the semester." See page 174 for an explanation.)

(16) I am sure that I will pass the TOEFL, which I have to score 500 on.
or
I am sure that I will pass the TOEFL, on which I have to score 500.

PRACTICE USING REDUCED ADJECTIVE CLAUSES

Exercise 1 Page 183

(1) In September 1991, a tourist hiking in the Italian Alps spotted something unusual in the snow.

(2) He found the frozen remains of the Stone Age wanderer now called "The Iceman."

(3) His age, determined by radio-carbon dating, is 5,300 years.
or
Determined by radio-carbon dating, his age is 5,300 years.

ANSWER KEY

(4) The discovery, opening a window on life in the year 3300 B.C., has given scientists new insights into our ancestors.
or
Opening a window on life in the year 3300 B.C., the discovery has given scientists new insights into our ancestors.

(5) Scientists studying the body and discovery site can only speculate about the Iceman's death.

(6) It is believed that he might have been a shepherd taking care of his sheep high in the Alps.

(7) For some reason still unclear to researchers, he separated from his group. (If you wish, you can use a comma after "some reason." See page 174 for an explanation.)

(8) A storm blowing up suddenly probably forced him off course.

(9) The Iceman, unable to find his group, probably fell asleep and froze to death.
or
Unable to find his group, the Iceman probably fell asleep and froze to death.

(10) Soon after his death, a storm dropped a lot of snow, protecting his body and keeping him intact.

PRACTICE USING ADVERB CLAUSES OF CONCESSION AND CONTRAST

Exercise 1 Page 186

There are many ways to complete the sentences for this exercise. The sentences below represent possible correct answers.

(1) Although Americans and the English have the same life expectancy, their doctors employ very different medical practices.

(2) American physicians tend to be aggressive, while British doctors are liable to be conservative.

(3) Despite the fact that there is no evidence for the effectiveness of the yogurt derivative lactobacillus, French doctors use it to treat stomach ailments.

(4) Whereas Americans visit their doctors on the average of 4.6 times a year, Germans see theirs 12 times.

(5) Even though medicine is usually thought of as a science, Lynn Payer considers it an art.

(6) Americans are no healthier than their counterparts in western Europe in spite of the fact that doctors in the United States run many diagnostic tests.

(7) Though the subtitle of the article refers to differences in medical practices all over the world, Payer only researched differences among Western countries.

PRACTICE USING ADVERB CLAUSES OF TIME, CAUSE-EFFECT/ REASON-RESULT, AND PURPOSE AND RELATED STRUCTURES

Exercise 1 Page 189

With all these sentences, you can write either the independent or the dependent clause first. (See sentences 1 and 2 as examples.) If the sentence begins with the dependent clause, use a comma.

(1) After (or when) I graduated from high school, I worked as a salesman.
or
I worked as a salesman after (or when) I graduated from high school.

(2) I participated in my school's science fair when I was a junior.
or
When I was a junior, I participated in my school's science fair.

(3) As soon as I finish my B.A., I will return home.

ANSWER KEY

(4) I will live here until I finish my studies.

(5) While I was working at Wang Computer, I was promoted three times.

(6) Before I flew to the United States, I bought life insurance.

(7) Since I came to the United States, I have eaten food from my country only three times.

(8) Once (or when, as soon as, after) I get used to the food here, I will feel more comfortable.

(9) I will never get used to the food as long as I am in this country.

(10) Whenever I see a fast food restaurant, I feel sick.

Exercise 2 Page 189

With all these sentences, you can write either the independent or the dependent clause first. (See sentences 1 and 2 as examples.) If the sentence begins with the dependent clause, use a comma.

(1) I worked as a computer programmer for three years because I wanted to get experience in that field.
or
Because I wanted to get experience in computer science, I worked as a computer programmer for three years.

(2) I will work for my government since my country needs trained computer programmers.
or
Since my country needs trained computer programmers, I will work for my government.

(3) I am studying at this university because I have heard that it is an excellent school.

(4) Since I was a research assistant in the chemistry department, I gained valuable skills in research techniques.

(5) I came to study in the United States because my aunt lives here.

(6) Now that I am studying at the university, I know I will reach my goals.

Exercise 3 Page 190

There are many ways to complete the sentences for this exercise. The sentences below represent possible correct answers.

(1) My major is architecture. I chose this field because my father is an architect and I have always been interested in his work.

(2) I would like to be a university professor because I want to share my knowledge with others in my country.

(3) Now that I am in the United States, I can read newspapers in English every day.

(4) In secondary school, I was a member of the cheer club because this was a way to meet other students.

Exercise 4 Page 190

(1) Because of its excellent reputation, this university attracts many international students.

(2) Many international students like to study in Florida because of its pleasant weather.

(3) Because of his extensive teaching experience, Mohammed was offered a teaching assistantship his first semester in graduate school.

(4) The famous Olympic skier Pirmin Zurbriggen was not able to win a gold medal in the Alpine Combined in 1988 because of his spectacular fall.

(5) Before the 1988 Olympics, U.S. skater, Debi Thomas, did not have much time to relax because of her very tight schedule.

Exercise 5 Page 190

(1) I decided to study computer science so that (in order that) I could get a good position as a programmer.

(2) I am studying English composition so that (in order that) I will be ready for university work next semester.

(3) I studied hard in the university so that (in order that) I would be successful in my courses.

ANSWER KEY

④ I plan to be a university professor when I return to my country so that (in order that) I can share my knowledge and expertise with others.

⑤ I chose this university so that (in order that) I could do research in the field of polymers.

Exercise 6   Page 190

There are many ways to complete the sentences for this exercise. The sentences below represent possible correct answers.

① I am studying English composition so that (in order that) I can handle my writing assignments in the university.

② I came to this university so that (in order that) I could earn a B.A. in history.

③ I chose my major so that (in order that) I would find a good job.

④ I hope to start my own import-export business so that (in order that) I will earn a good living.

Exercise 7   Page 191

There are many ways to complete the sentences for this exercise. The sentences below represent possible correct answers.

① I have to study all evening in order to (or to) prepare for my test tomorrow.

② People study English to (or in order to) improve their job prospects.

③ I write to (or in order to) communicate my thoughts and ideas to others.

④ People watch t.v. in order to (or to) escape their daily pressures.

PRACTICE USING REDUCED ADVERB CLAUSES

Exercise 1   Page 193

(Combined sentences from Exercise 1, page 189.)

① After graduating from high school, I worked as a salesman.
   or
   I worked as a salesman after graduating from high school.

⑤ While working at Wang Computer, I was promoted three times.
   or
   I was promoted three times while working at Wang Computer.

⑥ Before flying to the United States, I bought life insurance.
   or
   I bought life insurance before flying to the United States.

⑦ Since coming to the United States, I have eaten food from my country only three times.
   or
   I have eaten food from my country only three times since coming to the United States.

(Combined sentences from Exercise 2, page 189.)

① Wanting to get experience in computer science, I worked as a computer programmer for three years.

③ Having heard that this is an excellent school, I am studying at this university.

④ Being a research assistant in the chemistry department, I gained valuable skills in research techniques.

⑥ Studying at the university, I know I will reach my goals.

Exercise 2   Page 193

① While preparing for the Olympics, the athletes must train for several hours each day.

ANSWER KEY

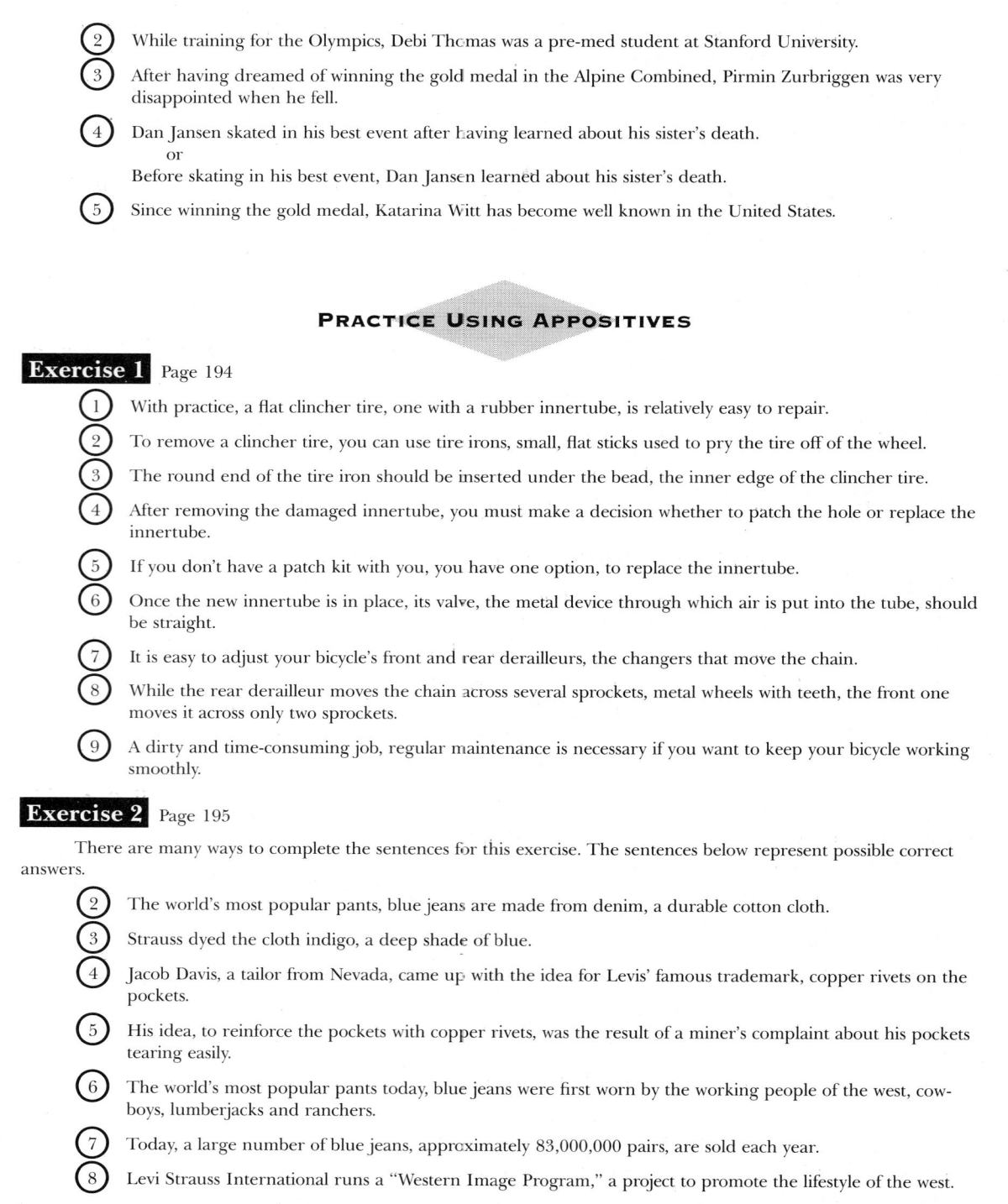

(2) While training for the Olympics, Debi Thomas was a pre-med student at Stanford University.

(3) After having dreamed of winning the gold medal in the Alpine Combined, Pirmin Zurbriggen was very disappointed when he fell.

(4) Dan Jansen skated in his best event after having learned about his sister's death.
or
Before skating in his best event, Dan Jansen learned about his sister's death.

(5) Since winning the gold medal, Katarina Witt has become well known in the United States.

PRACTICE USING APPOSITIVES

Exercise 1 Page 194

(1) With practice, a flat clincher tire, one with a rubber innertube, is relatively easy to repair.

(2) To remove a clincher tire, you can use tire irons, small, flat sticks used to pry the tire off of the wheel.

(3) The round end of the tire iron should be inserted under the bead, the inner edge of the clincher tire.

(4) After removing the damaged innertube, you must make a decision whether to patch the hole or replace the innertube.

(5) If you don't have a patch kit with you, you have one option, to replace the innertube.

(6) Once the new innertube is in place, its valve, the metal device through which air is put into the tube, should be straight.

(7) It is easy to adjust your bicycle's front and rear derailleurs, the changers that move the chain.

(8) While the rear derailleur moves the chain across several sprockets, metal wheels with teeth, the front one moves it across only two sprockets.

(9) A dirty and time-consuming job, regular maintenance is necessary if you want to keep your bicycle working smoothly.

Exercise 2 Page 195

There are many ways to complete the sentences for this exercise. The sentences below represent possible correct answers.

(2) The world's most popular pants, blue jeans are made from denim, a durable cotton cloth.

(3) Strauss dyed the cloth indigo, a deep shade of blue.

(4) Jacob Davis, a tailor from Nevada, came up with the idea for Levis' famous trademark, copper rivets on the pockets.

(5) His idea, to reinforce the pockets with copper rivets, was the result of a miner's complaint about his pockets tearing easily.

(6) The world's most popular pants today, blue jeans were first worn by the working people of the west, cowboys, lumberjacks and ranchers.

(7) Today, a large number of blue jeans, approximately 83,000,000 pairs, are sold each year.

(8) Levi Strauss International runs a "Western Image Program," a project to promote the lifestyle of the west.

ANSWER KEY

PRACTICE WRITING FACTUAL CONDITIONALS

Exercise 1 Page 197

There are many ways to complete the sentences for this exercise. The sentences below represent possible correct answers.

1. If you drop a raw egg, it breaks.
   or
   If a raw egg is dropped, it cracks.
2. If you cut your finger with a knife, it bleeds.
3. If a person touches a hot burner, he burns his finger.
4. If butter is heated, it melts.
5. If two hydrogen molecules are combined with one oxygen molecule, water is created.
6. If you keep water at 0° C, it freezes.
7. If you leave a piece of steel in the rain, it rusts.
8. If my refrigerator is empty, I go to the grocery store.
9. If I crave chocolate, I eat a candy bar.
10. If the phone rings in the middle of the night, I panic.
11. If someone calls during dinner, I ask him to call back later.
12. If I forget to water the plants, they die.
13. If a person has trouble falling asleep at night, he suffers from a sleeping disorder.
14. If my roommate plays the stereo too loudly, I ask him to turn it down.

PRACTICE USING CONDITIONALS TO GIVE ADVICE OR INSTRUCTIONS

Exercise 2 Page 198

There are many ways to complete the sentences for this exercise. The sentences below represent possible correct answers.

1. If you experience culture shock, you should not worry because it happens to many people.
2. If you do not make friends easily, you ought to join campus clubs or organizations.
3. If your friends speak your native language all of the time, try to convince them to speak English together.
4. If you have trouble studying in your apartment, go to the library to study.
5. If your friends have noisy neighbors, they should complain to their landlord.
6. If your friend is unhappy with his roommate, he ought to find a new roommate for next semester.

Exercise 3 Page 198

There are many ways to complete the sentences for this exercise. The sentences below represent some possible correct answers.

1. If you are a rule-learner, you should study the rules before class.
2. Try talking to yourself in French at home if you are inhibited about speaking in front of others.
3. If you feel uncomfortable with ambiguity, you ought to work on becoming more tolerant.

Answer Key

Practice Using Conditionals to Predict the Future

Exercise 4 Page 200

There are many ways to complete the sentences for this exercise. The sentences below represent possible correct answers.

1. If the world's population continues to grow, overcrowding will be a serious global problem.
2. If the number of cars increases, the level of air pollution in urban centers might become unmanageable.
3. If we do not conserve energy, we might find it difficult to maintain our current standard of living.
4. If communities develop good recycling programs, the need for landfills may lessen.
5. If more nuclear power plants are built, the threat of radiation pollution will increase.
6. Landfills will have to be closed if a solution to waste management is not found.
7. Water supplies will become contaminated if factories do not find safer ways to handle their waste.
8. The quality of air in large cities should improve if industries obey government regulations.
9. Future generations might have bigger problems if we do not solve our environmental pollution today.
10. We can have a cleaner world if we all work together.

Exercise 5 Page 200

There are many ways to complete the sentences for this exercise. The sentences below represent possible correct answers.

1. If Yen passes the TOEFL, he will go on vacation.
2. If he goes on vacation, he might go to Florida with his American friends.
3. If he travels to Florida, he will visit Disney World.
4. If he is in Florida, he should have great weather.
5. If he goes to Florida, he might go scuba diving.
6. If he goes scuba diving, he ought to see some exotic fish.
7. If he goes scuba diving, he may discover some buried treasure.

Practice Writing Present Counterfactual Conditionals

Exercise 7 Page 202

There are many ways to complete the sentences for this exercise. The sentences below represent possible correct answers.

1. If I were an English teacher, I could ban homework.
2. If students came to my class late, I might make them clean my car.
3. If a student asked a question I couldn't answer, I would consult with another teacher to find the right answer.
4. If my students were confused by the English verb system, they could review all of the tenses.
5. If my students hated to write, I would try to show them the power of writing.
6. If a student cleaned the blackboard in my room every day, he might get an A+.
7. If a student plagiarized, she would fail my course.
8. If I were 65, I could retire.

ANSWER KEY

⑨ I might give pop quizzes if my students seemed lazy about their homework.

⑩ I would give more homework if my students still didn't understand present perfect.

Exercise 8 Page 203

There are many ways to complete the sentences for this exercise. The sentences below represent possible correct answers.

② I review my lessons every day because it helps me learn the material faster. If I didn't review the lessons, I would forget everything I studied.

③ I don't speak English with my friends because most of them come from my country. If I spoke English with my friends, they would laugh at me.

④ I never ask the teacher for extra help because I am too shy. If I asked the teacher to explain the difference between simple past and present perfect, I might not be so confused.

⑤ My English class is not too difficult. If it were too difficult, I could move to a lower level.

⑥ My friends never correct me when I make mistakes. If they corrected me, I might become inhibited about my English.

⑦ My apartment is a wonderful place to study. If it weren't, I would go crazy.

⑧ My roommates are very considerate. If they weren't, I might move.

⑨ I do not try to create opportunities to use English because I am too shy. If I created opportunities to use English, I would be making faster progress.

⑩ I feel very comfortable living in the United States. If I were uncomfortable, I would go home.

PRACTICE USING PAST COUNTERFACTUAL CONDITIONALS

Exercise 9 Page 204

There are many ways to complete the sentences for this exercise. The sentences below represent possible correct answers.

① If yesterday had not been Friday the 13th, John might not have had so much bad luck.

② If John had been able to sew quickly, he would have repaired his pants.

③ If John had done his laundry Thursday night, he would have had some clean pants on Friday.

④ If John had not thrown the car manual away, he could have learned how to change his tire.

⑤ If the officers had not run his license through the computer, they would not have learned about John's unpaid parking tickets.

⑥ If John had paid his parking tickets, he could have avoided the court appearance.

⑦ John would have been able to change his tire if he had saved his car manual.

⑧ If John hadn't gotten a headache, he wouldn't have gone to the drugstore.

⑨ If the sign had not needed a new coat of paint, the painters would not have been there.

⑩ If John had not cleaned his car, he would not have thrown the car manual away.

⑪ If John had not broken his mirror, he would have been on time for class.

Exercise 10 Page 205

There are many ways to complete the sentences for this exercise. The sentences below represent possible correct answers.

① If Levi Strauss had not invented blue jeans, he would not have become rich and famous.

ANSWER KEY

(2) If Strauss had not immigrated to N.Y. in 1848, he might never have invented blue jeans.
(3) If Strauss' brothers had owned land, they would not have been peddlers.
(4) If Strauss had been happy with his life in N.Y., he might not have moved to California.
(5) If Strauss' sister had not sent him money, he could not have moved to California.
(6) If Strauss had not dyed the canvas blue, blue jeans might have been named "brown jeans."
(7) If Jacob Davis had not met Alkali Ike, he would not have heard Ike's complaint.
(8) If Alkali Ike had liked the pockets on his jeans, Davis would never have added the rivets.
(9) If Strauss had lived past 1902, he could have seen his company spread throughout the United States.
(10) If the careless construction worker had not been wearing blue jeans, he would have died.

PRACTICE WRITING MIXED COUNTERFACTUAL CONDITIONALS

Exercise 11 Page 206

There are many ways to complete the sentences for this exercise. The sentences below represent possible correct answers.

(2) If the explorers who settled in North America had come from Spain, we might be studying Spanish as a second language.
(3) If the American people had re-elected George Bush in 1992, he would live in the White House.
(4) If the United States had never started a space exploration program, the current space shuttle program would not exist.
(5) If Henry Ford had never built a Model T car, we might ride horses to school every day.
(6) If personal computers had never been developed, we might not have Nintendo.

Exercise 12 Page 207

There are many ways to complete the sentences for this exercise. The sentences below represent possible correct answers.

(2) My classmates could study my native language if they had moved to my country.
(3) I wouldn't speak English every day if I had stayed in my home country.
(4) We could write English fluently if we had learned it when we were children.
(5) I could afford to buy a new house and car if I had won the lottery last month.
(6) We might still be in our home countries if we had not had the courage to travel.
(7) My classmates and I would not be in English classes if we had already passed the TOEFL.

ADDITIONAL INFORMATION ABOUT CONDITIONALS

Exercise 13 Page 208

(1) In the event that you need corrective lenses to pass the vision test, your license will be restricted.
(2) In case you get a flat tire on the highway, pull the car off of the road onto the shoulder.
(3) In the event that the cabin of the plane loses pressure, the overhead compartments will release oxygen masks.

Answer Key

Exercise 14 — Page 208

1. Provided that you present the necessary documents, the deputy will give you a temporary permit application.
2. On condition that the applicants meet all of the entrance requirements, they will be accepted to the university.
3. As long as I pass the TOEFL, I can begin my studies next semester.
4. Provided that the benefits package includes comprehensive health insurance, I will take the job.
5. So long as you have filed the correct forms, you should receive your refund in about a month.

Exercise 15 — Page 208

There are many ways to complete the sentences for this exercise. The sentences below represent possible correct answers.

1. My friends and I are going to a movie tonight unless we have too much homework.
2. My sister will graduate from the university next semester unless she fails her calculus class.
3. You should not sign up for fifteen credit hours unless you are prepared to work hard all semester.
4. A student cannot take advanced geometry unless he has completed the prerequisites.
5. You will not graduate unless you fulfill all of the requirements.

ADDITIONAL PRACTICE WRITING CONDITIONALS

Exercise 16 — Page 208

1. future, prediction
2. present, counterfactual
3. future, advice
4. past, counterfactual
5. present, general truth
6. mixed, counterfactual
7. present, habit

Exercise 17 — Page 209

There are many ways to complete the sentences for this exercise. The sentences below represent possible correct answers.

2. If you are dictionary dependent, read on.
3. If you stop at every new word, you will lose the writer's train of thought.
4. If this happens, you might have to reread earlier sections of the text.
5. If your dictionary is fairly comprehensive, you can find thorough explanations of the words.
6. If you do not want to carry a 1500-page dictionary at all times, you should sometimes use a small pocket dictionary.
7. If you use your dictionary for every new word, you do not use another important reading strategy.
8. If you come across an unknown word, you ought to imagine that you are Sherlock Holmes.

Answer Key

Exercise 18 Page 210

There are many ways to combine the sentences for this exercise. The sentences below represent possible correct answers.

1. Some people in the United States get nervous when Friday falls on the 13th of the month because this is considered an unlucky day.
2. If they have something important planned, they postpone it until the 14th.
3. Elizabeth is one of these people who believe in the bad luck of Friday the 13th.
4. She developed this fear several years ago, when she had many bad experiences one Friday the 13th.
5. As soon as she woke up that morning, she saw a black cat outside her window.
6. If the cat had not been there, the day might not have started out badly.
7. When Elizabeth stepped out of the shower, she slipped on a piece of soap and fell down.
8. If the soap had not been there, she would not have fallen.
9. Although she hurt her shoulder and back, she felt good enough to go to school.
10. After she got dressed and ate breakfast, she walked out of her apartment building right under a ladder.
11. If the ladder had not been resting against the building next to her front door, she would have seen it in time.
12. When Elizabeth was crossing the street, a car almost hit her.
13. If the driver hadn't slowed down, he would have hit Elizabeth.
14. Elizabeth went to sit down on a park bench for a few minutes because she wanted to calm down.
15. When she sat down, she heard a "crunching" sound under her foot.
16. As she looked down, she saw a mirror that she had broken with her foot.
17. If she had not decided to sit and relax, she would not have broken the mirror.
18. Then she looked to her left and saw a "wet paint" sign on the bench, which city workers had painted early that morning.
19. If the bench had not needed new paint, the city workers would not have painted it.
20. All of these events, which happened one Friday the 13th, have made Elizabeth a very superstitious person.
21. Because she always thinks the worst will happen, she carries several good luck charms.
22. She carries a rabbit's foot, a four-leaf clover, a lucky penny, and a horse shoe.
23. If she carries these objects forever, she will have good luck.
24. Many of Elizabeth's friends think she is crazy because she carries all of these objects.
25. However, her family knows what happened to Elizabeth on that Friday the 13th, so they understand her fears.
26. If her family members did not know about her experiences, they would not tolerate her strange behavior.

PRACTICE IDENTIFYING AND WRITING PARALLEL STRUCTURES

Exercise 2 Page 215

There are many ways to complete the sentences for this exercise. The sentences below represent possible correct answers.

1. Many students in the United States wonder how they will cover the rising cost of tuition and living expenses.
2. Many students in the United States wonder how they will survive their academic programs and what they will do upon graduation.

Answer Key

(3) Not only is the tuition rising every year, but also the admission requirements are becoming stricter.

(4) Students are faced not only with higher tuition costs but also with larger classes.

(5) Some students will have to either work part time or borrow more money through student loans.

(6) The high cost of tuition, the problems of scheduling work and classes, and the lack of aid from the state and federal governments are making it more and more difficult for some students to get a higher education.

(7) Confronted with the decision to delay college, to borrow more money, or to give up the dream of earning a diploma, some students try to come up with creative solutions to the problem.

(8) For many students, neither student loans nor federal grants will be enough to ease the burden of the cost of higher education.

Practice Using Simple Coordination

Exercise 3 — Page 215

(1) I came to this university, for the chemical engineering program is world-renowned.

(2) I like living here, so I will stay for a few years.

(3) I like living here, but I will probably move back to my hometown after I graduate.

(4) Because this university does not offer computer engineering, I will transfer after next semester, or I will change my major.

(5) My advisor recommended that I take nine credit hours my first semester, for twelve would be too many to manage.

(6) For some people, living in a new country is exciting, and it helps them learn more about themselves and their native culture.

(7) For other people, living in a new country is not exciting, nor is it rewarding.

(8) When universities experience financial difficulties, they raise tuition, or they cut services.

Practice Using Correlative Conjunctions

Exercise 4 — Page 216

(1) Neither the hikers nor the initial rescuers realized the significance of the discovery.

(2) Both Austria and Italy claimed the Iceman as their own.

(3) The rescuers found not only the Iceman's body but also pieces of clothing and equipment.

(4) The Iceman left his group either to find material for tools or to hunt for food.

Exercise 5 — Page 216

There are many ways to complete the sentences for this exercise. The sentences below represent possible correct answers.

(1) Chris neither cleans nor cooks.

(2) Chris will either live with me or move back home.

(3) Both Chris and Terry study hard.

(4) Neither Chris nor Terry has lived with an international student before.

(5) Not only is Terry an excellent cook, but he also seems tidy.

ANSWER KEY

PRACTICE USING DISCOURSE THREADS

Exercise 3 Page 219

There are many ways to complete the sentences for this exercise. The answers below represent possibilities.

1. these fundamentals (or these ideas)
2. boats
3. They (or These)
4. The other
5. These boats
6. people (or navigators or sailors)
7. this sailboat
8. navigators
9. the sails
10. the wind
11. this position

Exercise 4 Page 221

There are many ways to complete the sentences for this exercise. The answers below represent possibilities.

1. These reasons
2. the pool
3. this
4. this experience
5. his fear
6. This story
7. this man
8. important
9. This (or This mistake or This error in judgment)
10. these questions
11. this technique
12. skill
13. my fear
14. this stroke
15. these strokes
16. these
17. swimming (or all of these strokes)

Answer Key

Practice Using Noun Clauses

Exercise 1 Page 227

1. Rescuers feared that the five cross-country skiers were lost in an avalanche.
2. That the skiers came out alive was amazing.
   or
   It was amazing that the skiers came out alive.
3. It seemed foolhardy that some of the skiers didn't bring waterproof gear.
   or
   That some of the skiers didn't bring waterproof gear seemed foolhardy.
4. The fact that they were all expert mountain climbers helped the skiers survive.
5. Many skiers do not realize that avalanches are often unpredictable.
6. Ski patrol squads urge that a skier stay within ski area boundaries.

Exercise 2 Page 227

1. Many people asked why the skiers went out in such dangerous conditions.
2. How they would shelter themselves at night posed a major problem for the skiers.
3. The first night out, the skiers decided where they should dig a snow cave.
4. The rescuers wondered when the weather would break.
5. Because of the weather conditions, the ski patrol was unsure about what they could do to save the skiers.

Exercise 3 Page 227

1. The rescuers wondered if the skiers would make it.
2. Whether a buried skier will survive an avalanche depends on how quickly he is found.
3. In the back woods, it is difficult to determine if the conditions are safe.
4. At the trailhead, a local resident asked whether the skiers had heard the weather forecast or not.
5. Whether the skiers acted carelessly or not was a matter of opinion.

Exercise 4 Page 227

There are many ways to complete the sentences for this exercise. The sentences below represent possible correct answers.

1. I suggest that your brother apply for his visa well in advance of his trip.
2. Your parents should insist that your brother call home after he arrives.
3. Your parents should request that your brother write a letter once a week.
4. It is important that you not worry too much about your brother.
5. It is vital that your brother take second language classes before he travels overseas.
6. It is best that you send your brother some money every month.

Practice Using Passive Constructions

Exercise 2 Page 230

1. The financial statement is signed by the applicant's sponsor.

ANSWER KEY

② The financial statement is being signed by the applicant's sponsor.
③ The financial statement was signed by the applicant's sponsor.
④ The financial statement was being signed by the applicant's sponsor.
⑤ The financial statement will be signed by the applicant's sponsor.
⑥ The financial statement is going to be signed by the applicant's sponsor.
⑦ The financial statement has been signed by the applicant's sponsor.
⑧ The financial statement used to be signed by the applicant's sponsor.
⑨ The financial statement had been signed by the applicant's sponsor.
⑩ The financial statement could have been signed by the applicant's sponsor.
⑪ The financial statement should be signed by the applicant's sponsor.
⑫ The financial statement has to be signed by the applicant's sponsor.
⑬ The financial statement must be signed by the applicant's sponsor.

Exercise 3   Page 231

① My visa application was mailed yesterday.
② My application has not yet been processed by the embassy.
③ A visa application must be approved by the consul.
④ The visa application will be approved by the consul tomorrow.
⑤ An I-20 will be issued by the English Program immediately.
⑥ Sixty I-20's were issued by the English Program last semester.
⑦ Ali was admitted by the university before he applied to the English Program.
⑧ Official records should be sent by the high school.
⑨ The financial statement is signed by the sponsor.
⑩ The financial statement can be signed by the applicant if he is independently wealthy.

Exercise 4   Page 231

① Christmas is celebrated in many different ways.
② On that day, a big meal is prepared in the evening.
③ Usually, turkey is served.
④ After dinner, the Christmas tree is decorated.
⑤ Ornaments and lights are put on the tree.
⑥ Like so many other families, my family celebrates Christmas this way.
⑦ However, last year, I celebrated Christmas eve in a strange way.
⑧ I spent December 24th in an airplane.
⑨ I had scheduled my flight home for December 23. (My flight home had been scheduled for December 23.)
⑩ However, my flight was canceled because of a heavy snow storm.
⑪ I was forced to stay in the airport for 24 hours.
⑫ On the 24th, the airlines announced a new flight. (A new flight was announced.)
⑬ The flight was scheduled to leave at 1:00 PM.
⑭ We were boarded at 12:30.

Answer Key

(15) However, the pilot discovered a mechanical problem.

(16) The plane had to be delayed for 12 more hours.

(17) When I finally arrived home on the 25th, my family had saved one small piece of turkey for me.

Practice Using Reported Speech

Exercise 1 Page 236

There are many ways to complete the sentences for this exercise. The sentences below represent possible correct answers.

(1) Robert Weatherall, the job-placement director at MIT, points out that the United States loses if it doesn't accept and encourage international students to study here (qtd. in Baker 1987, 74).

(2) Ching Bin Liaw, a Taiwanese student in mechanical engineering at the University of California, Berkeley, informs us that an advanced degree is a source of pride and respect in his country (qtd. in Baker 1987, 74).

(3) Roger Tougas, a Massachusetts state representative in 1987, argues that foreign students should cover the cost of their education because they gain so much (qtd. in Baker 1987, 73).

(4) Craufurd Goodwin and Michael Nacht contend that a department of the federal government should encourage the influx of international students (1983, 26).

(5) Goodwin and Nacht assert that foreign students bring a much needed global perspective to the education of American students (1983, 26).

(6) Lawson Lau, author of "The World at Your Doorstep," explains that today's foreign students will be tomorrow's world leaders in a variety of fields (qtd. in Rentz 1987, 10).

Exercise 2 Page 237

There are many ways to complete the sentences for this exercise. The sentences below represent possible correct answers.

(1) The Gentle Reader admits that he is not sure whom to look at when a foreign language translator is interpreting a conversation.

(2) Miss Manners explains that the speaker should look at the person to whom he is speaking but acknowledge the interpreter from time to time.

(3) Matt Clark adds that medicine is an art that mirrors the culture in which it is practiced.

(4) Clark reports that American medicine reflects the pioneer spirit on which the country was founded.

(5) Clark reports that when making a decision about how to treat a patient, French doctors rely more on theory than on practice.

Practice Using Sentence Connectors

Exercise 1 Page 239

There are many ways to complete the sentences for this exercise. The sentences below represent possible correct answers.

(2) They seek out opportunities to meet residents. For example, they join clubs and organizations.

(3) They make every effort to speak the new language. In addition, they attend community events, go to movies, and read local newspapers.

(4) The honeymoon stage can last several weeks. Next, the visitors experience the rejection stage.

Answer Key

5. During the rejection stage, the visitors feel anger and disdain for the new country. Consequently, they spend time with their fellow countrymen, speak their native language, and criticize the new culture.

6. The visitors often stay home. Moreover, they feel tired and bored.

7. They close themselves off from the new culture. For instance, they stay in their homes listening to music from their countries and reading books and magazines in their native languages.

8. They know they should practice speaking the language of their new country. Nevertheless, they speak their native languages every chance they get.

9. During the rejection stage, visitors face a conflict. On the one hand, they want to avoid the new language. On the other hand, they know they must practice the new language in order to learn it.

10. They want to distance themselves from the new culture. To do this, they surround themselves with signs and symbols of their native culture, things like food, music, and language.

11. In order to enjoy life in the new country, visitors must get through the rejection stage. Otherwise, they will be unhappy during their entire visit.

12. Fortunately, most visitors survive the rejection stage. Then they experience the adjustment stage.

13. During the adjustment and acceptance stages, the visitors begin to establish a routine. As a result they begin to feel comfortable.

14. In the acceptance stage, visitors acculturate. In other words, they feel like a member of the community in which they are living.

15. They do not lose their native culture. On the contrary, they come to understand and appreciate another culture.

D.M. - 642-3063